Machiavelli

A Man Misunderstood

MICHAEL WHITE

LITTLE, BROWN

A *Little, Brown* Book

First published in Great Britain by Little, Brown in 2004

Copyright © 2004 Michael White

The moral right of the author has been asserted.

A CIP catalogue record for this book is available
from the British Library.

ISBN 0 316 72476 9

Typeset in Caslon Old Face by M Rules
Printed and bound in Great Britain by
Clays Ltd, St Ives plc

Little, Brown
An imprint of
Time Warner Book Group UK
Brettenham House
Lancaster Place
London WC2E 7EN
www.twbg.co.uk

For our son Finley Albert,
born 26 September 2003

Contents

'We are much beholden to Machiavel and others, that write what men do, and not what they ought to do.'

Francis Bacon, *The Advancement of Learning*,
1605, Book II, xxi.9

Introduction: A Man Misunderstood

I'm beginning to see a pattern in the subjects I choose to write about. I have never attempted the life of a king or a queen, a pope or a statesperson, because for me the interesting subjects are not the leaders of men but those who have shaped our intellectual world. For me the rulers and monarchs, the pontiffs and presidents, are not the truly important historical figures who fill our past and our present. Some undeniably great figures led colourful, glamorous lives, filled with spectacle and show, and in a few exceptional cases their lives were filled with valuable deeds and great achievement (here I'm thinking especially of Churchill and George Washington). But, for all the bravura and fireworks of such lives, the true shapers, the real epoch-makers, are not those who waged war or passed laws but the men and women who discovered, portrayed and invented.

Almost all of these truly important people came from quite ordinary backgrounds, and a great many of them were never appreciated during their lifetime. Mozart and Leonardo da Vinci, Isaac Newton and Galileo, all came from modest homes. Dickens, Faraday and Dalton were born extremely poor. And while some of the most respected creators were acknowledged for their genius while they lived, we need only consider Mozart, Van Gogh, Copernicus or Mendel to realise that many other great figures were ignored until long after their death.

Furthermore, the truly great historical figures were often lowly servants of the puffed-up power brokers of their time. They enjoyed little influence and were granted few honours by those they served. One such great but powerless man was Niccolò Machiavelli. He came from an ordinary background but he achieved extraordinary things. He was a man who, more than most creative figures in history, had intimate dealings with the leaders of men, and he also suffered more than most at the hands of those born into privilege and bred to lead.

In his *Discourses* Machiavelli made the observation: 'Among all men who are praised, those who are most praised are those who have been chiefs and orderers of religion. Close behind them are those who have founded republics or kingdoms. After these, those are also worthy who, placed in the armies, have enlarged either their own kingdom or that of their homeland. Literary men are to be added to these.'[1] It was clear that he also realised that artists and creative individuals rarely held any form of power or influence, commenting in his comedy *Mandragola*, written in 1513 or 1514: 'For those without power, there isn't even a dog who will bark in your face.'

There are several surviving busts and portraits of Machiavelli, most of them produced about a decade after he became, in 1498, the Secretary to the Second Chancery in Florence. However, the picture that is probably most famous is the painting by Santi di Tito that now hangs in the Palazzo Vecchio in Florence, close to where Machiavelli worked for many years. Painted around 1505, it shows Machiavelli dressed in his formal gown of office, black overlaid on crimson velvet. In his left hand he holds his suede gloves, while his right hand is placed statesmanlike on a book set on a table. His clothes look as though they are several sizes too big for him and it is obvious that beneath them stands a scrawny body. His face is that of a small wild animal, a fox or a lynx perhaps, all skin and bone. His hair is receding and cut close, his eyes small and fathomless black. His mouth is interesting. He has thin lips and his fraction of a smile is almost impossible to read; it is merely a tightening of the facial muscles, a pulling in of the lips: it is a rather cynical smile. It is a pity that Niccolò's friend Leonardo da Vinci (whom he first met around the time of this portrait) could not have spared the time to paint him, because Machiavelli's face is every bit as enigmatic and fascinating as that of *La Gioconda*.

The fact that Machiavelli looked the way he did, a face so easily superimposed on a cartoon of the devil, a head crying out for a pair of horns to transform him into Mephistopheles, is one of life's strange little coincidences. Today the name Machiavelli is inextricably linked with the words 'Machiavellian' and 'Machiavellianism', words often written in the same sentence as 'evil', 'depot', 'tyrant', 'duplicity'. Indeed Machiavelli's ideas have become so famous that the man who described them and wrote about them is perceived by many as one who practised what he defined.

And yet nothing could be further from the truth. Niccolò Machiavelli was in many respects a perfectly normal man. He enjoyed the company of his friends and drank with them in Florentine taverns. He womanised and gambled, he married and fathered children. For fifteen years he got up each morning and did his job as a diplomat and civil servant. Then, after the government he served was ousted by the Medici dynasty, he was made a pariah; he lost his job, was imprisoned briefly and tortured, and for many years was unable to work in any official capacity. In exile he turned to writing and produced a collection of important works spanning history, politics and military analysis, as well as two comic plays and sonnets, songs and other verse. The most famous of his works is *The Prince*, a book that has been read widely for almost five hundred years and still sells hundreds of thousands of copies annually.

Contrary to popular belief, Machiavelli killed no one and was neither a politician who wielded power over the lives of others nor an evil adviser to an avaricious, scheming warlord. However, in his capacity as a Florentine diplomat he did rub shoulders with tyrants and fanatics, psychotic warlords and murderous popes. Being a great observer and analyst, and possessing a poet's mind, he resolved, when his life was shattered by the Medici in 1513, to turn his experiences and his learning into one of the most important books ever written.

The Prince was a radical treatise when it was written and it remains a radical treatise today. It is also one of the most misunderstood books in print, and those who misunderstand its intention also misunderstand the man who wrote it, tarnishing the name of the author along with the philosophy he describes. I can think of no other example of such an extreme misapprehension in all of literature, philosophy and politics.

Part of the problem derives from Machiavelli's character. As I have said, he was in many ways an ordinary man, but there was a controversial and unorthodox edge to him. He regarded religion as a human construct and he had no faith or spiritual convictions. He was a libertine who frequented brothels and gambling dens, rough taverns and debauched parties. He mixed with actors and whores as well as with kings and pontiffs, and he openly expressed a preference for the former. But his image also derives from the honesty of his writing.

Machiavelli's words are harsh and forceful, his ideas are like barbs, shards of steel; there is nothing warm and fluffy about Machiavelli's ideas. Naturally, a great many people have not liked this: the majority of those who read *The Prince* five centuries ago did not approve of it, and many who read it today do not approve of it. But none of this has any impact on the truths Machiavelli described; it is simply that, more often than not, people do not like being confronted with the truth.

As we read *The Prince* today it is sobering to realise that it has been read widely by generation after generation for half a millennium. And here again there is a great irony (the story of

Machiavelli is filled with them), for the only book that has been read by more people over a longer period of time in the Western world is the Bible, a tome that offers a vision diametrically opposed to the views expressed in *The Prince*. It is easy to think of books that have been read by more people, but it is not so easy to come up with titles that have been read by so many over such a long time. In compiling such a list we might consider Chaucer's *The Canterbury Tales*, Plato's *Republic*, the plays of Shakespeare (although these are rarely read as such). None, though, surpasses *The Prince*. I have also added the caveat 'Western world', for the Koran, as well as ancient books describing the teachings of the Buddha and the ideas of Confucius, rival the popularity of the Bible.

Machiavelli considered Christianity in a political context. He saw organised religion as simply a device, a tool for social control, but he also believed that it was damaging to the evolution of society because it made people more interested in a hypothetical afterlife than the reality of the here and now. To Machiavelli the Bible, like the works of many Classical writers, described the world through rose-tinted glasses. Plato's philosophy as it is expressed in the *Republic* is one Machiavelli used as an example of a set of ideas that do not define a real or practical world based on genuine human nature: the Greek philosopher built his ideas on an impossible ideal. Machiavelli viewed Christian morality in the same light as Plato's ideal system. To him the building blocks of Christian doctrine were unrealistic, unnatural, and therefore of little real value.

Such opinions were never going to make Machiavelli popular with the Establishment of his day, and indeed his name became anathema as soon as pirated and plagiarised editions of *The Prince* began to circulate a few years before his death in 1527. But by this time Machiavelli was well used to neglect and ignorance. Those who should have shown him respect, the very princes whose behaviour he dissected so brilliantly, were as energetically critical as those who had little grounding in the truths of the world. Such neglect was a perfectly Machiavellian display; it makes sense, after all, that most rulers and princes could feel little enthusiasm for a book that exposed their methods.

Today there is no genuine excuse for maligning the name of Machiavelli, and it is high time he was rehabilitated. Ignorance and ulterior motive drove the centuries-long darkening of his image. Today we should know better, for we have witnessed the accuracy of Machiavelli's icy words; we have all seen the true nature of men.

Michael White, Perth, Australia, July 2004

1

Love, Not Money

In May 1521, a few days after his fifty-second birthday, the former Florentine Secretary Niccolò Machiavelli was commissioned by the eight-member Otto di Pratica, one of the many councils that governed Florence, to travel to Carpi, a small town some sixty miles north of the city. The purpose of the trip was to discuss with the general assembly of the Franciscans, who had their headquarters in the town, a matter concerning clerical jurisdiction in the region around Florence.

It was a strange assignment for Machiavelli. For fifteen years he had served the Florentine government under the regime of Piero Soderini, but he had been cast out and left in the cold when the Medici family had dismantled the Republic and taken over in 1513. Since then he had been scraping a living from his country estate near Florence and occasionally taking on commissions from businessmen who were anxious to settle some dispute or other in a neighbouring city. By 1521 he was beginning to re-emerge from exile. He was acquiring a reputation as a serious writer – his book *The Art of War* was with the printers – and just a few months earlier the Medici pope, Clement VII, had awarded him a prestigious commission to write a history of Florence. But the commission to sort out a problem with the Franciscans was puzzling because Machiavelli was known to have no affinity at all with orthodox religion, and indeed many knew that he held the clergy in very low regard.

However, Machiavelli was in no position to spurn the offer, and so he set off on 11 May, stopping first at Modena, where he stayed a night with his friend Francesco Guicciardini, the papal governor of the region. On Machiavelli's arrival at Carpi, he and the head of the Franciscan council, Sigismondo Santi, took an instant dislike to each other. Perhaps the Franciscan had heard tales of his lifestyle and beliefs, but he also seemed irritated by the fact that it appeared to him that, in sending Machiavelli, the Otto di Pratica had appointed an official of low rank to deal with the issue.

Matters were not helped by the fact that Machiavelli was forced to attend regular services, including matins before dawn each morning, at the monastery where the council meetings were to be held. Furthermore, Santi was proving uncooperative and deliberately delaying proceedings in a rather pathetic attempt to show that he was in control of the situation.

One great source of relief for Machiavelli was the close proximity of his friend Guicciardini in Modena. Guicciardini was a man in whom he could confide and exchange letters in which he bad-mouthed the monks and poked fun at Santi. Guicciardini was a very powerful figure, an efficient bureaucrat, but also an insightful, intelligent ruler who was a devoted supporter of his friend Machiavelli.

Guicciardini paid for dispatch riders to carry the exchange of letters the twenty-five-mile round trip to Carpi, sometimes up to three times a day. After this happened a few times Machiavelli began to notice that the monks were starting to mutter and that even Santi was taking note of the fact that this seemingly unimportant civil servant from Florence was receiving inordinate attention from a powerful figure such as Guicciardini. It was then that he struck on the idea of playing a trick on the monks.

In a letter to his friend Machiavelli asked him to have his reply delivered by a crossbowman dressed in full livery, and asked that the rider should gallop the whole way so that when he arrived he and his horse would have worked up a sweat. Later that day a uniformed officer arrived on a sleek black horse wreathed in sweat and rushed to deliver a letter to Machiavelli, who was in discussions with the Franciscans.

It worked wonderfully. The monks were surprised to see Machiavelli being treated with such reverence and their curiosity was piqued. Santi, who was not so easily taken in and rather suspicious from the start, asked Machiavelli why he, of all people, should be sent urgent messages in this way, to a place so far off the beaten track. Without hesitating, Machiavelli retorted that these messages were extremely important dispatches concerning the Holy Roman Emperor and the King of France. Santi could hardly refute this explanation.

But, still not content with this deception, Machiavelli asked Guicciardini to repeat the trick the next day. His friend followed the instructions and even added a bundle of letters with a Zurich stamp across the front to give weight to the ploy. Then, on the following day, Guicciardini sent another bundle of official papers and documents, along with a pie, which the dispatch rider explained had been sent as a special gift to the Illustrious Machiavelli.

It was all good fun, but although Machiavelli and Guicciardini believed they had fooled the monks, they were never entirely convinced that Santi had fallen for it. In one letter, written while a group of monks stood around him convinced that he was imparting advice concerning great matters of state, Machiavelli declared: 'Holy dick! We are going to have to go carefully with this fellow, for he is as crafty as a thousand devils!'[1]

And indeed Santi, whom Machiavelli regarded as a malicious and naturally suspicious man, showed no softening of his dislike for Machiavelli. But the trick did serve another purpose. By the third day of dispatches the monks were so in awe of Machiavelli that Santi was beginning to feel his own authority being undermined by the Florentine emissary and he did his best to hurry the proceedings along so that he could bring forward his visitor's departure.

This amusing tale illustrates Machiavelli's mischievous nature, his healthy sense of humour and the cynicism that marked his attitude towards self-important bigots like Santi who prospered so well within corrupt institutions of the time. But it is also a sad story, for after a lifetime of commitment and achievement Machiavelli had been reduced to sorting out a trivial matter concerning a group of monks, and even in this task he received little respect from a relative nobody like Santi.

Machiavelli was aware of this irony but he made an excellent job of burying the pain of humiliation. To survive, he used humour: he was forever laughing at the unfairness of the world and the bad luck he had suffered. The exchange of letters with Guicciardini is filled with self-deprecation, along with the sharpened barbs he directs at Santi and his kind. 'I was sitting on the toilet when your messenger arrived . . .,' he wrote the day after he reached Carpi, 'and just at that moment I was mulling over the absurdities of this world.'[2]

But most ironic of all is the fact that, as Francesco Guicciardini was sending liveried horsemen to his friend in jest, his letters were filled not just with witticisms about the Franciscans but heartfelt comments highlighting the pathos of the game they were playing; for Guicciardini knew more than most the anguish Niccolò suffered. 'My dear friend Machiavelli,' he wrote in one letter:

When I read your titles as ambassador of the Republic and of friars, and I consider how many kings, dukes, and princes you have negotiated with in the past, I am reminded of [the Spartan general] Lysander, to whom, after so many victories and trophies, was given the task of distributing meat to those very same soldiers whom he had so gloriously commanded; and I say: You see that, with only the faces of the men and the extrinsic colours changed, all the very same things return; and we do not see any incident that has not been seen in other times.[3]

They were words meant to encourage, and perhaps they did, but with these simple observations Guicciardini had summed up Machiavelli's life, one filled with glory, glamour and pathos.

In a letter to a friend in 1513, the middle-aged Machiavelli declared: 'I was born in poverty and at an early age learned how to endure hardship rather than flourish.'[4] We should not take this comment too seriously. By the time he wrote this Machiavelli had grown rather used to rubbing shoulders with the super-rich of his day, and even if he was never wealthy himself, he had become more than a little accustomed to spending his time in a world of luxury and opulence. This close associate of men who in their day were the Renaissance equivalent of Bill Gates or the Sultan of Brunei had, when it came to a consideration of his own birthright, lost something of his sense of perspective.

Niccolò Machiavelli was in fact raised in a rather bourgeois Tuscan household. His family came from the patriciate (*popolani grassi*), approximately equivalent to the middle class of today, but although the branch of the Machiavellis into which he was born possessed the cachet of belonging to an old and respected family, they had lost their wealth a long time before his birth.

Machiavelli's ancestors had been one of the important Guelph families who had been engaged in violent struggle with another powerful group of Italian families, the Ghibellines, through much of the Middle Ages. After the battle of Montaperti in 1260 the surviving Guelph families were exiled and only returned six years later after an intercession by the Vatican. The Machiavellis were among the most respected of the Guelphs and were said to have once been closely related to the rulers of Montespertoli in the Val di Pesa, just south of Florence. This theory is supported by the fact that by the

fifteen century the family owed large tracts of land there. But
although Niccolò Machiavelli's cousins might have been considered noteworthy landlords in the region, the sole inheritance of his
father, Bernardo, was a small, rather tatty farmhouse at
Sant'Andrea, near San Casciano, that had come down to him
through the poorest and least successful branch of the family. (The
main street in San Casciano is now named Via Machiavelli.)

Machiavelli's country property still stands today, a sturdy clus-
ter of stone and tile buildings alongside which runs a small country
road. The main family home was in Florence, a small, cramped
house on the west side of a long street called Via Romana that ran
from the Ponte Vecchio to the gate (today called Porta Romana) of
the church of San Piero Gattolino. The configuration of the streets
has changed since Machiavelli was a boy and Via Romana now
approximates to Via Guicciardini and his boyhood home would
have been close to No. 16. This street lies in the heart of Florence
less than one hundred yards from the Ponte Vecchio and near the
Pitti Palace, which at the time of Niccolò's birth was in the earliest
stages of construction.

Remarkably, the Machiavellis' house survived until the Second
World War, when it was destroyed by an Allied bomb. But in
1469, when Niccolò was born, it comprised a small group of self-
contained dwellings, called *case*, arranged around a courtyard.
Essentially an apartment, each *casa* consisted of a large vaulted hall
on the ground floor and two more storeys above. The ground
floor was usually used as a shop or a work area. The middle floor
was often divided by wooden partitions and provided a living and
sleeping space, while the top floor housed the kitchen, so that the
smoke from the oven had only a short distance to travel to exit via
the roof.

The young Machiavelli was surrounded by relatives. On one
side of the courtyard lived his cousin Niccolò d'Alessandro, his
wife and their three children and his three brothers and sisters. On

another side the *casa* was shared by more cousins, the heirs of Machiavelli's recently deceased uncle, Nicholò d'Andrea Buondi. With them lived Piero, son of yet another cousin, Francesco Machiavelli, along with his wife and their nine children.

Florence was a noisy, crowded maze of narrow lanes and tall stone buildings. The city was divided into four quarters or *quartiere* – Santa Croce, San Giovanni, Santa Maria Novella and Santo Spirito – and the Machiavelli home was in the last of these. Each *quartiere* was more or less self-contained, with its own shops, churches, craftsmen and confraternities. Taxes were gathered from each of the *quartiere* by specially assigned collectors (one of Niccolò's cousins from the same building in Via Romana, Gherardo di Giovanni, was employed as a collector) and each quarter funded its own infrastructure and was in return granted a level of political and social autonomy within the government.

By the time Niccolò was born, on 3 May 1469, the family's little *casa* must have been getting rather crowded.[5] We know from the Florence City Registry of 1470 that Bernardo and his wife, Bartolomea di Stefano Nelli, also had two daughters: Primavera, five years older than Niccolò, and Margherita, two at the time of his birth. The register for 1480 shows that the situation had grown worse still because another son, Totto, had arrived in 1474.[6]

In September of that year Bernardo Machiavelli began a *libro di ricordi*, or diary. Discovered in the late 1930s, this invaluable document was restored and transcribed by a scholar named Cesare Olschki before its publication in 1954.[7] Chronicling the period 1474 to 1487, Bernardo recorded much of the minutiae of his life and family matters, from the sale of a donkey to the debts he seemed to be constantly struggling to pay off.

The diary helps us to add a little flesh to Niccolò's childhood and some colour to the figure of his father. We learn, for example, that Bernardo was born sometime between 1426 and 1429, that he had a doctorate in law but appears not to have practised his profession

for many years. There are intimations that he was born out of
wedlock, but he does his best to disguise it and there is no surviving evidence to support the hints. He also goes to great pains to
emphasise that all his children, including Niccolò, were legitimate.
This was extremely important to middle-class Florentines of the
time, but because record keeping was not then a precise science, it
was also an aspect of one's heritage that could be abused by others.
If illegitimacy could be proven, a citizen was prevented from joining most guilds, excluded from enrolling at the city's university and
they became ineligible for any government office.

One of the most revealing facts gathered from Bernardo's *ricordi*
is that he was a *specchio*, a tax debtor. This is significant because to
default on taxes was also perceived as bringing serious dishonour
upon oneself and one's family. The children of a *specchio* could not
serve in any government office, nor could a lawyer practise his profession if he was also in any kind of financial debt to the community.
The fact that Niccolò later served his government indicates that at
some point Bernardo's debt was completely cleared.

One of the most mysterious aspects of the Machiavelli family at
this time was exactly what Bernardo did. He was a trained lawyer
and his title of 'Messere' shows that he was a Doctor of Law (the
title was strictly applied in the fifteenth century), yet there is no
record of a practice. He is not mentioned in the registers of the
Florentine Guild of Judges and Notaries, there is no surviving
documentation linked with any cases in which he was involved and
there are no records of earnings. Indeed it appears that Bernardo's
sole source of income was the relatively small amount he earned
from the family's farm.

How he ended up in this sorry state is unclear. It is hard to
imagine the man we read about in Bernardo's diary, who clearly
loved his children and valued his social status, willingly slipping
into poverty. A serious block must have been placed on his aspirations by social convention or political incompatibility. The most

likely explanation is that Bernardo had worked as a lawyer when he was a young man, but got into debt with the tax authorities.[8]

For the young Niccolò, life in Florence was never dull. He played football and other games in the streets with his friends and witnessed the many pageants and carnivals in which the Florentines regularly indulged. These displays blended Christian and pagan rituals seamlessly and were designed to bring good cheer in the face of daily confrontation with death and hardship. One of the liveliest was the feast day of San Giovanni Battista, the patron saint of Florence, which took place on 24 June. It was a loud, joyful affair, the streets were decorated with ribbons, multicoloured banners and flowers and the noisy party lasted at least two days.

On festival days theatre companies performed plays and musicals in the streets and the piazzas. These were to make a lasting impression on Machiavelli, who, from an early age, showed a special interest in spectacle and the dynamics of the theatre. What he saw as a boy on the streets of Florence stayed with him and planted the seeds for the comic plays that made him famous half a century later.

The other side of life in Renaissance Florence was the dark underworld of death and disease, famine and war. Machiavelli, like almost all his contemporaries, was introduced to death young. A terrible plague in 1479 claimed the lives of neighbours and family friends. His own father became seriously ill and believed he was going to die. Before the plague reached its peak, the family were packed off to a country estate owned by the family of Niccolò's mother at Mugello, a few miles from Florence. Bernardo pulled through and joined them to convalesce a few weeks later.

Later that year, while the Machiavellis were staying at their own little country home, a Florentine mercenary army recently defeated at the battle of Poggio Imperiale was barracked in a nearby town during a lull in a conflict with Naples that had already cost the Republic many lives and a great deal of money. Some soldiers were

lodged in the family home and the ten-year-old Niccolò was fascinated with them and the stories they told. This experience too was
a significant influence on the mind of the adult Machiavelli, who
later campaigned for a Florentine citizens' army and spent time at
the battlefronts of Europe before writing his classic study of *The Art
of War*.

From the little we know of the domestic lives of the Machiavelli
family, the signs are that theirs was a happy home. Bartolomea had
been married before she met Bernardo, whom she wed in 1458.
Her first husband, Niccolò di Girolamo Benizzi, who died in 1457,
had been an apothecary, and by him she had a daughter named
Lionarda. The Benizzis lived a few doors away from where
Bernardo had grown up with his parents, and it appears that
Bernardo and Bartolomea began their relationship very soon after
Niccolò Benizzi's death. It is certain that Lionarda was raised by
her father's family, because there is no record of her in any of the
Machiavelli family tax records or other official documents.

Bartolomea is said to have been a pious woman who was fond of
poetry and music. At some point, when her eldest son was still
young, she turned her hand to writing *laudi*, or religious verse. A
fair copy of one of these poems dedicated to her son Niccolò was
later included in a book written by a descendant, Giovan Battista
Nelli.[9]

Niccolò's own flair for literature seems to have come from his
mother. However, Bernardo was also a highly educated, intellectual
man who in many ways embodied the spirit of his time. He had a
vivid interest in learning, and although he had no particular talent
for art, engineering or philosophy, he studied these fields carefully
and appreciated them. Perhaps more importantly, he loved books
and spent any spare money that came his way on acquiring the
latest works of Classical learning translated into Latin or the vernacular.

The printing press had been introduced in Florence in 1471,

when Niccolò was just two years old, and although his resources were modest Bernardo was one of the earliest and most enthusiastic customers of the city's founding press. A personal inventory of his collection to be found in his *ricordi* shows that he was a man with high-brow and discerning tastes. As well as possessing an extensive collection of printed law books, he owned works by Livy, Macrobius and Priscian, along with a commentary on Aristotle by a modern humanist and friend of Lorenzo de' Medici, Donato Acciaiuoli. He also borrowed books such as Ptolemy's *Cosmology*, Aristotle's *Ethics* and the writings of Justinus and Pliny.

Bernardo bought books in loose-leaf form and when he could afford it, he had them bound with the finest materials his budget would allow. When he could he added to his collection by bartering a few bottles of wine or a cheese from his meagre country estate in exchange for a copy of a Classical text. Bernardo's most valued book was Livy's *History of Rome*, a lavishly illustrated (and therefore expensive) volume, far beyond his means. He acquired it in exchange for compiling an index of place names for the Florentine publisher, a task that took him nine months.

As an adult Niccolò recounted how he had gone to the printer to collect for his father the extremely handsome copy of Livy, bound in the best calfskin and printed on the finest paper. It became the prize of Bernardo's collection, an item revered by the family. From this book Niccolò was to learn a great deal about history and it played such a significant part in moulding his intellectual progress that his own earliest writings were based on Livy's ideas.

Like most men of his class and education, Niccolò's father was a member of a confraternity. Bernardo's was called the Confraternity of San Girolamo sulla Costa, a religious society more usually referred to as La Pietà. Bernardo had little interest in religion, but it appears that he conformed to the social conventions of the time and played his part in the traditional ceremonies expected of him. La Pietà, which consisted of about 140 local businessmen and professionals, was more than a religious group because it had a political agenda and raised money for political purposes as well as for charity. It was a very important part of the social infrastructure of Santo Spirito, and only those who were involved in the confraternity could have a say in the running of the *quartiere*. Fortunately for the Machiavellis it was a brotherhood that did not exclude a *specchio* and it became a major influence on Niccolò, who joined the youth division, the Confraternity of Sant'Antonio da Padova, when he was eleven. At the age of twenty-four he moved on to the adult confraternity and this gave him the opportunity to mix with many of the important figures in his community.

Niccolò and his father were very close and Bernardo viewed his oldest son as the great hope for the future of the Machiavellis. Niccolò's sisters, Primavera and Margherita, went on to lead quite conventional lives. Primavera married Francesco Vernaccia, whose business was based in Constantinople, and the younger Margherita was wed to one Bernardo Minerbetti. The two women raised families, did what was expected of them and vanished into history. Of Niccolò's younger brother, Totto, little is known except that he became a priest and remained in Florence for most of his life. Machiavelli's surviving correspondence shows that the brothers stayed close and that when Niccolò became an important civil servant he did his best to help Totto's career in the Church.

There was much to draw Niccolò and his father together. They shared an irreverent sense of humour, a healthy cynicism towards many social conventions and an unusual lack of trust in the Church. This last must have irritated the pious and God-fearing Bartolomea, who took herself off several evenings a week to sing in the ladies' choir at the church of Santa Trinità and in quiet moments composed her religious verses. Bernardo meanwhile studied humanist tracts and, in private at least, professed quiet scepticism towards the Catholic faith and maintained a cynical disposition towards the institution of the Church.

Evidence of this outlook comes from the fact that when relatives died of the plague Bernardo wrote letters to report the events but never once used the language of the pious or indulged in exclamatory phrases or religious clichés about God guiding the souls of the deceased to heaven or cleansing their sins. He merely reported the facts as though religion played no part in his thinking. Nor is there any indication that he called on the services of a priest when he was himself close to death during the summer of 1479.

Oddly, though, for a man so much concerned with material matters and worldly affairs and who spent little energy on religion, Bernardo did enjoy a very close friendship with a group of friars at the Franciscan convent of Santa Croce, his local church. He often spent time talking and debating with them; and in his will he bequeathed the friars far more money than would have been considered the minimum that was socially acceptable.

Surviving letters show that Niccolò and his father enjoyed an almost fraternal relationship. Once, when Bernardo was staying at the family's farm, he sent his son a prize goose. In reply Niccolò wrote him a humorous sonnet that included the lines: 'Dear Bernardo, ducks and geese | You will have bought – yet eaten none of these.'

When Niccolò was a young man, father and son exchanged bawdy stories and smutty jokes, loved the company of other men and tavern talk and revelled in harmless pranks. Each was an attractive blend of scholar, man about town and adventurer.

Niccolò and Totto were given the best education Bernardo could afford and we know that they received tuition in the rudiments of language, mathematics and history. There is some confusion over Niccolò's knowledge of Greek as a boy. Some scholars claim that he began to learn the language when he was perhaps ten or eleven, while others suggest he was self-taught as an adult. Sadly, apart from a poem he wrote in Latin when he was about twenty-two, nothing earlier than 1497 written in Machiavelli's hand has survived. However, it is clear that he was well read for the time in which he lived; he was intimately familiar with the two most important Florentine writers, Dante and Petrarch. Almost certainly he enjoyed a conventional humanist education at the Studio Fiorentino, the precursor of the city's university, where he would have studied rhetoric, logic and literature.

The young Machiavelli demonstrated a flair for painting but was never more than a keen amateur. However, he had a gift for rhetoric and was supremely logical, eloquent and quick-witted. He was a natural strategist, by instinct a political animal, a man to whom the mechanics of statecraft came as readily as the execution of a landscape to Leonardo or a sonnet to Shakespeare. In middle age Machiavelli summed up his own mindset, and how his particular skills had led him away from many orthodox professions, when he confessed to his friend Francesco Vettori that fortune had so shaped him that he knew nothing of making silk or wool and had no interest in banking and trade nor any feel for profit or loss. His great skills lay elsewhere, far from the conventional talents of the craftsman or the banker.

Niccolò's first tutor was one Matteo, who taught the boy the rudiments of Latin. In his diary Bernardo dates this tuition as beginning on 6 May 1476, just after Niccolò's seventh birthday. The same diary tells us that a year later Niccolò had a second tutor, Battista da Poppi, of the church of San Benedetto, who continued with Latin and a few months later introduced the boy to basic mathematics. This tutor did not last long and in 1480 a third, Paolo da Ronciglione, took over Niccolò's education as well as that of his younger brother.

Much of 1481 and 1482 were spent outside Florence at the country estate at Mugello. Here Niccolò and Totto were taught by a string of local priests, medical students and retired teachers who lived in the nearby villages. When they were not receiving lessons the boys played in the local woods or in the nearby ruins of the castle of Montebuiano. Returning to Florence in the winter of 1482, Primavera married and the younger Margherita began to prepare for her own wedding. With the girls gone, the house in Via Romana began to feel a little roomier.

Little is known of Machiavelli's life during the decade and a half between this time and 1498, when he was elected to the position of Secretary to the Second Chancery of the Florentine Republic. We know that he studied at the Studio Fiorentino and spent some time at the Medici court, where he mixed with people from different professions and classes. We know also that he was considered an accomplished poet and wrote at least one sonnet that was published in a collection for the Medici around 1492. But, aside from this, there is almost nothing.

Clues from letters inform us that Niccolò read widely and studied the Latin poets. He was fond of Virgil and read Ovid and Tibullus. He knew his Dante and Petrarch, Livy and Boccaccio, but his favourite writer was Lucretius and he was particularly fond of the Roman poet and philosopher's *De Natura Rerum* (*On the Nature of Things*). This work, written around 60 BC, inspired many humanist manifestos of the Renaissance as well as fuelling the holism of Leonardo, Bruni and other iconic thinkers and artists of the period.

In 1496 Niccolò's mother, Bartolomea, died at the age of fifty-five. With his sisters long since married and living away from home, the house was left to the three men of Machiavelli's family. Bernardo, now around seventy, was absorbed by grief; Totto was nineteen and training for the priesthood; and Niccolò was almost certainly working in a relatively junior position in the Florentine civil service.

Up to this point there are no signs of even the embryo of Niccolò Machiavelli's extraordinary career. But then fifteenth-century Florence was fertile soil for the flowering of many extraordinary things, a place and a time that nurtured talent whatever its roots.

Machiavelli was a true son of Florence, a man of his age but a man who held within him a universal, timeless vision. There could be no better cradle for his intellect and his imagination than the city which, during the fifteenth and sixteenth centuries, was the epi-centre of the world's intellectual and political life.

2

Machiavelli's Europe

Florence was founded around AD 1000. Built on a settlement that had fallen to the armies of the Holy Roman Empire, it remained for a century or more a tiny city which had at its heart the cathedral of Santa Reparata and the church of San Lorenzo. However, from about 1120 Florence began to grow rapidly, soon becoming a trading centre and a cultural nexus that attracted artists and philosophers, merchants and bankers alike.

By the middle of the thirteenth century the city was an independent state with a population of about thirty thousand. It had its own currency, its own idiosyncratic political system and a growing reputation as one of the great creative centres of Europe. Dante was born in Florence in 1265, during the pre-dawn of the Renaissance. However, his time was scarred by internecine struggle in the city, which, coupled with disease and petty struggles with neighbouring states, severely reduced the city's population and for a while stunted its growth. But gradually Florence emerged from this time of death and darkness and entered an era of staggering achievement, a period during which it grew wealthy and famous. This came at a time when the whole of Europe was waking up to a new age of progress that unfolded faster and more fully than at any time since the Roman empire had foundered a millennium earlier.

There is no general agreement about the precise beginning or end of what historians have dubbed 'the Renaissance'. Those concerned with art and literature – by tradition the disciplines that define the period – would not apply the same dates as those more interested in politics, sociology, science or philosophy. The biographer of the great Renaissance artists Giorgio Vasari was probably the first to coin the term for the period during which he lived, referring to it aptly as a '*rinascita*', or rebirth, for we now think of the time as one during which Europe, having emerged from a particularly bleak and oppressive period in its history, experienced a new and astonishing vitality.

Fourteenth-century Europe had been a profoundly unpleasant place in which to live. Plague struck in wave upon wave, the most devastating outbreak coming during the first quarter of the century. This catastrophe, which left seventy-five million dead, about a third of the continent's population, truly earned the name 'the Black Death'. The century was also scarred by war. The Italian peninsula saw seemingly endless rivalry between city states, conflicts that drained the economy and depleted the population of those young men who had survived disease. And while Italy simmered with political intrigue and the politics of the sword, to its north France and England fought what has since become known as the Hundred Years War, a punctuated conflict that in fact lasted longer than a century, beginning in 1337 and ending in 1453. By contrast, the era between Machiavelli's birth in 1469 and the last decade of the fifteenth century was one of relative peace in Europe, eventually broken by the recurrence of French expansionism during the 1490s.

But although no great wars ransacked Europe during the late fifteenth century, the average life expectancy for a woman was just twenty-four and only a tiny fraction of people could read or write. Peasants lived in extended family groups, often twenty to a tiny, single-roomed hut, sharing the straw floor with their goats and pigs. Their diet was plain and one in four years saw a famine during which cannibalism was not uncommon. The nobility were insulated from some of the privations of the common folk, but not all: they too died of plague and their women succumbed in childbirth. And while the wealthy enjoyed a slightly better diet, they suffered from diseases of affluence, gout, liver disease, obesity. Syphilis was also widespread among that class; Catherine de' Medici, who married Francis I of France, lost both her parents to the disease when she was only three weeks old.

It was only as the horrors of the fourteenth century eased a little that people found the energy to be creative and play their role in advancing culture. During the thousand years between the final gasp of Rome and the fourteenth century, very little had changed. Only a tiny percentage of people in the world had any idea in which year they lived. Beyond the walls of the monasteries innovation was actively shunned and often anyone who suggested a way to improve life in even the most simple ways was regarded with suspicion. Many were excluded from communities as witches and wizards and a few met a worse fate still.

It is no coincidence that as life very slowly improved and Europe dragged itself from the mire of the Dark Ages, painting, literature and the advancement of ideas started to gain importance. Within a hundred years a wave of change had swept across Europe, transforming the intellectual landscape beyond the wildest dreams of those who had suffered grim recent history. The focal point of all this activity was Florence, a fact that prompted the humanist Leonardo Bruni to write at the start of the fourteenth century: 'Florence harbours the greatest minds: whatever they undertake, they easily surpass all other men, whether they apply themselves to military or political affairs, to study or philosophy, or to merchandise.'[1] Indeed the city was perceived by many of Machiavelli's contemporaries as perhaps the most beautiful on earth, inspiring one of them to write: 'Florence is the only town in the world . . . in which the eye meets nothing ugly, the nose smells nothing revolting, the foot treads on no filth.'[2] Although it is possible to accept the first assertion in this statement, one can only assume that fifteenth-century sensibilities were harder to offend than our own, and that this commentator described Florence so favourably because other cities were even filthier and smellier.

Almost all facets of culture were transformed dramatically during this period. It is startling to realise, for example, that in 1471, when the first printing press appeared in Florence, there were no more than about thirty thousand books in existence, yet by the time Machiavelli was working as Secretary to the Second Chancery, in 1500, an estimated eight million printed books were in circulation.

Machiavelli's youth was a period of burgeoning intellect, a time during which human creativity and endeavour flowered and began to influence all areas of life. When Niccolò was a child, Leonardo da Vinci was an apprentice at the studio of the artist Verrocchio a few hundred yards away, and within the same city walls Botticelli was already an successful painter. By the time Machiavelli was twenty-three, in 1492, Columbus had arrived in the New World and Nicolaus Copernicus, the father of modern astronomy, was a nineteen-year-old exploring the rudiments of the subject while a student of mathematics and optics.

This revolution in learning and dissemination of culture was kick-started by two linked factors. The first was the invention of printing with movable type, which led to the development of the printing press. The other was a realisation that a vast body of knowledge was locked up in the works of the great Classical writers of Greece and Rome. This discovery prompted a relatively small group of wealthy intellectuals to seek out these writings and to have them translated. The most significant contributors to this effort came from Florence, one of the primary reasons why this city became crucial to the development of culture, science and art during the Renaissance.

The search for surviving Classical manuscripts was really inspired by the humanist scholar Francesco Petrarch, who was born in 1304 in the little town of Arezzo, about fifty miles from Florence. As the most celebrated intellectual of his age, Petrarch gathered about him a collection of like-minded enthusiasts who shared their master's love for the Classical tradition. They believed there were perhaps hundreds of manuscripts and documents in the original Latin and Greek secreted away in private collections and hidden in the monasteries of Europe. Many of these men made it their life's work to search them out.

One of Petrarch's closest friends was Giovanni Boccaccio, who is credited with finding Tacitus's *Histories* and part of his *Annales*. He himself wrote several acclaimed books, including *On the Genealogy of the Gods*, and composed two biographical dictionaries, *On the Fortunes of Great Men* and *On Famous Women*.

Successive generations of scholars maintained the momentum created by Petrarch and Boccaccio, unearthing increasingly significant texts from the Roman era. Men such as Coluccio Salutati, Giovanni Conversini, Niccolò Niccoli and Poggio Bracciolini brought to the world of learning a lengthy list of some of the most important ancient works of science and literature, including *Astronomica* by the Roman writer Manilius, Lucretius's *On the Nature of Things* and several books about mining and agriculture, including *Silvae* by Statius and *De re rustica* by Columella, which were to influence such luminaries as Leonardo, Brunelleschi and Alberti.

What was significant about these finds was that they were written in the original Latin, so that, for the first time, the Florentine elite of the late-fourteenth and early-fifteenth centuries could read the words of the great thinkers of the Classical era exactly as they had been written, rather than as fragments crudely translated by semi-educated monks.

In itself this was a tremendous advance, but perhaps even more important is the fact that when these works were translated and interpreted it was soon realised just how much Roman scholars had based their work on an older source: the golden era of Greek learning of between 500 and 250 BC. The inevitable result was a new and intensified search for the original Greek sources of knowledge. Aware of the virtues of this ancient learning, many of the richest people in Florence began to send emissaries abroad to locate and purchase on their behalf anything they could find in the original Greek.

Until this time the only original Greek manuscripts in Western European hands were a few fragments of Aristotle and scraps of Plato, along with some quite substantial tracts of Euclid, all of which were either jealously guarded by monks or in the hands of a few devotees. Petrarch himself was reputed to own an original manuscript of Homer, but could not read a word of it. Acknowledging the authority of the Roman writers to whom he referred, he regarded Homer as a great poet and kissed the book every night before retiring to bed.

During the first three decades of the fifteenth century several hundred original manuscripts found their way to Florence, largely from the East: where once Crusaders fought for Christendom, Western emissaries now bartered and purchased intellectual capital from the Turks. A single Florentine agent, Giovanni Aurispa, returned after one particularly fruitful voyage in 1423 with no fewer than 238 complete manuscripts.

In this way the intellectual community of Florence acquired complete versions of Aristotle's *Politics*, the histories of Herodotus, Plato's dialogues, Homer's *Iliad* and *Odyssey*, the plays of Sophocles and the medical writings of Hippocrates and Galen, as well as some of the most important books from the Greco-Roman tradition (from the first centuries AD), which had found their way from the library of Alexandria to wealthy collectors in Asia. Alongside these was a clutch of books that became hugely influential in shaping the earliest scientific ideas of natural philosophy in Renaissance Europe. Most important were Ptolemy's *Almagest* and *Geography*, which were brought to Italy in 1406 by the Florentine merchant Palla Strozzi. The *Geography* described cartographic techniques such as the measurement of distances on the surface of the earth, a skill that had been forgotten in the West during the fog of the Dark Ages.

The Florentines were now in possession of the greatest works of humankind in their original language, but one problem remained: no one could speak or read ancient Greek. As early as the 1360s Petrarch and Boccaccio had tried to introduce the language into intellectual circles in Florence, and although neither of them had understood Greek themselves, they tried to establish a chair of Greek at the Studio Fiorentino. They had failed, but two generations later and prompted by the stunning collection of original works now at their disposal, the heirs of the men who had financed the original search for books finally sanctioned a chair there. This was soon occupied by an eminent scholar, Emmanuel Chrysoloras of Constantinople.

And so the first of the great factors of change had been set in place. With accurate translations of a growing collection of Greek texts came the startling realisation that everything the Florentines had so far achieved culturally had been surpassed almost two millennia earlier by the Greeks. But, far from acting as a destructive force, this discovery inspired them to emulate and even to seek to improve on the achievements of the ancients.

In 1428 a committee was organised to instigate a series of changes to the education system of Florence. The existing curricula consisted of medicine, astrology, logic, grammar and law, and now to these were added moral philosophy and a professorship of rhetoric and poetry. This provided a new syllabus for every student in Florence and laid the foundation for the system that was adopted

throughout Europe and remained in place in the universities of
Italy, France and England until the eighteenth century.

Concurrently with these sweeping advances, many promising
young scholars were moving from other parts of Italy, and from as
far afield as England and Germany, to study and teach in Florence;
most in demand were aspiring Greek-speaking professors. And, in
turn, the changes in thinking that this brought about among many
of the city's most wealthy and politically powerful citizens had a
dramatic effect on the social structure of Florence.

In Italy, as in all parts of Europe that were touched by the
Renaissance, an awareness of what could be achieved and a belief
that humanity could do better than it had already done was a
tremendous spur. It was an era of action, of participation. This
optimistic spirit led to the age of discovery and the beginnings of
modern scientific thinking, as well as providing a fertile ground for
the artistic endeavours we now see as emblematic of the time.

The importance of this shift in perception cannot be overstated.
With a few notable exceptions (such as the thirteenth-century scientist and philosopher Roger Bacon) people since the fall of Rome
had been paralysed by a deep-rooted sense of unworthiness. As a
result of the influence of Christian dogma most people perceived
humans as being mere creatures of God, pawns in a world where
the forces of nature and the Divine Will were everything. Theirs
was a world in which the individual was utterly without signifi-
cance. Such thinking could lead nowhere but to a stagnant society,
and although the belief that God controlled the universe and was
directly involved in all aspects of human existence persisted until the
Darwinian revolution, some of those with influence during the
Renaissance thought very differently from their counterparts of
only two or three generations earlier.

Far from feeling insignificant and powerless, the thinkers of the
Renaissance believed wholeheartedly in the idea that human intellect should be treasured and nourished. In this shift we can see the

impact of Platonic philosophy evolving into what has been called 'human virtue', a central tenet of active humanism. At the heart of Platonic philosophy is the concept that humanity can find God through unravelling the secrets of Nature. For Plato this was the foundation of 'inspiration', and it became a crucial element in the thinking of many of the best minds of the Renaissance. Machiavelli, although unorthodox in his religious ideas, understood and accepted this Platonic ideal even though he disagreed with many other aspects of Platonic philosophy. And although many intellectuals requisitioned the notion of 'virtue' and integrated it into orthodox Christian doctrine, its origins were purely Classical.

In his *Oration on the Dignity of Man*, one of the most important humanists of the age, Pico della Mirandola, describes the philosophy of humanism brilliantly when he has God declare to Adam: 'You may have and possess whatever abode, form and functions that you might desire. The nature of all other beings is limited and constrained within the bounds of law prescribed by us. But you, constrained by no limits, in accordance with your own free will, in whose hand we have placed you, shall ordain for yourself the limits of your nature.'[3]

This journey from acquisition of ancient knowledge to the development of wisdom as a human need we may picture as a path followed by pure intellect, but it was also a crucial, if esoteric, influence on Florentine culture. Such a rediscovery of human worth led to new ways of perceiving the world and played an enormous role in influencing the way Machiavelli considered the world, helping him to imbue his work with a very modern and quite revolutionary ethos.

The three most important figures in the intellectual world of Machiavelli's boyhood were Giovanni Pico della Mirandola, Angelo Poliziano and Marsilio Ficino. Pico della Mirandola was a renowned writer and humanist philosopher, Poliziano and Ficino were famed for their translations of Greek and Latin texts, and all were close friends of Lorenzo de' Medici, who could hold his own with these great thinkers and is said to have shown comparable intellectual versatility.

All three of these intellectuals (and indeed Lorenzo himself) were also fascinated with mysticism and metaphysics, an interest Machiavelli later shared. At this time astrology was extremely popular and alchemy flourished, while respected academics such as Ficino (whose father had been Cosimo de' Medici's physician) wrote books on arcane occult subjects that were considered in the same light as respected philosophical tracts. Indeed most people of the time – not just intellectuals, but also the largely uneducated public – subscribed to an odd confection of strict Catholicism, pagan leftovers and a hotchpotch of occult traditions and superstition.

So much for the intellectual backdrop to Machiavelli's life. But a factor of equal importance to him, and indeed to the entire development of Florence, was the political evolution of the city, a complex tangle of power games, commerce and military aspirations that found a nexus in one crucial family, the Medici.

Some have viewed the most prominent members of the Medici as dictators and point to corruption and self-interest. But there is no doubt they were *the* family of Florence, its most important and influential citizens for some three centuries. They guided its destiny and steered its sometimes stormy course through the unfolding history of Europe; without them Florence would have been a pale reflection of its real self.

The first of the line to emerge into public prominence was Giovanni di Bicci de' Medici, who, in the early fourteenth century, created a bank specialising in making loans to the Catholic Church. It was Giovanni who was responsible for taking the Medici from middle-class respectability to their status as one of the wealthiest families in the city, and when he died he left an estimated one hundred thousand florins to his descendants. (Conversions of ancient currencies into modern values can only be approximate, but this sum was certainly not less than about £50 million today.)

Cosimo de' Medici, Giovanni's eldest son, was born in 1389. Although he quickly demonstrated an acute business sense and a gift for numbers and ledgers, he was far more interested in books and the new learning. Between the ages of fourteen and seventeen Cosimo was taught by a scholar of Greek, Roberto de Rossi, who excited his taste for ancient intellectual property just as Giovanni was preparing him to take up the baton at the bank. Egged on by Rossi, Cosimo approached his father with the suggestion that he might embark on a journey to the East with his friend Niccolò Niccoli to search for a collection of ancient manuscripts they had heard about. Needless to say, the request fell on deaf ears. Giovanni possessed just three books, the *Gospels*, *The Legend of St Margaret* and an obscure sermon in Italian, and he saw nothing of value in his son's enthusiasm. Within a few weeks of his eighteenth birthday the reluctant Cosimo was part of the family firm.

Cosimo became a superb banker. In fact he surpassed his father in almost all ways. He led the family business, increased the family's wealth enormously and became the most respected and admired figure in Florence; but he also kept faith with his love for the arts. Throughout his life Cosimo patronised artists, writers and musicians. He sponsored seats of learning and paid for his servants to scour Europe and the East for ancient manuscripts before financing their translation and the production of copies. In his own way this financier, a man who at first glance may have seemed interested in nothing more than account books and interest rates, did as much for the Renaissance as Titian, Leonardo or Brunelleschi.

Machiavelli made it clear just how important Cosimo de' Medici was to the cultural evolution of Florence and indeed Europe when he wrote:

Cosimo was also a lover and exalter of literary men; he therefore brought Agyropoulos to Florence, a man of Greek birth and very learned for those times, so that Florentine youth might

learn from him the Greek language and other teachings of his.
He took into his home Marsilio Ficino, second father of
Platonic philosophy, whom he loved extremely; and that Ficino
might pursue his studies of letters more comfortably and that he
might be able to use him more conveniently, Cosimo gave him a
property near his own in Careggi.[4]

Although Cosimo never became the official leader of the
Florentine state, he was, in all but name, the head of state. He
served on many of the committees that made up the government of
the time and he was the most influential of all Florentines. In addition he did much to improve the political structure of Florence
and overhaul the city's finances.

Thanks to the ill-conceived taxation laws and the ineffectual
means of calculating and collecting revenue, at the time Cosimo was
taking over the Medici bank Florence was facing serious economic
decline. By the mid-1450s the situation had become so bad that 82
per cent of Florentines paid no tax at all. Cosimo believed it was the
duty of the wealthy to set the standards for all the citizens of the
state and so he pushed for new tax laws that affected the rich banking and mercantile families of Florence more than anyone.
Throughout his career, from the 1450s until the 1480s, the Medici
paid increasingly large tax bills. In 1457 alone, Cosimo's personal
tax liability was 575 florins, in a year when only three other house-
holds in the whole of Florence paid a hundred florins or more.
His revenue payment for that year was more than four times that of
his nearest business competitors.

Cosimo de' Medici also did an enormous amount to provide
Florence with political and social stability during his time as head
of the family. He formed strong political alliances with his neighbours, most especially Milan, but also with two other powerful city
states, Rome and Venice. Furthermore, he forged strong links with
the financial institutions of other countries, and during in his

lifetime the Medici bank opened branches in France, Germany and England, all of which brought increased prosperity to the citizens of his beloved Florence.

In return, Cosimo appears to have been loved by his people. When he died, in 1464, many grieved and the judicial body known as the Ten of Liberty drafted an edict to honour him with the title Pater Patriae (Father of the State). This was inscribed on his surprisingly ordinary tomb in the crypt of the church of San Lorenzo.

Cosimo's son Piero succeeded to the leadership of the family and assumed the political role vacated by his father, but he was in almost all ways the very opposite of the Pater Patriae. He was weak both physically and intellectually, possessed little charisma or adventurousness of spirit, and died prematurely, just five years after Cosimo. This left the guidance of both the Medici family and the city of Florence in the hands of a twenty-year-old, Piero's son Lorenzo.

But those hands turned out to be very capable. Lorenzo de' Medici took his place at the head of the family in December 1469, and although he was Piero's immediate successor by genes and blood, he was in fact a throwback to the thrusting dynamism of his grandfather, in every way his true heir. He even emulated Cosimo's reluctance to go into banking and politics: his elevation to the position of 'first citizen' and head of the world's most important and wealthiest bank had been quite unexpected and the very opposite of what he had wanted.

The portraits and sculptures of Lorenzo show that he was an exceptionally ugly man, long of nose with prominent lips and hooded eyelids, but what he lacked in looks he more than made up for in intellect and creativity. He was a gifted writer and could count as his closest friends the extraordinary triumvirate of Pico della Mirandola, Marsilio Ficino and Angelo Poliziano. A true exemplar of the Renaissance love of diversity and eclecticism, Lorenzo not only became a highly successful banker in the family tradition and leader of Florence, but he composed forty-one love sonnets, wrote several acclaimed plays, was an accomplished architect, played the lyre and the organ to accompany his own compositions, was the most admired patron of the Arts in Europe and became famous for his philanthropy.

Machiavelli wrote of the Florentine leader, often known as Lorenzo the Magnificent:

> He loved marvellously anyone who was excellent in an art; he favoured men of letters . . . Hence, Count Giovanni della Mirandola, a man almost divine, left all the other parts of Europe where he had travelled and, attracted by the munificence of Lorenzo, made his home in Florence. Lorenzo took marvellous delight in architecture, music and poetry; and many poetic compositions not only composed but also commented on by him are in existence. And so that the Florentine youth might be trained in the study of letters, he opened in the city of Pisa a school to which the most excellent men in Italy then were brought.[5]

Twenty years younger than Lorenzo de' Medici, Machiavelli grew up in a Florence completely dominated by the man. The city's magnificent leader and wealthiest citizen followed the example of his grandfather by doing all he could to maintain its peace and prosperity, but in spite of all his efforts, Lorenzo seemed destined to become embroiled in political intrigue.

This began in 1471, when he was twenty-two. That year a Franciscan monk named Francesco della Rovere from a poor rural family became pope, taking the name Sixtus IV. He had been in office no more than a matter of months before he began to clash with Lorenzo, the young banker who, by controlling much of the flow of money in Europe, had the power to encourage or to clip the wings of kings and pontiffs.

Sixtus believed he should become more than a religious leader and moral guardian. He perceived himself as a leader of a temporal state, a warlord as well as a priest. He was also an immensely greedy and avaricious man who possessed few moral scruples and considered the expansion of the papal states to be his first priority. Within months of ascending to the papal throne Sixtus had set his sights on buying or even taking by force large stretches of the north-eastern region of Italy known as the Romagna which he wanted for his nephew, Girolamo Riario, whom he planned to install there as a puppet leader. (The Romagna was never officially defined, but it was contained approximately by the River Po to the north and extending south almost to Rimini and west to the Apennines.) However, such a scheme cost money, and although in recent decades the papacy had become as rich as it had ever been (in no small part thanks to the guidance provided by the Medici bank), Sixtus was obliged to go to Lorenzo to ask for a loan of forty thousand ducats (in today's terms about £6 million).

As far as Lorenzo and the Florentines were concerned, Sixtus's plans were unhealthy and would not only compromise their trade routes, which for centuries had run through the Romagna to Venice, but also threatened to destabilise Italy after years of careful democracy and statesmanship had secured peace in the region. It quickly became clear to all that this new pope, in proposing his plans, was motivated solely by self-interest and had little concern for the subtle balance of power in Italy. For this reason Lorenzo felt entirely justified in turning Sixtus down.

In response Sixtus felt equally justified in sacking his banker, which he did straight away. But this was a move that did nothing to help his aims, and he knew he had lost the first battle. Frustrated and furious, he was unable to raise funds elsewhere for his scheme and retreated to lick his wounds. His simmering hatred for Lorenzo, whom he described as 'an evil, undutiful man who defies us', prompted him to declare publicly his wish to change the Florentine regime and have the Medici overthrown.

For six years friction between Rome and Florence chafed at diplomacy and the everyday course of Italian politics. Then, on 26 April 1478, an unseasonably warm, clear-skied Sunday, one week before his ninth birthday, Machiavelli, along with all the other sixty-thousand inhabitants of Florence, was stunned by the news that Lorenzo had almost been killed in an assassination attempt which, if not exactly engineered by Sixtus, had gone unopposed by the Holy See.

Four assassins had been hired by Sixtus's nephew, Girolamo Riario, and the plan had been hatched by two senior churchmen. One of these was the Pope's most loyal servant, Cardinal Raffaello, and the other was the Archbishop of Pisa, Francesco Salviati. Yet, in spite of the involvement of such powerful figures, the attempt on the life of Lorenzo de' Medici was an extremely amateurish exercise that was doomed to failure before it had even begun. This much is clear from the description Machiavelli himself wrote in his book *The Discourses* (*Discourses on the First Ten Books of Titus Livy*), in which he tells of the bungled start of the operation:

> The conspiracy of the Pazzi against Lorenzo and Giuliano de' Medici is familiar to all. The order given was that they give a breakfast for the Cardinal of San Giorgio and kill them at that breakfast, in which it had been assigned who had to kill them, who had to seize the palace, and who had to run through the city and call the people to freedom. It befell that when the Pazzi, the Medici and the cardinal were in the cathedral church in Florence for a solemn office, it was understood that Giuliano was not breakfasting there that morning. That made the conspirators assemble together, and what they had to do in the house of the Medici they decided to do in the church. That came to disturb the whole order because Giovambatista da Montesecco did not wish to share in the homicide, saying that he did not wish to do it in a church. So they had to change new ministers in every

action, who did not have time to firm up their spirits and made such errors that in its execution they were crushed.[6]

Having had their plan ruined, the assassins struck with daggers in the cathedral soon after Lorenzo and his younger brother, Giuliano, had attended mass. Giuliano died on the cathedral floor from his wounds, but a dagger thrust to Lorenzo's throat was deflected and it pierced his neck. Fearing the dagger tip was poisoned, Lorenzo's friend, Antonio Ridolfi, who had been attending mass with the Medici brothers, sucked the wound clean and, dragging Giuliano with them, they escaped through a secret passageway leading from the cathedral to the Medici palace.

There was pandemonium in Florence. Within hours everyone had heard the dreadful news and a manhunt for the murderers was underway. In his *Florentine Histories* Machiavelli tells us that 'there was no citizen armed or unarmed who did not go to the houses of Lorenzo in that necessity, and each one offered himself and his property to him'.[7] Although this was probably an exaggeration (an account designed to humour the Medici pope who commissioned the book some forty years after the event), the assassins had little chance and were soon apprehended.

That day riots broke out, and for about a week after the attack Florence teetered on the brink of civil war. But the Medici were too popular to be under any serious threat and when it was quickly discovered that some of the conspirators had come from the Pazzi, a rival family to the Medici, Lorenzo's position was greatly strengthened. The Pazzi, immensely rich and powerful in their own right, were ostracised for their involvement in the murder of Giuliano and the attempt on Lorenzo's life. The family name was struck from the register and their emblem destroyed. Surviving members of the family changed their names and it was not until some two decades later that the family was rehabilitated and accepted back into Florentine society.

The conspiracy failed in part because the Medici were the most popular leading family in the city but also because Lorenzo's advisers and protectors were swift and ruthless in the way they persuaded him to deal with the assassins. All the conspirators were executed except Cardinal Raffaello, who was discovered to have been an unwitting pawn in the whole affair; he was spared by Lorenzo himself. The true leader of the attempted uprising was Archbishop Salviati. He was caught attempting to escape the city, and after a cursory trial he was hanged, along with his hirelings, from the windows of the Palazzo della Signoria, the home of the city's ruling council of ministers. There he was left for several days until he began to stink and carrion crows had plucked out his eyes.

During the fifteenth century children were not spared the grisly facts of life, and so Machiavelli would certainly have seen the hanged man and, along with the other kids from the streets around the Signoria, he would have mocked the hated figure. Indeed very few in Florence missed the spectacle. Leonardo da Vinci, who in 1473 was studying under Verrocchio at the master's studio in Via de Agnolo, close to the cathedral and the Signoria, drew the archbishop dangling from a rope and the image has survived to this day in his notebooks.

Although the death of his brother was a tragedy for Lorenzo, this incident was an event that did much for his personal image and his credibility. During the remaining years of his life (he died at the age of forty-three) he continued to maintain stability in Florence and its dominions, and through diplomacy and intelligent political manoeuvring he won battle after battle with Sixtus. When the Pope died in 1484, Lorenzo became a close ally of his successor, Innocent VIII, and within thirty years his own son, Giovanni, had became pontiff, taking the name Leo X.

Under Lorenzo de' Medici Florence flourished and its people lived a better life than they had ever experienced before. This meant that the childhood of Machiavelli, although constrained by the limited fortunes of his father, was nevertheless a secure and stable one. It was a brief peaceful era sandwiched between revolution and wars and it ended with Lorenzo's death in 1492, a month before Machiavelli's twenty-third birthday.

The downside of benign leadership provided by successive generations of Medici was that Florence had grown complacent, its perception of the world and its place in it had been tainted by peace and relative prosperity. It was a gorgeous city, travellers tarried there long and its reputation as a great centre of learning, a womb for artists, writers, musicians and philosophers, was peerless and cherished by its citizens. But it was a city that was completely defenceless and open to abuse from without. While Lorenzo was in power Florence was steered carefully through the turbulent political changes of the era. When he died it suddenly became very vulnerable and at the same time the power of the Medici was greatly diminished.

Lorenzo's son and successor, the hapless Piero, had been thrown into the centre of a political whirlwind, and to ride out such a storm Florence needed a leader with far greater talent and personal resources than he could offer. Within months of Lorenzo's death, a French army led by King Charles VIII had crossed the Alps and was preparing to enter Florence. Piero immediately took the lead and organised a meeting to negotiate terms. In a bizarre encounter at San Stefano on 31 October 1494 the totally inexperienced Piero decided unilaterally to agree to every single one of Charles's demands without question or argument. Returning to Florence and leaving the French monarch stunned, Piero, who had expected a hero's welcome for having saved the city, instead found the gates of the Palazzo Vecchio locked to him. Bewildered, he then narrowly escaped being lynched by a justifiably furious mob before he fled to his palace. That night Piero, along with his two brothers, Giovanni and Giuliano, was spirited away into exile.

The turmoil Florence suffered immediately after Lorenzo's death was merely exacerbated by the fumbling ineptitude of his

son, and with the French bearing down on the city and the
Florentines in a state of near panic, it was a time during which
almost anything could have happened. In such circumstances it is
often the case that an individual with extraordinary charisma, a
strong message and some intelligence may grasp the reins of power
and rise far higher and faster than anyone could have dreamed
in simpler, calmer times. Such a man was the Dominican friar
Girolamo Savonarola, who arrived on the political scene in
November 1494.

Little is known of Savonarola's childhood or indeed his early
career. He was born in Ferrara in 1452 and was an adopted
Florentine, arriving in the city in 1481 after a spell at a Dominican
monastery in Bologna. From his earliest public appearances it was
clear that he was an extremist, but he was eloquent and forceful and
he came to prominence with perfect timing. With the city leaderless
and facing invasion, the Florentine nobles who formed the frac-
tured elements of government elected a group of representatives
to negotiate with Charles VIII a peaceful settlement to the crisis.
Savonarola was one of the five men sent on this mission and he was
closely involved with the truce that was quickly agreed. Shortly
after the group returned to Florence, an election was held and
Savonarola found himself the new head of state.

At first glance Savonarola's rise to power seems to have been a
curious anomaly, but on reflection it is easy to see how it happened. The city needed a figurehead who would appease the many
factions in the ruling class. As a religious man Savonarola was
seen as impartial, a man who apparently served a higher authority.
He had proven himself to be an able negotiator during the encounters with the French king and he was an extremely charismatic
man, described by Francesco Guicciardini in his *History of Florence*
as 'an eloquent speaker'. Most importantly, though, he had popular support from the citizens of Florence as well as from many of
the political elite.

Savonarola's charisma and his ability to captivate an audience should not be under-estimated as a factor in his success. Public oratory was an extremely important form of political control in Florence during this time. At the beginning of every new term of office the city's leader spoke in Tuscan from the balcony of the Palazzo Vecchio to large crowds assembled in the Piazza della Signoria, and the success or failure of this event could do much to shape popular opinion about the man then controlling the city.

Even though Lorenzo had done much to improve the image and the reputation of Florence and had brought the city great wealth and prosperity, Savonarola inherited a government that was in disarray. Amazingly for a city as sophisticated as Florence, there was no written constitution and the structure of government was unwieldy and open to corruption. Florence had been a republic since 1115 and its political structure was based very loosely on a primitive form of democracy that had changed little for nearly four centuries. The head of state, the gonfalonier, was leader of the Signoria, a council made up of himself and eight ministers. These ministers, or priors, came from the wealthiest and most honoured families from each of the four quarters of the city, and they were chosen by means of drawing names from a hat. As only the key rich and powerful figures were allowed in the running, the system had always been a closed shop.

Beneath this top tier of government there was a pair of assemblies: the Council of the Commune and the Council of the People, made up of two hundred and three hundred citizens respectively. These were elected by popular vote. However, the electorate was small, consisting of some six thousand men called 'citizens', all professional men aged over twenty-five and members of guilds. There was also a large number of separate elected councils that dealt with specific political tasks. These included the legislative body known as the Twelve Good Men (*Buonomini*) and the Ten of War (approximately equivalent to a department of Britain's Foreign

Office of today). Enamoured with the seeming modernity of this system, Leonardo Bruni, a great patriot and supporter of all things Florentine, declared in 1428 that in his native city 'equal liberty exists for all – the hope of gaining high office and to rise is the same for all'.[8]

Although Bruni's assertion was far from the truth, the Florentine system was, compared with any other state in Europe except for Venice, the most liberal and sophisticated of the Renaissance. Even so, it was badly flawed. First, the term of any political office was too short; a gonfalonier, for example, could serve for only two months. Second, the election of representatives was restricted to only the wealthiest and oldest families, who completely monopolised the system.

One of Savonarola's first acts as head of state was to establish a Great Council (*Maggior Consiglio*) and a new constitution modelled on the Venetian system. He kept the office of gonfalonier, which bore comparison to the Venetian Doge, except that in Florence the leader (along with the rest of the Signoria) was elected to sit for a term of just one year (rather than for life, as was the case in Venice). The Florentine system of councils was also revised under Savonarola, becoming a slightly more modern version of the Venetian paradigm in that the Great Council included middle-class, land-owning males and was no longer run exclusively by the representatives of a handful of elite families.

For all his efforts, Savonarola's government was far from united. In the Signoria different factions vied for power. The Whites (*Bianchi*) were pure republicans and the most vocal advocates of the new constitution, while the Greys (*Bigi*) were completely opposed to it and remained loyal to the Medici. Savonarola also had vehement enemies in the form of the 'Rabid' (*Arrabiati*), as well as close followers, the 'Monkish ones' (*Frateschi*), who clashed with the other three groups. This last faction had many nicknames, including 'the Blubbers' (*Piagnoni*).

Savonarola's theocracy lasted just four years. For many it began with promise, but it quickly degenerated into a horrible distortion of civilised government. Although Savonarola had risen on a groundswell of popular support, for many this had been simply a reaction to the fear and uncertainty of the times. Given a mandate and some temporary support, Savonarola applied his ideology in increasingly extreme form. He sanctioned the burning of books and his supporters led a witch-hunt against artists, writers and free-thinkers. Any work of art deemed to offer sacrilegious images was destroyed and all creative endeavours were purged.

As Savonarola expounded his political views from the gonfalonier's throne in the Palazzo della Signoria, he also continued to preach his ideas from the pulpit, his sermons moving from the extreme to the demented. His enemies were imprisoned and tortured, the irreligious and the heretical met the same fate as the books and paintings his new government deemed sacrilegious: all consumed in flames in the Signoria.

But Savonarola had some powerful enemies and they were soon to instigate his fall from grace. Not limiting his criticism to those Florentines he considered morally bankrupt, Savonarola attacked two parties who had huge influence and the ruthless energy needed to crush him. The first of these were the wealthy of Florence, whom Savonarola criticised for their materialism. He preached the belief that money and property should not be hoarded by the few and condemned tradesmen and merchants, small businessmen and the heads of banks and large companies, making enemies in almost every corner of Florentine society save the very poor, who had absolutely no power.

The second party to be offended by Savonarola was Pope Alexander VI. Savonarola had begun to criticise Alexander years before his election to the head of the Florentine government and had angered many in the Vatican. After acquiring power he had turned his unalloyed invective towards Rome, and backed it up with his new-found political clout, causing embarrassment among the cardinals and inciting the fury of the Pope himself.

In 1495, within a few months of becoming leader of Florence, Savonarola had been called to Rome. But he was familiar with Church history, and he was certainly no fool. He ignored Alexander and remained in Florence, where he defiantly stepped up his anti-papal commentary. By 1497 the Pope, unable to subject Savonarola to the hot poker and the strappado in his torture chambers in Rome, turned instead to the spiritual weapon of excommunication to try to bring the man into line. This edict forbade Savonarola from preaching and put in jeopardy the soul of anyone who ignored Alexander by assisting the friar in any way.

Even then, for a while at least, Savonarola was able to brazen it out. In the summer of 1497 he was elected back into government for a fourth term and survived thanks to the continuing divisions within the Signoria and because there was no one in Florence who could adequately oppose him. The Pope fumed and raged but, thwarted by geography, using purely ecclesiastical means he could no longer hope to win his battle with Savonarola.

Alexander's anger was exacerbated by political imperatives. He was opposed to the French, who he quite rightly believed to be a danger to the stability of the region, and as a consequence he disapproved of the stance taken by the Florentine government, who were following a policy of co-operation with the French. Later Alexander was to become a close ally of France for a short time, and his son, Cesare Borgia, was employed as a princely condottiere for Charles's successor, Louis XII. But in 1497 his distrust of the French, combined with his personal hatred of Savonarola, drove him to extraordinary measures.

Behind the scenes Alexander began to manipulate the political life of Florence in a way no other pope had succeeded in doing before. He knew that his greatest allies in the Republic were the elite families, who were enraged by Savonarola and fearful that they might lose their status and wealth if his theocratic government was to be allowed to survive much longer. Deftly fabricating a temporary alliance between this powerful group and other factions opposed to Savonarola, the Pope was instrumental in the rebellion against him that began early in 1498.

In the elections that spring Savonarola lost much of his political support, but, crucially, he was also becoming unpopular with the Florentine people. The final blow to his regime came on 7 April, when his most influential ally, Charles VIII, died suddenly, leaving the priest in the wilderness. Savonarola was arrested, tortured and, along with two of his closest supporters, Fra Domenico and Fra Silvestro, he was burned in the Piazza della Signoria on 23 May 1498.

With Savonarola gone, there was no repeat of the chaos of 1494. It was as though the city had awoken from a bad dream. Many of those who had supported the fanatical cleric readily cast off the spectre of the past four years as if they had snapped out of a trace. There was no gargantuan figure to take a grip on things and in spite of concerted efforts from the Greys within the Signoria, the citizens of Florence were in no mood to accept the return of the Medici.

The Florentines had seen little stability since the death of Lorenzo and they were tired of the upheaval. No one cherished the roller-coaster ride of political chaos, few businesses thrived during such uncertain times and the good people of the city craved peace so that they could get on with their own lives. In such an environment the ascension of conservative, steady leadership often goes unhindered, especially when there are no extraordinary political figures to take on an heroic role.

With the passing of Savonarola, the Florentine alliance with the French held good and many of the city's political elite returned to suspecting the motives and machinations of the Pope, whose interference they had needed but resented. The factions within the Signoria remained, altered only in the details, and a new government, a fresh and prosperous republic, took the place of the theocracy that, in such a short time, had done so much damage to Florentine society.

Within this government there were many new faces, men who had risen through the ranks unsullied by Savonarola as well as new bright stars in the political firmament who appeared to have sprung from nowhere. One of this latter group was the new Secretary to the Second Chancery, a young man named Niccolò Machiavelli.

3

In at the Deep End

Machiavelli had been no fan of Savonarola. In a letter to a friend dated 9 March 1498, less than three months before the friar's execution, he described attending a sermon given by Savonarola in which the preacher delivered one of his typical fire-and-brimstone tirades. Although impressed by the man's delivery and his genuine passion, Machiavelli was sceptical of his motivations and aims. 'He has changed coats,' he wrote. 'Now that he understands that he no longer needs to act in this way [afraid of his adversaries because matters had already gone too far]. So, he urges them to the union that was initiated, and he no longer mentions the tyrant or the wickedness of people; he seeks to set all of them at odds with the Supreme Pontiff and, turning toward him and his attacks, says of the Pope what could be said of the wickedest person you might imagine.'[1]

Machiavelli makes his judgement even clearer in *The Prince* when he dismisses Savonarola with the observation:

Moses, Cyrus, Theseus, and Romulus would not have been able to have their institutions respected a long time if they had been unarmed, as was the case in our time with Fra Girolamo Savonarola who came to grief with his new institutions when the crowd started to lose faith in him, and he had no way of holding fast those who had believed or of forcing the incredulous to believe. Men such as he have considerable difficulty in achieving their ends, and the most dangerous time for them is when they are still striving; but once they have succeeded and begin to be venerated, having destroyed those who were envious of their abilities, they stay powerful, secure, respected and happy.[2]

In Machiavelli's eyes Savonarola had made two major mistakes: he had not created a militia to protect himself and he had not destroyed, nor could he have destroyed, all those opposed to him, most especially Pope Alexander VI.

As Savonarola's regime was folding in on itself, Machiavelli would almost certainly have made clear his opinion of the cleric, who had made so many mistakes and caused such chaos. Indeed the fact that Machiavelli was never perceived as a supporter of Savonarola served him well. Just four days after the friar's execution and with a new government in place, the Council of Eighty (a group of senior officials responsible for advising the Signoria and appointing high-ranking government representatives) and the Great Council of the Republic of Florence made him Secretary to the Second Chancery.

This was an extremely important job. As Secretary, Machiavelli was effectively head of the Second Chancery. The First Chancery, which was considered senior to the Second, was responsible for foreign affairs and matters of war, while the Second Chancery dealt with all matters relating to internal affairs and domestic bureaucracy. However, although the roles played by the two different chanceries were originally clearly delineated in this way, by the time of Machiavelli's appointment, in June 1498, their remits often overlapped. Because of this, the best way to describe the functioning of the First and Second Chanceries at this time is to say that between them they dealt with all matters of state, both domestic and foreign, but that for much of the time not even the secretaries and staff of the two departments could have stated accurately who was officially responsible for what.

Like most political positions within the Florentine government, that of Secretary to either chancery (or Florentine Secretary, as the post was sometimes called) was subject to an annual re-election after a first term of office of two years. The holder of the position could remain in power for many years if they performed well and were popular. The only way career politicians who were well liked, efficient and successful might lose their jobs was through a dramatic regime change.

The primary role of both Secretaries was to support the gonfalonier and the eight ministers of the Signoria. They read and filtered correspondence and other documents, prepared summaries and drafted letters of state. They dealt with the mundane matters of government and prepared and primed the leading politicians of the day. In order to perform these functions each Secretary was given a large staff of civil servants and scribes.

Both Secretaries were well paid, but the fact that the First Chancery was regarded as superior to the Second was reflected in a higher salary. The head of the First Chancery, a man of considerable power and influence within the Florentine government, was at this time Marcello Virgilio Adriani, who was paid 330 *fiorini di suggello* or florins (today equivalent to about £150,000) a year. He had two assistants, each paid eighty florins. Machiavelli received a salary of 192 florins (about £90,000) and had two assistants, Agostino Vespucci and Andrea di Romolo, who drew salaries of ninety-six and sixty florins respectively. In addition, there were scores of other executives working under these senior figures within each chancery.

For historians, the greatest mystery of Machiavelli's early life is how exactly he managed to land such a prestigious job. The position of Secretary to the Second Chancery was usually reserved for highly regarded and experienced lawyers and doctors who had been working within the political forum for many years. For example, Machiavelli's assistants at the chancery, Vespucci and Romolo, were both youngish men in 1498, but each was a practising lawyer and had worked his way through the ranks to become an experienced and seasoned civil servant.

Machiavelli was not a trained lawyer and probably had only a limited experience of politics. But what the young Machiavelli did have was a set of very useful contacts and a talent for networking. Furthermore, he was an eloquent, likeable, extremely quick-witted man who knew the importance of making himself popular.

The key to Machiavelli's surprising elevation into the upper reaches of government lies in the confraternity of which he and his father were members, and in the many good friendships Bernardo Machiavelli had cultivated over the years. Through the confraternity Niccolò rubbed shoulders with members of the elite families of Florence, and as a young man he would have played some small role in the political life of his *quartiere*. However, the most crucial factor in Machiavelli's elevation to a political career was first his father's and then his own close association with certain key members of the Medici family.

It is known that Bernardo did not support many of the political views held by Lorenzo de' Medici, but he was never openly opposed to the regime. One of his closest friends was the humanist politician Bartolomeo Scala, who had been the Secretary to the First Chancery from 1464 to 1497, a remarkable term of office which had seen him in the service of three different heads of state, Piero de' Medici, Lorenzo the Magnificent and Savonarola.

Clearly Scala served as an invaluable link between Bernardo's aspirations for his son and Niccolò's successful election, and it is almost certain that in the years leading up to his appointment Niccolò had worked closely with him at the Palazzo Vecchio, learning the ropes and acquiring many of the skills he would need for the future. Scala also provided an entrée into the Medici inner circle.

Niccolò certainly knew and mixed with the younger members of the family and there is compelling evidence to support the idea that he was at one time a member of the Medici court. In or around 1492 Machiavelli composed a set of three poems that were included in a little booklet in which there also appeared ten poems by Lorenzo and one by the famous intellectual Angelo Poliziano. One of Machiavelli's poems is dedicated to the adolescent Giuliano de' Medici, who was thirteen in 1492, and this dedication implies that Giuliano and Niccolò knew each other, even if they were not necessarily close friends.[3]

The Medici offered the link Niccolò needed to find support from other rich families. Key figures in his elevation included the lawyer (and later diplomat) Agostino Vespucci, who became a lifelong friend. Another was a young notary and nobleman named Ugolino de Martelli. Both Vespucci and Martelli worked for Niccolò when he took up his position as Secretary to the Second Chancery.

Even more important was Alamanno Salviati, the son-in-law of Piero de' Medici and one of the most influential and respected men in Florence. Salviati was to remain an invaluable ally and supporter of Machiavelli for many years until the two men fell out in 1506, some eight years after Niccolò's election.

Equally influential was Niccolò's immediate superior, Marcello Virgilio Adriani, who had replaced the elderly Bartolomeo Scala at the First Chancery. Adriani had been appointed to the post of Secretary to the First Chancery during the last Savonarola election in January 1498 and he had remained in power for over two decades, always surfing with skill the tides of political change that swept over Florence during his lifetime. He had been an academic and it is possible that he had taught Machiavelli at the Studio Fiorentino. Adriani was another close ally of the Medici and a friend of Bernardo Machiavelli.

Further evidence that Niccolò and Bernardo had links with some influential people comes from the oldest surviving fragment of a document in Machiavelli's hand. This is a pair of letters written in Latin in which, at the age of twenty-eight, and some seven months before becoming Florentine Secretary, he appears to have taken on the role of representative for the Machiavelli family. The letters, dated 1 and 2 December 1497, concern a dispute over the appointment of a family member, Francesco Machiavelli, to a church property outside Florence. It appears that he had been granted the appointment by the regional church authorities, but that this was then contested by the rich and powerful Pazzi family (who had returned to their former respected position after the failed assassination attempt on the life of Lorenzo two decades earlier). The Pazzi wrote to the Cardinal of Perugia, Giovanni Lopez, to lodge their complaint and threw their considerable weight behind an annulment of Francesco Machiavelli's appointment.

The letter of 2 December is a formal appeal to the cardinal to reject the claims of the Pazzi, but the letter of the day before is more interesting, not only for its wording but also for the fact that here Machiavelli is clearly making an appeal for help from an influential Florentine figure. It begins with respectful mentions of the help already provided to the Machiavellis by whoever the intended recipient might have been. Then Niccolò continues:

> I shall write nothing other than to encourage, beg and pray that you do not cease until our efforts have a happy outcome. Towards this end I ask that you show your might, and use all your might; for if we, mere pygmies, are attacking giants, a much greater victory is in store for us than for them. For them inasmuch as it is base to compete, so it will be a very base thing to give in; we on the other hand, shall consider it not so ignominious a thing to be beaten, as it is honourable to have competed, especially having a competitor at whose nod everything is done immediately. Wherefore, whatever outcome Fortune may reserve for us, we shall not regret having failed in such endeavours.[4]

This letter is intriguing for many reasons. First, it shows that Niccolò, not his father, was considered the family representative; this was almost certainly because of the shadow that still lay over Bernardo's past. More importantly, it casts light on Niccolò's view of the world shortly before he was placed in one of the most senior positions in the Florentine civil service. To him, families like his were mere 'pygmies' compared with the likes of the Pazzi, who were 'giants'. Such a statement shows clearly how Machiavelli understood well his place in the scheme of things, but it also illustrates how he resisted it. He was already aware that he had to fight for what he believed was right and that he could never simply lie down and let 'giants' walk all over him.

Frustratingly, the identity of the intended recipient is open to question, but it was probably a person of similar rank to the Pazzi, quite possibly a senior Medici, who would perhaps help his friend Niccolò covertly. If this is true, it dovetails neatly with the evidence that the Medici were the prime movers in placing Machiavelli in his surprisingly lofty government position little more than half a year after this incident.

In fact it was on his second attempt that Machiavelli acquired the job of Secretary to the Second Chancery. In February 1498, while Savonarola was clinging to his last vestiges of power, the annual election had brought one of the friar's supporters to the position, Alessandro Braccesi. In that election seven candidates had stood, one of whom was Machiavelli. When Savonarola was deposed and executed, a new government under the influence of the Medici (but not led by a Medici family member) was hastily created after an extraordinary election.

Machiavelli took to the job as if he had been born to it. Surviving letters that passed between him and his staff during their early days working together show that he was well liked and trusted. Furthermore, he appears to have encountered no trace of enmity among his colleagues, which is perhaps surprising given his promotion over the heads of men who were older and far better qualified. There is also no escaping the impression that Machiavelli emerged from the shadows fully formed as a great political figure, a supreme diplomat and organiser. Before 1498 we see only flashes of him, visions of a boy playing on the streets of Florence with the others of the neighbourhood, running through fields around the family's country home, or as an adult joking with his father. Then we catch snatches of him playing a role in his confraternity, writing poetry at the Medici court, taking on responsibility for the family's bureaucratic entanglements. But from 1498 everything is brought into sharp focus. From this time on everything is documented. We have hundreds of letters, we have diaries and memoirs, we have recollections documented in later life to add flesh to his career, and we have the accounts and comments of others close to him. Suddenly Machiavelli's vital presence may be felt, and he comes alive.

Machiavelli's earliest biographer, Pasquale Villari, wrote a description of how he perceived Niccolò to be as he took up the role of Florentine Secretary, and it offers us a clear image of the man. 'Of middle height, slender figure, sparkling eyes, dark hair, rather a small head, a slightly aquiline nose, a tightly closed mouth. All about him bore the impress of a wry accurate observer and thinker,' Villari wrote. 'He could not easily rid himself of the sarcastic expression continually playing around his mouth and flashing from his eyes, which gave him the air of a cold impassible calculator; while nevertheless he was frequently ruled by his powerful imagination; sometimes led away by it to an extent befitting the most fantastic of visionaries.'[5]

For a year Machiavelli had plenty to do adjusting to the job and dealing with matters close to home, most especially the work needed to stabilise the state after the political and social unrest of recent years. A month after his appointment to the Second Chancery Machiavelli was made Secretary to the Ten of War, the government committee most directly responsible for dealing with foreign affairs, diplomatic relations and military campaigns. This role was absorbed into his job at the chancery with no extra salary or benefits, but it added to his workload and offered greater responsibility. It was also the part of the job that led him to travel widely as a roving ambassador, a diplomat at large for the Florentine Republic.

Machiavelli's first mission outside Florence came in March 1499, when he was sent to resolve a conflict that had arisen between the Signoria and a military commander, Jacopo d'Appiano, Lord of Piombino, a small coastal town some sixty miles south-west of Florence. D'Appiano had demanded an increase in funding and more men at arms under his command in order to fulfil his role as condottiere for the Florentine state. Machiavelli was to talk to him and make it clear that there was no more money available and no reinforcements on their way; but at the same time he needed to do everything he could to prevent him feeling alienated or his services in any way abused.

Machiavelli found Lord Piombino to be a surprisingly unsophisticated character, and described him as a man who 'spoke well, judged ill, acted worse'.[6] D'Appiano proved no match for Machiavelli's diplomatic skills and after two carefully steered discussions held at a military camp at Pontedera, a small town near Pisa, the Florentine envoy was able to report back to his government that matters had been smoothed with d'Appiano, who had accepted the fact that there was no more money to be had from the Republic.

This was a gratifying success for Machiavelli and did much to build his confidence. However, his second foreign assignment, a visit to the court of Caterina Sforza Riario, Countess of Imola and Forli, proved to be much more of a challenge.

Caterina, the illegitimate niece of the Duke of Milan and widow of Count Girolamo Riario, was an astonishing woman and Machiavelli came to have enormous admiration for her. (Girolamo Riario had been one of the conspirators behind the assassination attempt on Lorenzo de' Medici and with the help of his uncle,

Sixtus IV, he had taken control of the city of Imola some two decades before Machiavelli's visit to Caterina.) In the mould of Boudicca and with a touch of Joan of Arc about her, Caterina was a famous beauty even as she entered middle age, but she was a woman who was constantly let down and abused by the men with whom she associated. Her husband, Riario, had been an avaricious thug who was murdered by a faction of his own militia. But Caterina had the courage and the brains to defend herself against the enemies of her family. Under threat from these conspirators and realising that the key to their success in taking over her dominion lay in the occupation of a particular fortress at Ravaldino, she persuaded them to let her enter the fortress alone, claiming that she would hand it over to them. The conspirators did not trust her and demanded she leave her children with them as hostages. She agreed to this, but as soon as she entered the fortress she took to the battlements and turned on her enemies, declaring she would exact her revenge on them. When they threatened her with the execution of her children, she lifted her skirts, showed them her genitals and declared that they could go ahead, she had the means to make more of them.

Remarkably, the bluff worked, Caterina won the day and the rebellion was put down. By 1499, when Machiavelli met her for the first time, her children had all grown up and she had ruled Imola and Forli alone for almost a dozen years. However, her kingdom was small, barely able to hold its own and wholly dependent on the Florentines for protection against greedy neighbours on all sides.

Caterina had been on friendly terms with Florence for many years, but she had no liking for the French, who in the summer of 1499 were poised ready to attack and conquer her uncle's kingdom of Milan some 160 miles to the north-west. She knew she was in an extremely vulnerable position, but one of her greatest assets was her son Ottaviano, who was a renowned and respected condottiere with a small but well-trained and well-equipped army. He had been fighting as a mercenary for Florence and during the past two years he had helped it to win a series of important campaigns. The reason for Machiavelli's visit was to renegotiate Ottaviano's contract with the Signoria. However, the matter was complicated by the fact that the cash-strapped Florentine government was trying to make Caterina and her son agree to a cut in his salary.

Caterina was a woman motivated almost solely by principle and she was not best pleased with the suggestion that Ottaviano, who had done so much for Florence, should be treated as a mere servant and have his contract altered for the worse. But, equally, she was in a dangerous position and needed Florence to offer at least some protection should the French turn her way or if she came under threat from elsewhere. The grip of the acquisitive Cesare Borgia, the captain general of the papal army, on central Italy (funded and supported by his father, Alexander VI, as well as by the French) was growing tighter by the day.

It appears that from the start Machiavelli and Caterina got on very well, and two decades after their first meeting he wrote highly of her in both *The Art of War* and the *Florentine Histories*. Machiavelli spent a week at Caterina's court, where he was treated with honour, but his efforts were hampered by the fact that the Signoria would not sanction officially any guarantees to protect the cities of Imola and Forli should they be attacked. This was a crucial condition for Caterina, and because Machiavelli could do nothing to alter the policy of the Signoria, she broke off the negotiations, leaving him with no choice but to return to Florence empty-handed.

Although he had failed to produce a happy outcome for all concerned, this unsuccessful mission did Machiavelli no harm. The Signoria preferred to lose Ottaviano rather than increase his salary. But for Caterina it was to prove a disaster. Within six months of the meeting with Machiavelli, Imola and Forli were conquered by the armies of Cesare Borgia and Caterina was sent to Rome in chains. The Pope, who called her 'the Amazon of Forli', kept her locked up for a year until she finally renounced her rights over her twin cities and moved to Florence. There she married Giovanni di Pierfrancesco de' Medici and by him had a son, Giovanni delle Bande Nere, who became the founder of the only ducal line of the Medici family to survive to this day.

For the following year, between the summer of 1499 and July 1500, almost all of Machiavelli's energies were concentrated on a conflict that had been recently rekindled between Florence and Pisa, some forty miles to the west. The conflict had really begun almost a century earlier, in 1406, when Florence had taken the city by force. Pisa was a hugely important resource for Florentine trade, providing the Republic with access to major sea routes. Since then it had became a pawn in the struggles between greater powers. Venice had been eyeing this key region of Tuscany for years, and with its huge naval resources it could have taken Pisa quite easily had it not been held in check by the French.

In 1494, as Savonarola was taking over the leadership of Florence, a French army had invaded northern Italy for the first time. Florence bowed to their military superiority and as part of the negotiated peace Charles VIII handed Pisa back to the Pisans. This caused great resentment within the Republic, and when Charles died Florence immediately pushed for Pisa to be returned to it. Understandably, the Pisans, who under the French had been granted a significant degree of autonomy for the first time in a century, resisted, and so began an expensive, bloody struggle that was to drag on for years and cost the lives of thousands.

Since the fall of Savonarola and the change of regime in the summer of 1498, Florence had been preoccupied with internal affairs and had left the problem of Pisa to simmer. But once Florence had found some form of political stability the government decided it was time to flex its muscles. However, because there was no such thing as a Florentine citizens' army, the Signoria was obliged to hire expensive and often inefficient mercenaries. The Pisan resistance, an army of Pisans fighting for their very survival, put up a solid defence and pushed back the mercenaries, forcing the Signoria to order an expensive and frustrating siege.

By the late summer of 1499, after only a brief respite from his earlier foreign missions, Machiavelli was sent to the battlefront to try to find a way to break the Pisans. In his capacity as Secretary to the Ten of War, he now took on the joint role of diplomat and military observer, with orders to make a clear assessment of the situation and devise possible solutions.

The Signoria proposed that the French might act as intermediaries and could push the Pisans into submitting to Florence. But, after visiting the region, Machiavelli quickly realised this plan would have no chance of success and offered the view that the only way to regain Pisa would be to launch a direct military assault on the city. The Signoria agreed and, early in August, Paolo Vitelli, the commander of forces based close to Pisa, was ordered to attack. However, Vitelli, who made a rapid advance to the very walls of the city and could have taken it with a final decisive move, inexplicably pulled back at the last moment and threw away his advantage. The Florentines were outraged. Vitelli was recalled, put on trial, found guilty, tortured and beheaded.

Machiavelli's role in the Vitelli affair is ambiguous. He was certainly a senior member of the committee that tried Vitelli, but some historians interpret the surviving memos and reports from the trial as unambiguous evidence that he was a major player in handing down the punishment to Vitelli and influencing the decision to have him executed. Others say the very opposite, that he did not agree with the fate meted out to the commander.[7]

What is clear is that Machiavelli considered Vitelli a huge failure who caused his city a great deal of harm. At the time of the trial he wrote that Vitelli 'deserves endless punishment'.[8] And he believed that by throwing away an easy victory the commander had cost

Florence the dominion of Pisa. Many believed the condottiere was
not just a failure but a traitor, a man who had deliberately and
knowingly left Pisa to the defenders. Machiavelli may have shared
this view because he referred to Vitelli's actions as 'a betrayal'.[9]
Many years after these events he wrote about the reaction of the
Florentine government to their commander, saying of the Signoria:
'shortly following the rude deception, you took full revenge . . . by
putting to death the one who caused such harm . . .'[10]

The Florentine government was frustrated, but, embarrassed
by this military shambles, it then made matters much worse.
Against Machiavelli's advice, it agreed to pay the French the exor-
bitant sum of fifty thousand gold scudi to both hire five thousand
Swiss infantrymen and to cover the expenses of a further ten thousand men at arms whom France wished to hire in order to attack
Naples as part of a new move to regain a footing in the peninsula.

These mercenaries, led by an incompetent French commander,
Hugh of Beaumont, turned out to be cowardly and wholly unreli-
able. But this bad situation was made even worse when a
cash-strapped Signoria decided to supply the soldiers with inferior
food and supplies and to delay their pay. It is not surprising that the
Swiss troops refused to fight and threatened to withdraw from the
region and allow the siege to break.

Machiavelli made several trips to Pisa during the winter of 1499
and the spring of 1500, and he was back there in the thick of things
when the Swiss mercenaries mutinied in July of that year. His main
role had been to assist two commissioner-generals who had travelled
to the troubled region in an effort to find a way in which Florence
could save the campaign and appease the wishes of the hired troops.
One of the commissioner-generals, Giovambattista Ridolfi, was a
man with whom Machiavelli had already worked closely, and who,
like him, had been vehemently opposed to the idea of hiring the
Swiss in the first place. Ridolfi was a senior figure and a great
diplomat, but soon after reaching the battlefront, at the walls of

Pisa, he fell ill and returned to Florence, leaving Machiavelli with the other commissioner-general, Luca degli Albizzi.

By the time Machiavelli and Albizzi started to find a diplomatic resolution to the problem, it was far too late. The hired soldiers, desperate for their salaries and contemptuous of the Florentines, took Albizzi captive and threatened to kill him if they were not paid a ransom. Narrowly avoiding capture himself, Machiavelli at once set off for Florence, but before he could push the repeatedly wrong-footed Signoria into taking appropriate action, Albizzi (a man who understood well the ineptitude of his government) succeeded in ransoming himself for thirteen hundred ducats and was freed. The Swiss then vanished into the night, leaving the Florentine campaign in tatters, the Signoria even more frustrated and embarrassed than before and the government considerably poorer for the effort.

The Pisans were elated by the turn of events and Machiavelli later wrote wisely and presciently: 'The Florentines being completely without forces, hired ten thousand Frenchmen to reduce Pisa; because of which decision they incurred more dangers than at any time during their troubles . . . Auxiliaries are fatal, they constitute a united army, wholly obedient to the orders of someone else.'[11]

The real source of the recent troubles lay in the fact that Florence did not possess an army of its own and had always relied on mercenaries who could never be trusted and were ruinously expensive. Machiavelli had realised this problem shortly before the farcical Pisa campaign, but the embarrassment he now felt for his own country added substance to his convictions and fuelled his determination to make his government realise the folly of this approach.

Fortunately for Machiavelli, he again came out of a failed mission with his reputation untarnished. Indeed, in the aftermath of this shameful debacle he was viewed as a rather cool customer who had advised against the actions that had caused such problems for the Republic. And although his superiors also managed to cleverly sidestep any blame that might have attached to them, they accepted that he had remained level-headed throughout the conflict. In recognition of this, he was rewarded a bonus of six gold florins (about £3000), a gift which was, according to the Signoria: 'In payment of his labours on this occasion and of the dangers he ran.'[12]

Meanwhile the diplomatic fallout from this political farce was considerable, and the Florentines felt justifiably aggrieved over the behaviour of their French partners in the campaign, whom they accurately perceived as treacherous and avaricious. They also needed to pass the blame to cover up their own naïvety and indecisiveness.

Within days of Machiavelli's return to Florence, the Signoria sent him to France to meet the French king, Louis XII, in an effort to claw back something tangible for the money they had spent. Commanded to 'go with all possible speed, riding post while you have the strength to do so,' the Secretary to the Second Chancery and to the Ten of War, accompanied by another Florentine emissary, Francesco della Casa, was on the road by 18 July. The two men had been given the fastest horses in the stables of the Signoria, and each carried nothing more than a small bag containing a few personal items, his passport and a set of state documents.[13]

They were riding away from confusion and a city that seemed to be in the hands of amateur politicians. Ahead of them, the only certainty was that they would face danger around every corner. At the turn of the fifteenth century the French were the most powerful nation on earth, their military might second to none and their wealth matched only by their Spanish neighbours. And in Louis XII, who had succeeded Charles VIII in 1498, they had a focused, greedy, strong monarch who was also guided by clever, ruthless advisers.

In complete contrast, Florence was at such a low ebb economically that the government owed its richest citizens some four hundred thousand ducats (about £60 million). In addition it had been humiliated at the walls of Pisa and had witnessed nothing but political upheaval since the death of Lorenzo nearly a decade earlier. Its leaders seemed incapable of taking the sort of single-minded determined action that men such as Machiavelli knew was necessary for a modern nation state to survive.

To complicate things, the French were not the only ones to watch. Florence was surrounded by enemies and untrustworthy, fair-weather allies. Throughout 1499 and the first half of 1500, Louis had been financing the campaigns of Cesare Borgia (who had been given the title Duke Valentino in 1498). The Pope had aligned himself with the new French king in order to help carve out his own worldly dominion in Italy using his psychopathic son Cesare Borgia as his instrument. The latter had accepted this role with enthusiasm and it had allowed him to cut a swath through the Romagna, swallowing up weak city states such as Caterina Sforza Riario's Imola and Forli. It was clear to all that he had his sights set on Florence, which meant that in spite of their anger, the Florentines needed the French as allies.

Although Machiavelli was the perfect man for the mission to the French court, his task was a formidable one. His most important objective was to have altered the terms of the debt Florence owed France for the hired troops who had let them down so badly. But at the same time he needed to renew bonds of friendship between Louis XII and the Florentine government, and if possible, acquire guarantees of protection against any possible attack by Duke Valentino.

None of these aims was going to be easy to accomplish. To begin with, the French were not at all well disposed towards Florence. As much as the Florentines considered the French greedy, Louis XII placed the blame for the embarrassment of Pisa squarely at the door of the Signoria, whom he suspected of deliberately withholding payment both to him (for the troops hired to attack Naples) and to the mercenaries he had provided. However, the Florentines had not paid up because they had overstretched themselves and were now desperately trying to salvage the situation and at the same time encourage Louis to protect them against the threat posed by Duke Valentino. Weak, ineffectual and out of their depth, the members of the Signoria were relying on Machiavelli to get them out of a very dangerous situation.

For Machiavelli this was a huge challenge. He was only too aware of what was at stake, but he was also facing a personal crisis. In 1500, two months before this mission and as the Pisa campaign was drawing to an ignominious close, his father had died, leaving Niccolò and his brother as sole occupants of the house in Via Romana. Machiavelli had no time to properly organise his father's burial, let alone to grieve, and while he was away from Florence he was obliged to rely on Totto and other family members to put Bernardo's affairs in order. For Machiavelli, now the head of the family and a man who had adored his father, this was a painful and trying time, for he had no choice but to meet his obligations to his country, namely to leave home and bargain with the French.

The journey to France should have taken them no more than three days, but it was punctuated by delay after delay. Within a day of leaving Florence Machiavelli and Francesco della Casa received instructions to stop at Bologna to consult, on behalf of the Signoria, the lord of the city, Giovanni Bentivoglio. Then, between Parma and Piacenza (less than a hundred miles from Florence), they heard word that a contingent of more than a thousand mercenaries from the Pisa campaign was camped out in the mountains and should be avoided at all costs. This meant a lengthy detour. To make matters worse, in the heat of summer, plague was a constant danger. In France it had become so dangerous that Louis had been obliged to keep on the move, remaining mainly in the country and avoiding the disease-ridden cities.

Exhausted and disorientated, the two Florentine emissaries eventually caught up with the French on 26 July, in Lyons. At first they were received politely and treated well, but it soon became clear to them that their hosts considered Florence a third-rate state of little real importance. Matters were made worse by the fact that, thanks to the petty-mindedness of their own government and the parsimony of the wealthy of Florence (who sanctioned the release of expenses to civil servants abroad), they had to struggle to present an appropriate image at court. They had been given an allowance for expenses, but the French provided them with nothing but a room and basic meals, and because they had rushed to the rendezvous on horseback, they were obliged to buy fresh horses and clean clothes and to hire servants. Within two days their allowance had gone and they were dipping into their personal funds to pay their way. To compound the problem, because the French court was constantly on the move, Machiavelli and della Casa had to pay for expensive horses to keep pace with the king's swift carriages and military horsemen.

Machiavelli quickly learned the form at Louis XII's court. It soon became clear that the way to the king was through his favourites and that many of these, notably his closest advisers and military strategists, had already been bribed into aligning themselves with other Italian states. And so, for the next few months, Machiavelli and della Casa worked their way into the court structure, making as many friends as possible and trying to attract the king's attention.

Even though they were official emissaries who carried letters from the gonfalonier and the Signoria, these documents cut little ice with the arrogant French, and it was thanks only to Machiavelli's great diplomatic skills and his gift for communication that he and his colleague eventually managed to gain the ear of the most powerful of Louis's advisers, Georges d'Amboise. This man, the Cardinal of Rouen, became the most useful contact they had in their efforts to make the French king understand the Florentine position.

The fact that the situation was almost untenable frustrated

Machiavelli immensely, but he could do nothing but persist. Throughout the autumn of 1500, as the court moved first to St Pierre le Moutier, then Nevers and Montargis, before stopping at Nantes and Tours, he tried desperately to reach a compromise whereby Florence would compensate the French as best they could while obtaining a written guarantee of French protection against Duke Valentino.

Yet it seemed the harder Machiavelli and della Casa worked, the worse things became. By early October the French were rapidly losing their patience, so that even Georges d'Amboise had turned against them. On one occasion, as Machiavelli tried to convince the cardinal that any day a spokesman for the Signoria would arrive from Florence with good news, the Frenchman replied threateningly: 'That is what you said, it is true; but we shall all be dead before the spokesmen come. However, we shall see to it that others die first.'[14]

Even under such pressure and with the mission folding around him, Machiavelli was being hamstrung by his government. By mid-October the situation had become so bad that he and della Casa could not afford to send their messages to Florence by special courier, with the result that days were wasted waiting for responses from the Signoria.

To add to his misery, Machiavelli learned around this time that his sister Primavera had died suddenly after a brief illness at the age of thirty-five. A few days later della Casa fell ill and travelled to Paris for medical attention, leaving Machiavelli alone to face the implacable French court.

Then, in late October, just as the mission hit rock bottom, the Florentine government finally came to its senses and secured the funds to pay off its debt to the French and to the Swiss mercenaries involved in the ill-fated campaign against Pisa. This reversal of fortune had been prompted by aggression. Just as Machiavelli was making his last desperate efforts to gain better terms for the

Signoria from an intransigent French king, Duke Valentino's forces had overrun Rimini and besieged Pésaro, both on the coast less than seventy miles east of Florence.

It is easy to imagine how relieved Machiavelli must have felt at this news. He was homesick, and longed to get back to his job at the Palazzo della Signoria. He was concerned that his position was under threat from other, ambitious members of the Second Chancery and he had a fervent wish to help his family through what had been a disastrous year for them. However, he was expected to stay on at Louis's court to finalise the agreement between France and Florence and to ensure that he came home with a written guarantee of French military protection.

By 4 November he had obtained copies of a royal letter signed by Louis and sent to Duke Valentino warning him not to make any form of incursion into Florentine territory. The Signoria wished Machiavelli to stay on longer at the court in order to nurture the relationship after the agreement had been finalised and to form strong diplomatic links with certain key figures within Louis's inner circle. To this he reluctantly agreed; but without telling his superiors at home, he made arrangements to leave France before Christmas.

Machiavelli set off in the last week of November and took a long, leisurely route home. Just before Christmas and halfway back to Florence, he received orders, sent out on 12 December, relieving him of any further duties at the French court. On 14 January 1501, after almost seven months away from his desk at the chancery, and missing terribly the welcoming glow of his own home, he passed through the city gates tired but relieved that he had concluded his mission successfully, and that, for a while at least, Florence had, through clever diplomacy, once more avoided subjugation.

4

Running with the Devil

Machiavelli learned many lessons from his mission to the French court. On a personal level he discovered, from the affectionate letters of his friends and assistants in Florence, just how much he was liked at the Second Chancery. They missed his wit and rapier intellect, his camaraderie and his insightful intelligence. As a political observer and analyst he also gained much. But perhaps the most important thing he had learned was just how vulnerable his beloved city had become. He had seen at first hand how the major players of Europe acted and how the Florentine approach was amateur by comparison. Prompted by these revelations, Machiavelli had already begun to consider ways in which Florence could improve its position, how it could better protect itself, how it could bolster its power and influence in Europe. But he knew that he would have to bide his time before he could use these ideas to help facilitate change.

In 1500 Machiavelli was thirty-one and had been in his job for just two years, but he was quick to gain confidence and already quite aware of his extraordinary abilities. Although he was a natural diplomat, he sometimes found it impossible to hold his tongue on subjects that inspired him, even if he knew his opinions would cause offence. Having spent months negotiating with the French, he felt he had the measure of them and believed he understood their policies. He had gained some insight into their strategies as well as their weaknesses.

As Machiavelli had made ready to leave France for his long-awaited return home, the Cardinal of Rouen, Georges d'Amboise, had commented sarcastically that the Italians knew nothing of war. Machiavelli responded that this might be so but it was equally true the French knew nothing of statecraft. Not content with this retaliation, he then felt the urge to deliver a lecture to Amboise (effectively the second most powerful man in France) in which he explained that if Louis XII really wanted to dominate the Italian peninsula he should heed the example of history. To conquer a nation with customs and cultures different from one's own, he declared, the king should protect and utilise the friendship offered by those states naturally inclined towards him, namely Florence, Bologna, Ferrara, Mantua and a few others. He should then work with these allies to suppress the threatening power of cities such as Venice and most especially the Vatican. But, above all, he should do his utmost to prevent the Spanish (the only power to rival France) from gaining any sort of foothold in Italy.

Georges d'Amboise was a gentleman and he admired Machiavelli's intellect. He listened politely and then gave the curt response that His Majesty the King was 'exceedingly prudent'. Machiavelli remembered this exchange and recounted it in *The Prince*:

I had a word on this subject with Rouen, at Nantes, when Valentino was occupying the Romagna. When the Cardinal of Rouen said to me that the Italians did not understand war, I retorted that the French did not understand statecraft, because if they understood it, then they would not let the Church become so great. And the course of events in Italy has shown how the greatness of the Church and of Spain has been caused by France, and how the ruin of France has been caused by them. From this we can deduce a general rule, which never or rarely fails to apply: that whoever is responsible for another's becoming powerful ruins himself, because this power is brought into being either by ingenuity or by force, and both of these are suspect to the one who had become powerful.[1]

With hindsight it is clear that Machiavelli was absolutely correct in both his analysis and his suggestions. Louis almost certainly heard nothing of his opinions, and Amboise, as smart as he was, probably forgot the advice soon after he heard it. The French did the very opposite of what Machiavelli could see to be the best course of action for them, and as a result their attempts to conquer Italy brought only temporary success. Writing some fifteen years later and having observed the consequences for Italy of France's strategy, Machiavelli was able to state in *The Prince*:

Louis had, therefore, made five mistakes; he had destroyed the weaker powers [Milan and others]; increased the power of someone already powerful in Italy [the Church]; brought into that country a very powerful foreigner [Spain]; stayed away from Italy himself; failed to establish settlements there. Even these mistakes, if he had lived, need not have been fatal if there had not been a sixth; his dispossessing the Venetians of their state. If he had not made the Church strong, or brought Spain into Italy, it would have been reasonable and necessary to crush the Venetians. But having taken those steps, he should never have let them be ruined; because while they remained powerful they would always have prevented the others from moving against Lombardy.[2]

Back in Florence in January 1501, Machiavelli immediately

returned to the old routine he had enjoyed before his departure. His responsibilities had remained unchanged while he was away and his assistants, most especially his close colleague and intimate friend, Biagio Buonaccorsi, maintained Machiavelli's office during his absence. Biagio and Niccolò had been friends before they began working together. They had joined the chancery on the same day and quickly established a productive working relationship there. Biagio knew Machiavelli's mind, and while his master and confidant was away they corresponded almost daily. Reading these letters, one immediately understands their relationship. Machiavelli was Biagio's superior but they were also close friends. Biagio was quite unreserved in his letters and told Machiavelli exactly what he thought of him, often in the most crude terms; but at the same time he was also a reliable, trustworthy, honest and completely dedicated assistant.

In private, each of them displayed an endearing lack of reverence for the powerful figures who controlled their lives, but they were also superb at playing the diplomacy game that stood as the central pillar of their careers. Biagio was fond of caricaturing those with whom he worked. So there was 'Snail', one Antonio della Valle, who was a middle-ranking politician, and in Biagio's eyes at least, something of a pedant. Another name Biagio had for him was 'Tight-arse', presumably after a request for funds or expenses had been turned down. The letters Niccolò and Biagio exchanged during the former's long absences are filled with gossip and in-jokes, and coded references to contemporaries only they would appreciate; and although it is clear that Biagio was envious of Machiavelli's position and covetous of his abundant talents as a writer, he was also in awe of his older friend.

Machiavelli needed his friends and assistants to look after his domestic affairs while he was away on extended trips. Biagio Buonaccorsi and Agostino Vespucci were frequently called on to pay bills or to collect personal items and clothes that were then to be sent to wherever he was working. They also helped to run the family home in Florence as well as the country estate of Sant'Andrea. In a letter written in 1506 Vespucci tells his boss: 'I have just come back from your house, I took care of everything . . . They are all well, very well. Marietta [Machiavelli's wife] was anxious for me to give you her and the children's regards . . . only Bernardo [the couple's son] is a little cranky.'[3]

Machiavelli had others that were close to him at the Palazzo Vecchio, men with whom he exchanged friendly letters while he was away and who accompanied him to taverns, gambling houses and brothels when he was in Florence. Most prominent in this circle, apart from Biagio, were Niccolò's fellow workers Andrea di Romolo and Giuliano della Valle, and among these friends he was known, in a play on his name, as 'Il Machia', the Man.

It was an entirely apt nickname, for Machiavelli was a commanding presence in any company. He was cool, calm, astute, probing and wise. He could size up others very quickly and identify any weaknesses with very little to go on. Most of the time he played his cards close to his chest, but he was never afraid to express a sincerely held opinion. He was a diplomat *par excellence*, but he was no pushover. He understood how the world worked, how civilisation functions, and he could make piercing critical judgements with apparent ease. But what his friends liked about 'the Man' was his wit, his irreverent sense of humour, his daring, his *joie de vivre*. He loved his work, but he also liked to play hard. He was a cerebral man, but he loved to drink wine, eat fine food, throw dice, and he fell in love easily, letting the poet in him sweep him away.

In the spring of 1501 Machiavelli was coming up to thirty-two. He was now the head of the Machiavelli family, but with his younger brother Totto training for the priesthood and their father, mother and sister Primavera dead, he lived alone in the house in Via Romana. It was clearly time to consider marriage.

There is no record of Machiavelli's courtship with his wife

Marietta, the daughter of one Luigi Corsini. We know from her modest dowry that Marietta's family were of a similar class to the Machiavellis – there was very little intermarriage between classes in fifteenth- and sixteenth-century Florence – but there is no surviving account of how they met or when. It is most likely that Marietta lived close by and that the Corsinis had known the Machiavellis for a long time. If there was any correspondence between Marietta and Niccolò while the Florentine Secretary was in France, no trace of it has survived.

Sadly, there is also no record of the marriage itself, but the ceremony probably took place in the autumn of 1501, perhaps in late September or early October. This is supported by a letter dated 25 August of that year from Machiavelli's friend and colleague Agostino Vespucci, who had become the Florentine emissary to Rome. Vespucci writes that 'when his Beatitude the Pope comes here [Florence], you and any others who want a dispensation either to take or leave a wife, shall have it willingly . . .'[4]

It is difficult to judge exactly what Vespucci means by this. It could be simply a reference to the developing wedding plans as the big day approached or it could be a witticism typical of the sort of banter exchanged by Machiavelli and his friends, implying that if Niccolò was already tired of his wife he could have the marriage dissolved.

In many ways Machiavelli must have been a difficult man to live with. He was self-motivated and independent. He chased women and did as he pleased. He was most definitely a man's man and although he clearly had a deep affection for his wife and they remained together until death separated them, their marriage was, for him at least, a convenience, almost an obligation. This meant that during their first decade together, as he carved out a career, his role as a husband and father was very much a secondary aspect of his life. Looking at the marriage from a different perspective, there is no denying that Niccolò was something of a catch for Marietta.

Her new husband was a rising star in the government, one of the most trusted emissaries of the Signoria, a diplomat of growing influence who was commanding a substantial salary and could keep his wife and family in some comfort.

There was little either of them could have done about the nature of Niccolò's work and Marietta had to accept that her husband would be around only rarely. She fumed and complained about it, and while he was away she conveyed these feelings to him through the letters from their friends. Even so, it is likely he missed the birth of their first child, in the early summer of 1502, a daughter they named Primerana, because at that time he was travelling between Florentine dependencies on diplomatic missions. He was also absent for the birth of their second child, Bernardo, born the following year. In fact he was away so much his friends ribbed him that it was a miracle he had found time to father the children. When Bernardo was born, a friend, Luca Ugolini, wrote: 'My very dear *compare* [old pal]. Congratulations! Truly your Madonna Marietta did not deceive you, for he is your spitting image. Leonardo da Vinci would not have done a better portrait.'[5]

It was a most demanding job, but for a Florentine emissary there could have been no better or more exciting time in which to work. In 1501 the ongoing struggle to regain Pisa was put to one side temporarily because the Signoria was distracted by the potentially more dangerous rise in the fortunes of Cesare Borgia, who was rapidly becoming the most powerful military figure in Italy; a man who could not be ignored.

The portrait of Cesare Borgia by Gianfrancesco Bembo now hanging in the Accademia gallery in Carrara is a starkly revealing rendering of one whom many consider to have been the embodiment of pure evil. It offers the image of a handsome man with small menacing eyes, of whom an Italian historian of the period wrote: 'The Pope loves his son . . . and has great fear of him.'[6]

However, modern historians are divided on the accuracy of this statement. Cesare was seventeen when his father, Rodrigo Borgia, became Pope Alexander VI, and father and son formed a powerful double act for the entire period of the pontiff's tenure at the Vatican. The power and influence of the Borgias stretched far beyond the nerve centre of their operation in the Vatican so that between them (and in league with Louis XII) they utterly dominated political life throughout Italy.

Alexander VI has himself entered the history books with an image every bit as reviled as his son, for he was perhaps the most debauched and murderous of all popes, a man who leads a crowded field of those who have most besmirched the name and the image of the papacy. The compilers of *The New Advent Encyclopaedia of Catholic History* refer to Alexander rather transparently as a man in whom 'were combined rare prudence and vigilance, mature reflection, marvellous power of persuasion, skill and a capacity for the conduct of the most difficult affairs'. They then go on to admit that he had 'a passion for card-playing, but . . . was strictly abstemious in eating and drinking, and a careful administrator who became one of the wealthiest men of his time'.[7]

He was certainly good with money, and his 'power of persuasion' cannot be denied. However, the gloss applied by Catholic historians is absurd. During a thirty-four-year career as first cardinal and then vice-chancellor (effectively number two in the Vatican) Rodrigo Borgia had accumulated a vast fortune which he used to buy the papacy in 1492. Copying his predecessor the wonderfully misnamed Innocent VIII, he rigged the votes with bribes and promises, some of which he immediately reneged on, and once installed as head of the Holy Roman Church he wielded absolute power and lived a life of total debauchery and indulgence, often ignoring even to feign any semblance of holiness or piety. Machiavelli was later to write of him: 'Alexander VI never did anything, or thought of anything, other than deceiving men; and he always found victims for his deceptions. There never was a man capable of such convincing asseverations, or so ready to swear to the truth of something, who would honour his word less.'[8]

Not content with maintaining a harem of forty courtesans at the Vatican for his private and personal pleasure and another prepared by his hosts on his arrival in any city he visited, with advancing age Alexander grew increasingly interested in lavish pornographic displays.

'The Pope is always at his illicit affairs . . .,' wrote Vespucci to Machiavelli in 1501 (by which time Alexander was in his seventy-first year), 'every night twenty-five or more women, between Ave Maria and one o'clock. They are taken into the palace, a few at a time, so that manifestly the whole palace is turned into a brothel. Other news I will not give you now, but if you reply to me I will tell you some fine things.'[9] And in other letters written soon after this, the Florentine emissary to Rome made veiled references to His Holiness's predilection for murder and his use of poison to rid himself of anyone who stood in his way.[10]

However, quite who was in charge and who dominated whom, the Holy Father or the warlord son, remains open to debate. According to some contemporaries, Cesare Borgia made very public displays of his fearlessness and his arrogant disregard for any mortal, including his own father. 'He was the haughtiest man that ever was seen,' reported the diplomat Branca Tedallini. 'Among other things he gave audiences to no one, neither to cardinals nor ambassadors nor lords; no one may speak to him save Michelotto, who is his executioner.'[11] Another historian, Alessandro Luzio, described how, on 12 November 1501, Borgia 'in anger made passes with a dagger at the breast of an ecclesiastic in the presence of the Pope and many prelates, and being severely reproved by the Pope, replied angrily with the threat that if he did not hold his peace he would do the same to him'.[12]

So who was Cesare Borgia, the man Machiavelli immortalised in *The Prince* as the model of the perfect leader? Who was this man whose very name conjures powerful images of dark deceit and corruption?

Born illegitimately in 1475 (or possibly 1476), probably in Rome, Cesare was raised as Rodrigo Borgia's legitimate son after a Bull relating to his birthright was issued by Sixtus IV in 1480. This Bull succeeded one that had designated him the legitimate son of Sixtus's favourite mistress, Vannozza de Catanei, and Domenico d'Arignano, and simply stated that Cesare Borgia was exempt from any need to prove the legitimacy of his birth. Crucially, this also meant that Cesare was entitled to benefices from various offices to which Sixtus, under pressure from Rodrigo, could bestow on him. In consequence, when he was seven he was made Prebend of the Cathedral Chapter of Valencia and a year later he became Apostolic Protonotary in the city. By the age of nine he had also received the titles of Rector of Gandia and Provost of Albar and Jativa. For his tenth birthday Cesare was made Treasurer of Cartagena.

Long before he became pontiff, Rodrigo had engineered his son's education with great care so that the boy might be of greatest service to the family. Tutored in Perugia, Cesare then studied theology at the University of Pisa. By 1493, a year after Rodrigo had transmogrified into Alexander VI, his eighteen-year-old son was made a cardinal.

Cardinal Cesare Borgia is thought to have committed his first murder soon after ascending to the Holy College. His victim was his younger brother, Giovanni. The brothers had attended a dinner together and after leaving the venue, the pair, along with their servants and friends, began their journey back to the papal palace. At some point along the way Giovanni apparently decided to take a detour with his manservant in order to visit a friend. The following morning his body was dragged from the River Tiber; he had been stabbed more than a hundred times.

The Pope was mortified by the death of his son and retired into isolation for several weeks. Meanwhile Cesare's enemies in Rome began to build an argument that showed he had murdered his brother. The reason, they declared, was that Cesare was jealous of Giovanni's growing secular power, he was frustrated with the religious restraints placed on him and he yearned for his brother's freedom and status.

The evidence against Cesare was circumstantial. Several independent witnesses described two men attacking Giovanni and his groom in a dark alley. One of the men fitted Cesare's description. Other witnesses claimed they had known of a secret plot to kill Giovanni. Knowing Cesare Borgia's character and later deeds, it is easy to believe he was his brother's murderer. It is also clear that the Pope himself believed these stories, because there was a very noticeable chilling of the relationship between Alexander and his son for at least twelve months after this incident. Yet, even if Alexander had known for sure that the murderer was his eldest son, he could have done nothing about it without damaging the reputation of the Borgia family irreparably.

The claim of Cesare's enemies that he had committed the murder out of jealousy of his brother's status gained greater support when, a year after the incident, Cesare succeeded Giovanni to all the key positions of state he had controlled and acquired all his brother's lands and possessions. Even so, avarice may have been only part of the motive. At least two contemporary historians, Marino Sanudo the Elder and Francesco Guicciardini, postulated that Cesare killed his brother out of sexual jealousy over their sister, thirteen-year-old Lucrezia.

Whatever the motive, Cesare survived the crime unscathed and used his gains to gradually build a power base at least comparable to his father's. Furthermore, because he worked with the Pope and also aligned himself with the all-powerful French, he was free to extend his influence far beyond Rome. By 1498, when he was twenty-three, Cesare had reached the conclusion that he should put all his efforts into emulating his namesake and become a true

'Caesar', grabbing as much territory as he could and embracing the lifestyle of a Roman emperor.

That year his father gave Cesare the title Duke Valentino, and for the following three years he was often away from Rome with his army acquiring any city states and dominions susceptible to invasion. However, Cesare was no warrior. He did not like to become involved in real battles. Instead he conquered through deceit and treachery. He used his agents to murder important opponents and paid enemy commanders to turn traitor on their leaders. Cesare cultivated betrayal and ruled by division, moving in through the back door. One chronicler of the Borgias' methods, Raffaello Matarazzo, said of him: 'In those days the duke was the first captain in Italy, but not at all by reason of his great understanding of arms, but by means of treachery and the power of money; he had reduced war to betrayal, which every man had learned of him.'

Beyond the arena of conquest and war, Cesare also made sure he always had his way. Before dozens of witnesses he stabbed to death a young servant who had been seduced by Lucrezia (and who may have fathered her first illegitimate child). He also arranged the murders of two of his sister's husbands, along with a string of her lovers. Most infamously, one of Cesare's thugs strangled Lucrezia's second husband, Alfonso, Prince of Bisceglie, in his bedchamber, within the very walls of the papal palace.

When Cesare was in Rome he often grew bored and as a form of entertainment he liked to go out in the streets in disguise. Protected by his henchmen, he picked fights with locals in taverns or coaxed them into saying something disparaging about the Pope or his family. According to the historian Johannes Burckhard, who wrote a history of the Borgias, Cesare once cajoled a man into making a derogatory remark about the Pope's son. Then, after revealing his true identity, he had the man arrested. Before the large crowd that had gathered he cut off one of the man's hands, cut out his tongue and had the tongue attached to the bloody stump of the victim's arm, then made the man walk the streets of Rome for two days as a warning to the people of the city.

Such stories became almost legends, folklore of the era, and the name Borgia, particularly that of Cesare Borgia, was not just unsavoury to many rulers of small Italian states, but was a name to be feared. By the summer of 1501, through the employment of stealth and shameless deceit and treachery (as well as by keeping his father and Louis XII constantly on his side), Cesare, or Duke Valentino as he now was, had occupied entire regions of Italy. He was racing at full throttle towards the fulfilment of what he saw as his destiny. Believing himself to be the new Caesar, he had adopted the motto '*Aut Caesar aut nihil*' (Either Caesar or nothing).

However, Cesare Borgia was never entirely satisfied. As a young boy he had been struck by the meaning of his own Christian name: he had believed unquestioningly that his destiny was to be a great ruler. Unfortunately for him, although his father was the absolute spiritual leader of Christendom and in today's terms a multi-billionaire, Alexander was still little more than a vassal for greater temporal powers. The real players in Europe in the early sixteenth century were the French, the Spanish and the Holy Roman Empire. The Pope had given his strongest allegiance to Louis XII, who kept Cesare Borgia on a tight leash, constantly wary that if the man was not a servant he had the potential to become a very dangerous enemy. Consequently, although Cesare was supplied with money, men and arms by his father and the French, Louis and his advisers also made sure to curb his ambitions. (Cesare Borgia was naturally aware of this and frustrated by it. He did all he could to strengthen his hand and to loosen the reins of control. By 1503 he had even succeeded in marrying a French Princess, Charlotte d'Albret, with whom he fathered a legitimate daughter he named Louise in honour of the French king. But his ambitions were always curtailed by the French unless his plans suited them.)

Florence was caught between the ambitions of the Borgias and the wiles of the French, who were solely interested in accumulating greater wealth and power. Through his advisers and military strategists, Louis understood well the city's weaknesses and failings and was keen to prise open political crevices in Italy in order to further his aims. To Florence, Cesare Borgia's aims became all too clear during the summer of 1501. As the family of Marietta Corsini made arrangement for her wedding and her betrothed, Niccolò Machiavelli, dashed from city to city conducting the work of the Signoria, Cesare's troops advanced through the Romagna and reached Campi, a short ride from the gates of Florence itself. It was only then that stern words from the French king forced the Pope's son to withdraw at the last moment.

It was a terrible position for Florence to find itself in, and its people knew it. One ordinary citizen, Francesco Pepi of the Santa Croce quarter, declared of the situation: 'The illness of the city is so severe that we do not have much time for medicine.'[13]

The crisis precipitated by Duke Valentino's advance to within sight of Florence was a perfect example of the power struggles that controlled the Borgias' plans and threatened the very survival of the Florentine Republic. Louis's intervention had been facilitated with money. There was no other reason for the French to demand that Duke Valentino move his soldiers away and retreat from all Florentine dependencies. To Machiavelli this was a further illustration of just how vulnerable Florence had become. He could see that such a policy of appeasement and the system of buying help from more powerful states was unsustainable and perilous not to mention dishonourable.

It was not as if the Signoria lacked information or intelligence. In Rome, Agostino Vespucci was as much a spy as a diplomat. His letters to Machiavelli alluded to the machinations of Alexander and his fearful ambitions, and what he conveyed to the Signoria in coded dispatches was a set of undiluted reports giving a very clear warning that Florence was in danger from papal expansionist plans.

But the Florentine government continued to play its dangerous game, almost as if it felt that Florence somehow stood above the murky pastimes of lesser cities, that it could never become subject to anything so sordid as an invasion; that it was beneath its dignity to copy everyone else and create an army of its own. Machiavelli knew that this was the attitude of his superiors and he privately predicted that such a stance would eventually destroy the Florentine Republic. Yet he could do nothing but watch as the government continued to follow the capricious moods of the French king while constantly watching every move made by Valentino.

Then, in the early summer of 1501 came a reprieve. Forced to keep his hands off Florence, Duke Valentino decided to turn elsewhere and make easier conquests which he knew, for the moment at least, the French would tolerate. Intent on grabbing as much as he could before Louis again clipped his wings, he captured town after town beyond the borders of Florence, fully aware that, although he would be forced to give back most of his gains, he would still be able to make advances in the long term. But this fraught situation could not go on for long and in June 1502 the Republic decided to attempt some form of negotiation themselves and arranged a meeting between Duke Valentino and their most trusted emissary, Niccolò Machiavelli.

On this mission Machiavelli was accompanied by the Bishop of Volterra, Francesco Soderini, who was a senior diplomat and the brother of the future gonfalonier of Florence, Piero Soderini. The two men set out from Florence on 22 June, expecting to meet Duke Valentino at his camp close to the city of Urbino. En route, at the town of Ponticelli, they met a monk who was fleeing towards Florence. He informed them that Urbino had fallen and that the duke was already establishing a base there.

Several months earlier Vespucci had warned the Signoria that Urbino, a close ally of Florence, was under threat. Now it had become another territory in a growing list of conquests made by

Duke Valentino since the winter, a list that included the towns of Monte a San Savino, Cortona, Castiglione, Anghiari and Borgo San Sepolcro. In April, shortly before the fall of Urbino, the strategically valuable state of Arezzo had been taken by one of the duke's captains, Vitellozzo Vitelli. Urbino was a great prize. It had been a duchy in the hands of one of the most respected figures in Italy, Guidobaldo da Montefeltro, and it was a great asset for any conqueror.

As usual, Borgia had taken Urbino not by force of arms but by deceit and deception, in this case by bribing key members of da Montefeltro's household to turn against their master, and when Machiavelli learned of this grave news he sent a message to the Signoria before leaving for the meeting with the duke: 'Your lord-ships should take note of this stratagem . . .,' he warned, 'and this [Valentino's] remarkable speed combined with extraordinary good fortune.'[14]

The first meeting between Machiavelli and Cesare Borgia was a fraught affair. The emissaries reached Urbino on 24 June at 'the second hour of the night' (two hours after the evening Angelus bell), and they were escorted immediately to the newly conquered ducal palace, where Valentino was already beginning to make himself at home. The duke trusted very few people and he was sceptical of Florentine intentions. A master manipulator and strategist who was at the height of his powers, he took great pleasure in intimidation and political game playing. He had Machiavelli and Soderini brought to him straight from their horses; the doors to the meeting room were locked from the inside and a guard was placed at each exit. All of this was done to unnerve his visitors.

Machiavelli described his first encounter with Duke Valentino in a letter written to the Signoria immediately after the meeting: 'This lord is most splendid and magnificent and is so vigorous in military matters that there is no undertaking so great that it does not seem a minor thing to him. He never ceases from seeking glory or enlarging his state, and he fears no effort or danger: he arrives in a place before it has been noticed that he set out from another; his soldiers love him; he has recruited the best men in Italy: and all of this makes him victorious and formidable, to which we should add that he is perpetually lucky.'

The duke wasted no time in explaining his position to his visitors. To him the sole purpose of having them in his palace was to make clear his demands. He did not like the current government in Florence and he wished to reinstate Piero de' Medici and his family, who since his exile had been working for him. Piero would be a puppet leader, while he pulled the strings. He also wanted a large sum of money to act as a very superior condottiere, defending Florentine interests in the region. 'This government of yours does not please me, and I cannot trust it . . .,' he declared, 'you must change it and give me a pledge that you will observe everything you promised; otherwise you will soon realise that I have no intention of going on like this, and if you do not want me as a friend, you will find me your enemy.'[15]

It is easy to see why Duke Valentino wanted these things. He wished to get rid of a government that was in thrall to the French and to use Florence as a centre of operations from which he could extend his influence throughout Italy. Indeed it is striking how close his plan was to the stratagem Machiavelli had advised the French to pursue. He wanted to form alliances with Italian states and to drive his own wedge between Italian power and French interference. Louis he viewed simply as a meal ticket.

Machiavelli had been quite aware of the man's abilities and his ruthless drive long before meeting him, but this first encounter sealed his belief that the Pope's son was perhaps the most dangerous man alive. The French were a constant threat to Italian peace, but they were tempered by the Spanish in a superpower stand-off. The Pope himself was a vile slug of a man possessed of unlimited greed, but the papal states were always obliged to rely on more powerful allies to fight alongside them. This meant that in any military campaign they had only a minor say and received only a modest reward for any victory in which they were involved. Through his megalomaniac son, Alexander had the potential to one day wield real temporal power and become a player in Italian affairs. And if his son could create his own power base, Cesare might dispense with his fair-weather friends.

Machiavelli realised this and he could visualise the danger the younger Borgia represented. He respected the man's powerful character and dynamism. He knew that the politicians of the Republic would be no match for him and that, without France, Florence would be quite unable to stop his forces. Such realities were made clear immediately to Machiavelli and Soderini during the evening of 24 June, and in response to Duke Valentino's demands the emissaries could do nothing else but bluff their way through the negotiations by exaggerating the friendship between Florence and France. But the duke was not easily taken in. 'I know better than you what the king has in mind,' he responded. 'You will be deceived.'

Privately, Machiavelli found himself in agreement. He had some experience of the way the French behaved and how they viewed Florence, and he had little faith in the altruism of Louis. The French understood Cesare Borgia's intentions and his formidable abilities, but they were confident they could contain his ambitions, which meant that Louis would only protect the Republic if there were enough gold in it for him and if it suited his broader political desires. Fortunately for Florence, the Signoria trusted no one and was at least wary of Duke Valentino.

The day after the meeting the duke sent two of his most trusted aides, the brothers Giulio and Paolo Orsini, to speak with the Florentine emissaries. (A third Orsini, Francesco, along with Paolo, Vitellozzo Vitelli and Giampaolo Baglioni, was later to break with Duke Valentino.) At this meeting the Orsinis claimed that the French king would stand back while their master levelled Florence and murdered its citizens, and that their master had been assured that as long as any attack on Florence was swift, the French could be persuaded to slow any rescue efforts they might undertake.

Machiavelli and Soderini were as unconvinced by this as Cesare Borgia had been by their claims of French support. But they needed to tread carefully. In this delicate game of bluff and counter-bluff Machiavelli would have to use all his analytical and negotiating skills to get the best result for Florence. At a second meeting with Cesare the next day the duke seemed irritated and frustrated that the Florentine emissaries were not immediately acceding to his wishes. Florence had four days to comply with his demand for an alliance, he told them. The Signoria must pay him a tribute of thirty-six thousand ducats and the government must stand down and hand power back to the Medici. If these conditions were not met, he said by way of conclusion, his forces would advance on the city at a time of his choosing.

Racing back to Florence and leaving Soderini to continue negotiations, Machiavelli delivered the ultimatum to the Signoria, which was finally propelled into informing the French king of the duke's threat. Within two days French troops had advanced on Arezzo and were moving troops to the border: Duke Valentino's bluff had been called. Happy to accept Florentine cash and angered by the duke's threatening megalomania, Louis flexed his muscles, declaring that his intention to stop him was 'as pious and holy an expedition as any against the Turk'.[16]

Thanks to this astute political manoeuvring, Florence had escaped again. The Republic had bought itself some time, but if anyone within the government believed that Duke Valentino's ambitions had been quashed for long, Machiavelli could have happily disabused them of the idea. He had seen him in person, faced up to him across a desk, looked him steadily in the eye; Duke Valentino, he knew, would be back, and soon.

Realising he had overreached himself, Cesare Borgia hurriedly set about salvaging something from the situation. Throughout the summer and autumn of 1502 he played a delicate diplomatic game. Intent on mending the rift with Louis, he travelled to Milan and met him on 5 August.

But, before he had reached the French court, many of Cesare Borgia's enemies had rushed to Louis to curry favour. The Duke of Urbino had been there, as had Pietro Varaon, one of the sons of the deposed Lord of Camerino. Giovanni Sforza of Pésaro and Francesco Gonzaga of Mantua had also visited to air their grievances against Duke Valentino and to ask for French help in reclaiming their lands.

Louis had made each of them a promise, in exchange for gold. But the French were also aware that they needed to maintain a balance of power within Italy and that although he had to be kept constantly in check, Cesare Borgia was valuable to them. Because of this, when he arrived in Milan he was well received and given due honour. Indeed the duke was treated so well that the Florentines were shocked by Louis's behaviour and some observers began to suggest that the French were about to double-cross the Republic.

Such a sudden turnaround in the attitude of the French towards Duke Valentino also confused and alarmed his own senior commanders. Uncertainty over what lay behind the relationship was particularly disturbing for four of his most powerful and influential captains, Paolo and Francesco Orsini, Vitellozzo Vitelli (who still clung on to Arezzo with French troops at his door) and Giampaolo Baglioni. While their commander languished in Milan, the four men organised a secret meeting at which they decided to break with him and to unite their forces in moving against him at the most auspicious moment.

Duke Valentino heard of this conspiracy as he was arranging to leave the French court and he finally set out from Milan on 2 September, heading for a new centre of operations in one of the

cities he had snatched from Caterina Sforza, Imola, some fifty miles
north-east of Florence. Before the duke left, Louis supplied him
with two and a half thousand foot soldiers and three hundred men
at arms to accompany his own hundred-strong lances.

The Orsinis, Vitelli and Baglioni had assembled a far greater
force, some nine thousand foot soldiers and one thousand horsemen, and they also had time to prepare. But for all their fine ideas,
the conspirators possessed neither Cesare Borgia's ruthlessness nor
his intelligence. As the duke was on his way to Imola, the Orsinis
approached the Florentines to propose an alliance, but the idea was
rejected. Then they turned to the Venetians, who were certainly not
well disposed towards Valentino; but, wary of making an enemy of
France, they too rejected the overtures of the conspirators.
Incompetent and unable to even trust each other (let alone any
weighty ally) during September 1502, Cesare Borgia's new enemies
wasted every opportunity to strike at their old master before he was
fully prepared for them, and by the end of the month he was out of
danger and the conspirators' moment had passed.

In October 1502 Machiavelli was sent by the Florentine government to meet Duke Valentino again. At this second meeting
Machiavelli found him greatly changed since their first encounter
four months earlier. Where the duke had once been arrogant and
demanding, he was now conciliatory and patient. His self-confidence had not diminished in the slightest, but he had adopted the
guise of a reasonable man who wanted to discuss rather than to
insist, to negotiate rather than to foist. He also seemed more
relaxed, revitalised by his successful discussions with Louis. Now
there was no mention of the Medici or money, and he was more
interested in co-operating with the Florentine government.

There were two purposes to Machiavelli's mission to Cesare
Borgia's court at Imola. Officially he was there to continue discussions with the duke in an effort to construct some form of workable
relationship, an alliance that suited Florence and offered the chance

of a lasting peace in the region. The other, equally important, reason for his presence there was to spy for the Signoria.

It was immediately clear to Machiavelli that Borgia had made exactly the right moves at Louis's court. It had been clever of him to snatch as much land as possible during the summer of 1502, and even though he had been obliged to return most of it he was better off than he had been beforehand. Machiavelli was also aware of how the duke had not only avoided the danger his conspirators represented but was quickly using them to his advantage. Never shy to boast of his successes, he told Machiavelli, waving under his nose a letter in which the French king had promised to supply him with three hundred lancers: 'Imagine what I can get to defend myself against those men whom I have convinced the king are his enemies as well as mine . . . Believe me that this thing is to my advantage, and the [conspirators] cannot reveal themselves at any hour when it will damage me less.'[17]

The duke was boasting, but he was also telling the truth. In the space of just a few short months, he had reversed his fortunes with almost miraculous skill. It is small wonder Machiavelli was impressed by the man, for he was everything the Florentine leaders were not.

Machiavelli's mission to Imola lasted almost three months. It was a time during which he learned much about Cesare Borgia and the refined political world in which he was a major performer. It appears from surviving letters that Machiavelli's talents were in turn much appreciated by the duke. 'I am sure, by God, that you are held in great honour there . . .,' Agostino Vespucci wrote from Rome, 'you, whom the duke himself and all the courtiers favour, so that they heap praise on you as a prudent man, surround and flatter you.'[18]

It was a mission that piqued Machiavelli's intellectual interest more than any other he had so far undertaken, and when he realised that he would be at the Imola court for some time he set out to make

a close study of Borgia, to analyse his methods, to observe the techniques he employed and to explore the ways in which he gave
substance to his plans. He noted how the man was almost paranoid
about secrecy, how he used disinformation to fool those who tried to
second-guess him. He watched and recorded how almost all of his
conquests were achieved by deception, by taking advantage of the
moral weaknesses of those around him, the greed, avarice and self-
ishness of those he could identify as men of influence. Borgia was
clearly fearless, possessed of innate self-confidence, and he had
powerful allies. He was also not averse to dirtying his hands dealing with the dregs of humanity, men he employed for his nefarious
purposes. Yet he rarely displayed any physical courage, and the
times he took up arms and fought were rarer still. To Machiavelli
such methods, quite at odds with the traditional approach of most
leaders of men, were the key to his uniqueness and his success. Far
ahead of his time, Machiavelli realised that few leaders were suited
to fight the good fight alongside their followers, that there was
another breed of warlord, the man who thrived on intrigue, the
chess master who moved the pieces rather than taking up positions
on the board himself.

In every practical sense this mission was another difficult commission for Machiavelli. In a repeat of the situation he had faced in
France two years earlier, he was underfunded by the Signoria and
was obliged to dip into his own savings to subsidise his lifestyle at
Borgia's court. As before, he was nervous about his position at the
chancery and almost completely dependent on his friends (especially Biagio Buonaccorsi) to keep him informed of events within
the cloistered world of the Signoria and to help him manage his
domestic affairs.

This last factor was a major consideration for him. In early
October, as he had prepared for the journey to Imola, he had told
his wife that he would be away for no more than two weeks, but as
October dissolved into November and the weeks passed,

punctuated by far fewer letters home than she had hoped for, Marietta grew steadily more irritated with him.

Her frustration was exacerbated by the fact that for almost a year after their marriage and with their first child a few months old, Machiavelli had not yet paid Marietta her dowry in full. During the early part of the mission Marietta had tried communicating with him through Biagio, sending him messages of love and telling him how much she missed him. But then, as the commission dragged on and there was no news of when he might hope to return home, she began to withdraw and eventually became frustrated and angry with her husband. 'Madonna Marietta is angry and does not want to write to you. I cannot do anything else,' Biagio informed Machiavelli in late November.[19]

A month later, with Marietta's dowry still not paid and no clear idea of when the mission would end, Biagio reported: 'I go wallowing about and I am waiting for you, by God, very anxiously, and I can't wait. Madonna Marietta is cursing God, and she feels she has thrown away both her body and her possessions. For your own sake, arrange for her to have her dowry like other women, otherwise we won't hear the end of it.'[20]

By this time Biagio himself was growing impatient with Machiavelli. Only the day after this latest friendly letter, his mood had changed, presumably because his last letter had crossed with a businesslike missive from Machiavelli. 'Stick it up your ass,' Buonaccorsi declares in a letter of 22 December. 'We are sending you money and cloth and what you ask for, and Madonna Marietta is desperate.'[21]

But there were compensations. Most importantly, the seeds for *The Prince* were planted during the autumn of 1502 and these were nurtured during Machiavelli's many meetings with Cesare Borgia. The Borgia court was also an exciting place which, for a short time, lay at the epicentre of Italian politics. Great leaders, military experts, cardinals, aspiring diplomats and politicians were all drawn to

Cesare Borgia like moths to a flame; he was the man of the moment.

One of those attracted by the excitement of it all and the potential it offered him was Leonardo da Vinci. Then fifty years old, Leonardo was at the peak of his powers, respected throughout Italy as a master artist, and he was enjoying a growing reputation as a military engineer of genius. He had probably first been introduced to Cesare Borgia by Louis XII, who had met the artist when the French had invaded Milan in 1499, but some historical commentators have seen Leonardo's brief liaison with Borgia as strange, and wonder how this vegetarian pacifist artist could have even considered working for a man who was renowned for his ruthlessness and his insatiable hunger for power. But this is to ignore the fact that Leonardo, like almost all artists of the era, was dependent on patronage for his livelihood. For some fifteen years he had served the dictator Ludovico Sforza, and like any other creative spirit of the Renaissance, he could ill afford to be too choosy about the morals of his employers.

During much of 1502 Leonardo travelled through Italy as Cesare Borgia's engineer, a job that took him from one city to another, where he would suggest improvements that could be made to fortifications and where he developed ideas for defensive systems. It was an immensely satisfying time for Leonardo and in a little notebook (now called *Manuscript L* and kept in the Institut de France in Paris) he recorded designs for defensive devices and curious weapons, questioning such things as the best profile for a buttress or a defensive wall. At the same time he pursued elaborate investigations into how best to build walls that would deflect arrows or protect defenders from projectiles and fire. In addition he created movable defences, bridges that could be dismantled and transported long distances, plans for secret escape tunnels and fortresses with self-contained inner chambers that would remain hidden even after the ramparts had been breached. Alongside these ideas, the notebook contains descriptions of such eccentric inventions as sword-eating shields and schemes to create 'defensive curtains' that could deflect any known weapon.

It is likely that Machiavelli first encountered Leonardo in November 1502 in Imola, and they were to meet on many subsequent occasions in Florence and Rome. In letters written to the Signoria, Machiavelli mentions 'a friend' at Cesare Borgia's court and 'another who is also acquainted with the Lord's [Borgia's] secrets'.[22]

At first glance it seems that Leonardo and Machiavelli had little in common. They were in many ways quite different in temperament, for Machiavelli was drawn to an area of human activity that stood diametrically opposed to the aims of the artist. He was interested in society and military power, his ideas governed by bureaucracy and the pursuit of order. But, looking beneath the surface, we may see many points of compatibility between the two men. They were born some seventeen years apart, but Machiavelli had grown up within a few streets of the studio in which Leonardo had served his apprenticeship. They were both Florentines, and shared a history, a culture, a stance. But, more than this, they came from the same social class. Leonardo's father had been a lawyer, but his opportunities had been blighted by the fact that he was illegitimate, and so he had faced similar constraints to Niccolò, whose father had been a tax debtor. Machiavelli had been a poet at the Medici court, but his family had not supported their politics. Leonardo had not been liked by Lorenzo the Magnificent, and later he was largely ignored by the Medici, who instead favoured his great rival, Michelangelo.

Machiavelli was a man of action, a heterosexual drinker and womaniser, while Leonardo was a homosexual teetotaller who did not frequent either inn or brothel. But Machiavelli was also cerebral and literary with a razor-sharp mind. He was witty, charming and a wonderful conversationalist. Like Leonardo, he was an autodidact, and although his outlook was very different from Leonardo's inspired way of seeing the world, it is extremely likely that Machiavelli found the artist and inventor's freedom of thought, his intensity and his drive, inspiring. The two men worked in very different fields, and throughout his life Leonardo appears to have felt nothing but apathy towards politics and the schemes of princes, yet nevertheless he would have appreciated Machiavelli's clarity of vision and his 'scientific' objectivity towards human behaviour as he was later to express it in *The Prince*. (The meeting at Imola was probably brief, but the two men remained friends and Machiavelli recommended Leonardo to the Signoria as both an artist and an engineer.

By the last weeks of 1502 Machiavelli, aware of the genuine feeling behind the imprecations of his wife and his friends, and feeling homesick, was beginning to believe that Cesare Borgia and the government of Florence could never work closely together. Having reached this conclusion, he requested permission to return to his duties at the Palazzo Vecchio as soon as possible, but each request was denied and he was told he had to continue observing the duke and report back with every scrap of information he could obtain concerning the man and his movements. However, in one letter written in late December, the gonfalonier, Piero Soderini, told Machiavelli that 'someone will be designated to come to take your place there . . . you will continue in your duties to keep a good watch on affairs over there and you must write often'.[23]

Then, just as Machiavelli was beginning to despair, the duke moved unexpectedly against the conspirators who had threatened him a few months earlier. After months of secret planning he was ready to exact his revenge on Vitelli and the others. Machiavelli left Imola with the duke's forces on 20 December, travelling on horseback and heading for Cesena, about thirty miles to the south-east. When he arrived in the town, a message from the gonfalonier was awaiting him which said: 'Maintain the diligence you have exercised up to now.'[24]

Machiavelli hardly needed reminding of this, and soon he found himself a witness to a bloodbath. This began on 22 December. Duke Valentino's army was about to leave Cesena en route for Fano when he ordered the murder of his own right-hand man, Remirro de Orco. De Orco was a ruthless captain and no less psychotic than the Pope's son. Since the duke's occupation of the Romagna in 1500, he had terrorised its citizens and was both feared and loathed. De Orco was cut in two and dumped in the town square.

Machiavelli was stunned by this savagery. In a letter to the Ten of War in Florence he declared that 'the duke shows that he can make and unmake men at will according to their merits'.[25] He realised immediately that in taking this action Duke Valentino was not only demonstrating his autocratic power, he was presenting the mutilated body of the detested de Orco as a gift to the people who had suffered under him. A decade later he used this incident as an example of how a strong leader maintains order among his underlings:

> So he placed there Remirro de Orco, a cruel, efficient man, to whom he entrusted the fullest powers. In a short time this Remirro pacified and united the Romagna, winning great credit for himself. Then the duke decided that there was no need for this excessive authority, which might grow intolerable . . . He determined to show that if cruelties had been inflicted they were not his doing but prompted by the harsh nature of their minister. This gave Cesare a pretext: then, one morning, Remirro's body was found cut in two pieces on the piazza at Cesena with a block of wood and a bloody knife beside it. The brutality of this spectacle kept the people of the Romagna for a long time appeased and stupefied.[26]

From Cesena, Borgia headed south again, a day's ride to the coastal town of Fano. As he was leaving, he had heard reports that Paolo and Francesco Orsini and Vitelli had also moved their forces. They had taken and sacked the small town of Sinigaglia. The duke reached Fano, took it effortlessly, and with a small force he set out for Sinigaglia to meet the conspirators.

Sending ahead messengers, Duke Valentino declared that he wished to broker a peace between himself and his erstwhile colleagues. Perhaps unaware of how strong a force he had at his command, Vitelli and the Orsinis were lulled into a false sense of security and agreed to meet him on the road between Fano and Sinigaglia. At this meeting the duke convinced the conspirators that he wished to end the conflict and form a new alliance.

It was the worst and the last mistake the rebels made. Once they were inside the city gates, they were seized by the duke's men and held prisoner. Dubbing them the '*dieta de falliti*' ('assembly of failures'), Borgia had them all strangled.

After witnessing the disposal of Remirro de Orco at Cesena, Machiavelli had acquired some measure of Borgia's ruthlessness. After following the duke and his men to Sinigaglia, the Florentine Secretary found himself in the thick of things as the duke carried out his treachery. On 31 December he wrote to the Ten of War: 'The town is being sacked, and it is 11 o'clock at night. I am extremely worried. I don't know if I shall be able to find anyone to take this letter. I will write at length later. My opinion is that they [the conspirators] will not be alive tomorrow.'[27] The next day the duke's forces had moved on to Corinaldo. On 3 January 1503 the entire force reached Gualdo. From there the army moved on to take Assisi by the 8th and Torciano on the 10th.

By the end of January it seemed to Machiavelli that Borgia was now losing any wish to work with Florence. The emissary had spent three months trying to create a workable agreement between the duke and the Republic and it had come to nothing. He was also homesick and concerned for his position in the Palazzo Vecchio. After numerous requests had fallen on deaf ears, the Signoria finally approved Machiavelli's return to Florence and acceded to Duke Valentino's request to be allowed to negotiate with a member of the government itself. Machiavelli headed for home just as Jacopo Salviati, one of the leading figures within the Signoria, took over the thankless task of trying to forge an alliance between the duke and the Florentine government.

Machiavelli returned home on 23 January and did his best to make his peace with Marietta and to spend a little time with Primerana, who was only four months old when he had left for Imola. Back at the chancery, he was debriefed by Piero Soderini and his colleagues, and when he could find time he began to untangle the amazing web of events he had just experienced. From this contemplation came an early template for *The Prince*, a detailed account of the events at Sinigaglia entitled *Descrizione del modo tenuto dal Duca Valentino nell'ammazzare Vitellozzo Vitelli* . . . (*Description of the Method Used by Duke Valentino to Kill Vitellozzo* . . .). A document written in matter-of-fact, almost journalistic style, it makes for chilling reading.

The danger presented by the Borgias had not passed, but was merely lying dormant for a while. For quite how long, no one in Florence knew. The Pope desired closer ties with the French and wanted them to launch a military campaign to push back the Venetians, who were once more making infringements into the war-torn Romagna. By the spring of 1503 Alexander was growing impatient with Louis and complaining of the king's intransigence. Meanwhile France and Spain were in conflict over Naples, and the Pope was beginning to make clandestine overtures towards the Spanish. Machiavelli believed this to be a very dangerous development that had the potential to destabilise the fragile balance of power. Through Agostino Vespucci in Rome he made strenuous efforts to warn his masters of the trouble brewing, but his views were largely ignored.

Misreading the fact that the major powers appeared to have lost interest in Florence, the Florentine government, much to Machiavelli's disgust, decided to raise an army to turn against its old adversary Pisa and to waste money and resources in another attempt to regain its lost dominion. The Signoria was ignoring the bigger picture, and as the summer advanced, Alexander's scheming intensified. By July he had made it clear that he had switched his allegiance to Spain and was discarding the French. Vespucci kept the Signoria appraised of these moves, but it ignored him.

It was obvious that the Pope was preparing for a showdown – what would have become one of the most incendiary campaigns of the era. By trying to play one superpower off against the other, he was inciting conflict, and if fate had not taken a hand his actions might well have precipitated a pan-European war in 1503. On the night of 10 August, in an attempt to poison one of his political opponents, Cardinal Adriano di Corneto, during a dinner party in Rome, Alexander instead succeeded in killing himself and making his son Cesare desperately ill. The Pope took seven days to die in abject agony, while Cesare fought a fever and excruciating stomach pains. He pulled through but was greatly weakened by the poison.

Machiavelli, who heard all about the incident in detail from Vespucci, realised immediately that it was a significant event, and, convinced that the Signoria should send him as an emissary (and a spy), he made ready to leave. But, in typical style, his government saw no particular urgency in the situation and decided against sending any emissary or other representative to the Vatican.

Other powers were not so slow in responding to the shock of Alexander's sudden death. Louis had immediately mobilised his forces, diverting them from a planned move on Naples to instead confront the Spanish. Within days of the Pope's death a large French force was camped just outside the walls of Rome waiting for the results of the conclave, the assembly of cardinals charged with electing his successor.

The cardinals were thought to be considering a choice between three prospective candidates for the papacy: Georges d'Amboise, Giuliano della Rovere and Ascanio Sforza. But the election of any one of these men would have been controversial and dangerous and so, when the vote was made, the College decided to elect a compromise candidate, the prematurely old and ill Cardinal Francesco Piccolomini. On 22 September he took the name of Pius III in honour of his uncle and was crowned on 8 October. Ten days later he was dead.

The death of Pius sent shock waves through Europe and even the Signoria responded quickly. Within twenty-four hours of this news reaching Florence on 20 October, the Ten of War had drawn up Machiavelli's orders to travel to Rome and he was on the road by daybreak on 24 October. Officially his mission was to observe and to report on the election of the new pope, but he had letters of introduction to all the key players in Rome, including the three prime papal candidates, Giuliano della Rovere, who was now the favourite, Georges d'Amboise, whom he already knew well, and Ascanio Sforza, the brother of Ludovico Sforza (Il Moro), the deposed Duke of Milan. The real agenda for Machiavelli was to watch Cesare Borgia like a hawk and to report back to the Signoria every detail of his movements, for it was clear that the outcome of the election would seal the fate of the duke and with it the future of the Florentine Republic.

Machiavelli found Rome cast in aspic; all matters of state had been put on hold while the cardinals sat in conclave. As the son of the dead pope, a power broker with influence at the French court and a cardinal in his own right, Cesare Borgia was at the very centre of this political maelstrom. 'Duke Valentino is much cultivated by those who wish to be Pope . . .,' Machiavelli reported to the Ten of War soon after arriving in the city, 'the Spanish cardinals, his favourites, and many other cardinals have been to talk to him every day in the castle, so that it is thought that whoever becomes pope will be indebted to him, and he lives in the hope of being favoured by the new pope.'[28]

Borgia was aware that the outcome of the election would both change the face of Italian politics and determine his own future. He knew, as Machiavelli knew, that this would be the fight of his life. Yet from the start there seemed to be something not quite right about the young duke. Something had changed. Probably for the first time in his life, he had become indecisive, unsure.

Machiavelli was stunned by this change of character and confused by Borgia's deliberations over the election. He believed the duke should have put his weight behind a little-known cardinal, a man he could manipulate for his own purposes. Failing that, support for Louis's favourite, the king's right-hand man, Georges d'Amboise, would perhaps have gelled Borgia's relationship with France and brought him the king's favour. But, to the surprise of everyone, the duke instead used his influence to help elect Cardinal Giuliano della Rovere, a man who had loathed the Borgias, a grudge bearer who had been wronged by Cesare and Alexander on numerous occasions.

Machiavelli knew this was a terrible mistake and later wrote of it: 'The duke deserves censure only regarding the election of Pope Julius, where he made a bad choice . . . Not being able to get a pope to his liking he could have kept the papacy from going to one who was not; and he should never have allowed the election of one of those cardinals he had injured, or one who would have cause to fear him. Men do harm either because they fear you or because they hate you.'[29]

Cardinal Della Rovere was elected pope on 31 October, taking the name Julius II. Like many popes before and after him, he was a corrupt man who was far more interested in temporal power and influence than in leading his flock. To those who assisted his election he had promised so many things that he could not have possibly honoured a fraction of them, even if had wanted to. It is believed that Cesare Borgia's price had been the entire Romagna as his princedom. Della Rovere had convinced him this would be his; but he was lying and set on a course of betrayal.

To Machiavelli's bewilderment, Borgia, a man renowned throughout Christendom for his treachery and corrupt methods, had placed his fate in the hands of a man he knew to be a deadly enemy of his family and had convinced himself that the cardinal would keep his word. 'The duke allows himself to be carried away by his brave confidence, and believes that other people's words are more to be relied upon than his own were,'[30] he reported to the Ten of War.

November 1503 was a black month for Borgia, and Machiavelli could do nothing but watch astonished as the man whom he had considered 'a most splendid and magnificent lord' seemed to have become rudderless, confused, easily manipulated and abused by the new pope. 'The duke's affairs have suffered a thousand changes . . .,' he observed, 'and it is true that they have continuously gone from bad to worse.'[31]

Machiavelli was not the only one to witness the sudden degeneration in Borgia's fortunes. The Cardinal of Volterra, Francesco Soderini, visited the duke shortly after the election of Julius II and found him 'variable, irresolute, and suspicious, and incapable of consistency in any opinion . . . whether is thus by nature, or whether these blows of fortune may have stupefied him'. Another visitor wrote that 'he was out of his mind, for he himself does not know what he wants to do, so wrapped up in himself is he, and so irresolute'.[32]

Gradually Machiavelli's confusion turned to contempt. He had once considered Cesare Borgia to be the very model of the all-conquering, ruthless prince, but now he saw him as an extinguished flame. Towards the end of November, only three months after the death of his father, Cesare was, Machiavelli observed, a man whose sins 'have brought him little by little to penance. And so, inch by inch, the Duke slips into the tomb.'[33]

Borgia knew the game was up. As rumours circulated that he had been murdered, that his body had been dragged from the Tiber or that he had fled Rome to regroup with his army, he was in fact trying to cling on to the last vestiges of his power. After fraught negotiations with Julius, he had agreed to return his dominions in the Romagna to the rulers he had defeated only a year or two earlier.

During the last days of November, Borgia finally fled Rome. Outside the city he met up with a small but well-armed army of loyal supporters. Yet, even then, he could not decide what to do, and his indecision cost him dear. His many crimes and those of his evil father were at last coming out into the open in Rome, and across Europe deposed noblemen, church leaders, vengeful victims and righteous leaders were calling for him to be strung up and flayed alive. In a letter to his government, Machiavelli made clear that Borgia's arrest would be to their advantage. 'As soon as he is taken . . .,' he declared, 'whether dead or alive, it will be possible to think of one's own affairs.'[34]

Borgia's escape bid failed miserably, just as everything else had failed for him that unforgiving season. To the delight of the gloating Julius II, he was arrested not far from the city walls and brought in chains to Rome. With unalloyed irony, this new pope, a man perhaps only slightly less debauched than Alexander or Cesare, declared: 'Now that he is taken, there is an opportunity for us to reveal all the cruel robberies, homicides, sacrileges and other endless evils which for eleven years had been committed in Rome against God and man.'[35]

Machiavelli was there looking on as the prisoner was flung into the Vatican prisons. By this time he had his orders to return to Florence and was preparing for his long journey north. The entire drama of his experiences so closely shadowing one of the most infamous men of his or any age had passed in little more than eighteen months. Cesare Borgia's black life was approaching an end, and within four years he was dead, murdered in 1507 by brigands on the road to the court of his brother-in-law, the King of Navarre, where he had been sent in exile by Julius, the man he had foolishly entrusted with his fate.

For Machiavelli the entire adventure had done more to shape his thinking and to mould his political vision than anything he had experienced up to this time. For him the Borgia who would act as the immutable model for his prince was the dark lord who had strutted arrogantly through the Romagna. The pathetic broken man who had been damaged by poison and then brought down by powerful enemies who had employed the very tools he had once himself used was not part of the picture.

The day Cesare Borgia was imprisoned, 5 December 1503, was also the day of Julius's coronation. In spite of fears concerning an outbreak of the plague, Machiavelli tarried in Rome just long enough to witness the event. The ceremony over, he concluded his affairs in the city, fulfilled his final obligations as a diplomat by organising future meetings between the Signoria and the new power brokers at the Vatican and set off for Florence.

By this time Machiavelli was keen to get home. He had been away for almost eight weeks. During that time Marietta had given birth to their second child, whom they named Bernardo, in honour of Niccolò's father. The city Machiavelli now left behind him had altered radically during the three months since the death of the Borgia pope, and with it the entire political map of Italy had once more been redrawn.

Machiavelli had enjoyed the privilege of witnessing the bridging of two eras. The Borgias' power in Italy had crumbled with shocking ease. The Florentines were understandably relieved by Duke Valentino's unexpected fall, but Machiavelli remained justifiably cautious. The transition between eras was, he understood, a dangerous time, one filled with political instability and uncertainty, and Florence, he also knew, had in recent years experienced its fair share of close shaves. Because he could see and analyse with such clarity he could never rest easy, nor, after all he had learned, could he feel confident about the ability of Florence to always escape intact the vicissitudes that lay around every corner.

5

Machiavelli's *Cause Célèbre*

During the summer of 1502, between Machiavelli's two missions to the court of Cesare Borgia, Florence had gone through a long-overdue constitutional change. The government of the city had been based loosely on the Venetian system whereby small councils were answerable to a group of ministers, the Signoria, headed by a gonfalonier. The most influential figures in the political life of the city, the wealthy landowners and nobility – referred to as the *ottimati*, or principal citizens – were keen to refine the political system and adopt a form of government that was even closer to the Venetian paradigm in having a gonfalonier who enjoyed lifelong tenure.

Some of the *ottimati* favoured a complete overhaul of Florence's governmental system, including the scrapping of many of the councils and committees and a streamlining of the structure, perhaps resulting in a two-tier government. But it was agreed that such reforms would have proved too radical, so instead, believing that such a system could better guide the Republic in modern Italy, they established a form of presidency in which a head of state would hold the position for life: in effect, it was the adoption of the role of the Venetian Doge.

Recent events had crystallised the thinking of the radical members of the influential *ottimati* and had accelerated the move towards reform. The city had gone through some of the most violent and disruptive times in its history. Since the loss of the Medici, who had themselves been lifelong leaders without an official mandate, the Florentines had suffered the tyranny of Savonarola, the dictates of the French, the threats of the Borgias and a constant stream of military and political humiliations. Machiavelli had realised long before that part of the cause of these woes was the system of government favoured in Florence. Only now, with such misery behind them, could the reformists begin to bring about change.

The man chosen from a field of 236 candidates and elected to the position of the first gonfalonier for life was Piero Soderini. Born in Florence in 1452, five weeks after Leonardo da Vinci, Soderini had been involved in politics from an early age. The family had been great rivals of the Medici; Piero's father, Tommaso, had been gonfalonier five times during the previous century, and his uncle, Niccolò, had headed an ill-fated uprising against Cosimo de' Medici in 1465. Although some of the other *ottimati* viewed his election by the Great Council as something of a compromise, Soderini was a popular choice with the people of Florence. 'Seeing his services used more than anyone else's, and not considering that the reason was that his equals avoided office,' the contemporary historian Francesco Guicciardini commented, 'they thought that he must be more able than the others.'[1] In other words Soderini was considered an able politician and had not been chosen simply because, as often happened in Florentine politics, no one else wanted the responsibility.

For Machiavelli the election of Piero Soderini was to prove one of the most important events in his career. Machiavelli was already a good friend of the gonfalonier's brother, Francesco Soderini, the Bishop of Volterra. They had travelled together to the court of Cesare Borgia in June 1502 and Francesco did much to promote the Secretary's career and push forward his ideas. Before becoming the gonfalonier, Piero Soderini had been one of the most powerful figures in the Great Council, and he was a man who appreciated not only Machiavelli's political acumen but also his eloquence and the literary ability he often demonstrated in official papers and correspondence during his foreign missions. Within weeks of coming to power, he was calling on Machiavelli for help and employing his skills as both an analyst and a writer. The respect for Machiavelli felt by the Soderini brothers is clear to see in surviving correspondence. While Piero wrote to Machiavelli instructing him to watch every move made by Cesare Borgia, Duke Valentino, during the emissary's time at the Imola court, he also wrote personal comments and referred to his most trusted aide as 'dear friend' and frequently used the familiar 'tu'.[2]

One of Soderini's first tasks was to reorganise the political system as thoroughly as the constitution would allow. He, perhaps more than anyone apart from Machiavelli himself, realised that many of the problems the city had faced and barely survived in recent years had been caused by political amateurism. In a letter to Machiavelli he admitted: 'We have found the city very disorganised in respect to money, allotments and many other things.'[3] However, he also realised that things had been made worse by the inability of his peers to communicate properly with influential Florentine citizens who were not in government.

To Soderini's great credit, he was quick to realise the value and scope of Machiavelli's skills and used him to influence the thinking of his government and the nobility who elected it. In November 1502 the gonfalonier delivered a speech to the Great Council written by Machiavelli and called *Words to Be Spoken on the Law for Appropriating Money, after Giving a Little Introduction and Excuse*. Soderini needed to generate funds to finance his plans for reform and hoped that a combination of his own powers as an orator and Machiavelli's gift for language would win over his peers.

The collaboration was a success and Soderini got approval and funding. But Machiavelli, fired up by this success, saw this achievement as merely a stepping stone. Acquiring money and approval to improve the machinations of government was, he realised, an important move forward for Florence and a great improvement on the clumsy system that had been employed before this reform, but he knew that Florence's political weakness derived primarily from its military impotence. With Soderini now in power and on his side, he believed the time was right for him to begin to lobby for more radical reforms.

Machiavelli once claimed that *The Discourses* had been shaped by his 'long experience of modern things'. But, many years before he could say this of his most famous treatise, he could have applied the statement equally well to justify his conviction that Florence needed a well-funded and well-trained citizens' army. He had seen how the army of Cesare Borgia had so easily swept through Italy. He had witnessed at first hand the immense muscle of France, the sophisticated army of a pan-European superpower, and he could see how Venice, the only other republic in Italy, had used its powerful army and navy to great effect.

Although Venice employed foreign condottieri, most of its military forces were under the control of Venetian commanders and all were closely and carefully supervised by the ruling council and the Doge. In 1495 Venice, a city with a population of some 200,000, boasted an army of 15,500 horsemen, 24,000 infantrymen and 3300 members of what would now be called 'special forces'. Coupled with this, the city supported 36,000 naval personnel, manning forty-five fully equipped galleys with 16,000 shipwrights working at the Arsenal and other naval bases.

During the first decade of the sixteenth century Florence had a population less than a quarter that of Venice, and even Machiavelli never imagined his city could compete militarily with the Venetian Republic. What he wanted was an independent force, made up of

Florentines, to protect Florence. He made this point clear in *The Prince* when he wrote: 'I say that, in my judgement, those princes can stand alone who have sufficient manpower or money to assemble an army equal to an encounter with any aggressor.'[4]

Knowing that it would prove extremely difficult for him to persuade the Florentine government that a militia was necessary, Machiavelli grasped every opportunity to convey his opinion to the people of influence in Florence. His versatile and direct method was to write speeches for the gonfalonier. 'Every city, every state ought to consider as enemies all those who can hope to take possession of her territory and against whom she cannot defend herself,' he told the Great Council through Soderini.[5] 'Fortune does not change her decision when there is no change in procedure . . .,' he declared in another speech written for the gonfalonier, 'and the heavens do not wish or are not able to support a city determined to fall. Such a fall I cannot believe in, when I see that you are free Florentines and that your liberty rests in your own hands. For that liberty I believe you will have such regard as those who are born free and hope to live free always have had.'[6]

Employing another Soderini speech to the Great Council, Machiavelli hammered home his point by offering the councillors a slice of recent history dished up as a parable. The story came from the fall of Constantinople to the Turks in 1453. Shortly before the Turkish forces attacked, the emperor beseeched his people to provide through taxes the funds he needed to build up the city's army so they could defend themselves against the invaders. But, instead of support, all he received was ridicule and mockery. A few months later, as Turkish cannonballs rained down and the city walls were breached, the citizens of Constantinople ran to their emperor offering him as much money as he wanted: 'Go away and die with your money . . .,' he told them, 'since you have not wished to live without it.'[7]

Piero Soderini's brother Francesco was Machiavelli's most

dedicated supporter over the proposal for a citizens' militia, but he was aware how the people of Florence were resistant to the notion. In May 1504 he wrote to him declaring: 'The argument against the militia is not good in a thing so necessary and so sound, and they cannot be suspicious of the force, which will not be raised for private but for public convenience. Do not give up, for perhaps the favour that is not given one day will be given another.'[8] These were encouraging words, and Machiavelli felt confident he could bring about reform.

But then, in the autumn of 1504, his plans seemed to founder completely, for Piero Soderini's support had cooled and even those councillors who seemed to have been coming round to the idea were backing off. The reason for this is clear from Francesco Soderini's letter and his claims as to why there should be no objection to Machiavelli's scheme. It came down to the fact that the people of Florence were suspicious of anyone who might gain the potential to establish a dictatorship. They now had a gonfalonier with a lifelong tenure and they were nervous about the idea that he might wish to create an army for his own ends rather than for the benefit of the city. Francesco Soderini had described it as 'a force raised not for private but for public convenience'.[9] But it was almost two hundred years since Florence had kept its own army and some prominent and influential Florentines feared that the gonfalonier might use such a force, as one nobleman stated, 'to remove the citizens who were his enemies'.[10]

Machiavelli had been appealing to the Florentines through parable, through example, and with his piercing, carefully worded logic, but their resistance was not intellectual. Instead it derived from fear and misinterpreted memory. Since the death of Lorenzo de' Medici they had seen Savonarola establish himself as a dictator, and they could glance over at Milan and see the way in which Ludovico Sforza had established his autocratic state. In all this somehow they chose to ignore the example of Venice.

Piero Soderini was placed in the bind all politicians experience at some point in their career. He supported Machiavelli's ideas and had done much to advance them, but during the summer and autumn of 1504 he began to realise that the majority of councillors were utterly opposed to the concept of an independent Florentine army and knew that in order to save his political career he needed to distance himself from Machiavelli's scheme.

Francesco Soderini, now a cardinal, made excuses for his brother in private letters to Machiavelli. 'Concerning recruitment,' he wrote in October 1504, 'we are of the same opinion, but we are afraid that the person whose enthusiasm you say has cooled off [Piero Soderini] has done so to take away the opportunity from those who want to speak and do ill and to interpret the public good as if it were private good.'

A master political analyst, Machiavelli was aware of this without Francesco Soderini having to spell it out for him, but such knowledge did nothing to change the dangers Florence faced if it continued to ignore the shifting sands of modern politics. As Machiavelli had once told the Great Council through Soderini: 'Fortune does not change her decision when there is no change in procedure.' And indeed fortune was soon to help Machiavelli to convince all but the most stubborn and suspicious that the time had come to at least give his scheme a chance.

Pope Alexander VI's death in 1503 had changed many more lives than that of his beloved son. Italian politics, always a volatile blend ready to ignite from the smallest of sparks, was thrown into disarray by the election of Julius II. The delicate stalemates and the carefully monitored power balance had shifted, and the greedy and the avaricious immediately grabbed at opportunities for personal gain. Through them, states were moved to act and new uncertainties affected the life of every citizen throughout Europe.

The stability of the Florentine Republic was once more under threat from outside forces. With Cesare Borgia effectively neutered by Julius II, the Venetians, who had always considered the Romagna as almost an extension of their state, had no qualms about sending their forces into the region to take advantage of the new power vacuum. The old rulers of the region, the petty noblemen who had been ousted by Duke Valentino, were naturally anxious to take back their lost dominions and many had received promises to this effect from the new pope himself. However, having made his promises, Julius was now contemplating grabbing the Romagna for himself.

To complicate the situation further, as Venice and the Vatican looked likely to clash head on, late in December 1503, within three weeks of the coronation of the new pope, the uneasy peace between the two superpowers of Europe, France and Spain, had ended with the Battle of Garigliano, near Cassino, in southern central Italy.

In part because of the superiority of the Spanish infantry, but also thanks to the skills of their commander, Gonzalo Fernández de Córdoba, the Spanish had won a resounding victory at Garigliano. (Garigliano has been the site of numerous crucial battles since ancient times. Six hundred years before this conflict, in 915, an alliance between Empress Zoe Carbospina and Pope John X led to a resounding victory at the Battle of Garigliano which ended the Arabic threat to Italy. Almost five hundred years after the great Spanish victory against the French, between November 1943 and May 1944, a series of battles between Allied and Axis forces near Garigliano eventually allowed the Allies to drive on to Rome and the eventual liberation of Italy.) Because Florence had forged such close ties with Louis, the defeat of the French caused shock and dismay in the Palazzo Vecchio. And coming as it did just as fresh fears were growing over Venetian interest in the Romagna, which posed a direct threat to Florentine interests, it meant Florence was once more facing peril. The optimists supposed that the French would want to create closer ties with Florence and other powers to forge alliances to resist the Spanish, but others believed they would turn inwards to protect their own interests, allowing Florence's enemies, especially the Venetians, to do what they liked.

Amid such turmoil the Florentines again decided to make things worse for themselves by returning to their old grievance against Pisa. The squabbling over the city had been simmering for years as more serious military concerns precipitated by the Borgias, Louis, the Pope, the Venetians and the Spanish took centre stage. But suddenly the question of Pisa was intimately linked with the brewing crisis in the Romagna, because it was clear to the Signoria that Pisa lay wide open to attack from Venice, and if it fell it would mean disaster for Florence. This prompted the Signoria to place Pisa at the top of its list of priorities and to attempt to dispense with the problems it caused once and for all.

Using the customary expensive mercenaries, in April the Florentines laid siege to Pisa, burned the countryside around the city and retook the nearby town of Librafatta. Realising that no siege of the city could succeed unless the Pisans were denied supplies coming from the sea, which they were acquiring from the Genoese, who were keen to make a quick ducat, the Florentines placed their own ships at the mouth of the River Arno, which flows through Pisa. But even then the Pisans showed no sign of capitulation. Months passed and the Florentines began to feel frustrated with the stalemate. It soon became apparent that the siege was failing, and having little stomach for an all-out attack on Pisa that might expose them to their more powerful enemies on all sides, the Florentine government saw it had reached an impasse. It was then that someone proposed the radical idea of diverting the Arno so that instead of flowing through Pisa it would turn towards Leghorn and transform the land around Pisa into a marsh.

It is possible that Machiavelli was the source of the idea, but although he was vocal in his support for the project and worked hard on it throughout the summer of 1504, there is no documentary evidence to prove it was his brainchild. What is certain is that in desperation the government embraced the idea wholeheartedly. It was encouraged in this both by Machiavelli and the man who designed the method for diverting the river, Leonardo da Vinci. In June 1504 Leonardo visited the area around Pisa and drew maps of the region, and although the Signoria spent some time considering plans and proposals from a number of engineers, it was, thanks largely to Machiavelli's influence, Leonardo's scheme that was eventually implemented.

Leonardo had been thinking about using natural resources in warfare for many years, and in 1500 he had proposed to the Venetians a method of defending themselves against the Turks by flooding the Isonzo valley by damming the river. To the Pisa problem, Leonardo applied similar thinking and suggested that the Arno be diverted a few miles from Pisa. This would, he argued, have the twin effects of depriving the town of water and cutting it off from its harbour, which together, he reasoned, would end the siege far quicker than the methods already tried.

The scheme was begun in August with all the resources the Signoria could divert from other fronts. It involved building a huge wooden barrier across the Arno and digging two enormous channels some eight miles long which would divert the water to a large lake and then on to the sea, cutting it off before it reached Pisa. In a report written a few months later, Machiavelli's assistant Biagio Buonaccorsi described the commencement of the project:

> At this time it was considered taking the Arno River away from the Pisans in order to conduct it into the Stagno di Livorno, for it was shown with good reasons that besides depriving the Pisans of their source of life, those who were undertaking this project were to benefit our town immensely, therefore the decision to undertake the project being taken, the camp was set up at Riglione after having cut the forage, and a Maestro d'Acque Colombino was summoned, who was asked to state what was

necessary to complete the undertaking. He asked for two thousand labourers a day equipped with wood necessary to construct a weir in order to retain the river and divert it into two big ditches through which the Arno was to flow. It was planned to go all the way to the Stagno; and he promised that the undertaking could be carried out with thirty or forty thousand works [man days], and so, provided with such a hope, the project was undertaken on 20 August . . .[11]

With hindsight it is evident that this scheme would almost certainly have worked, but it was too radical for most of those involved in raising the finance, and it was also opposed by those who believed that such efforts were in some way an intrusion into God's dominion. A friend of Machiavelli's, Ercole Bentivoglio, who was with the army besieging Pisa, expressed the second view when he declared: 'Certainly, as far as human judgement can see, we cannot hope for anything but ill, if He that saved the people of Israel from the hands of Pharaoh does not open up for us in the midst of this tossing sea an unexpected road to salvation, as that one once was.'[12] At a crucial moment, and in spite of Machiavelli's protestations, the Signoria began to pay attention to men like Bentivoglio. Leonardo's methods were scrapped and the Signoria opted for a cheap version which proved to be quite inadequate and was plagued with problems from the start.

Under this new scheme the walls of channels kept collapsing, the barrier could not be built properly with the manpower made available, and the work quickly fell badly behind schedule. Then the weather turned against the workforce just as the Pisans began carefully planned raids attacking the workers as they dug. Still confident of success, Machiavelli continued to help raise money and to divert men to the Arno project, but by the middle of the autumn the battle was lost, and the government made an about-turn, cancelling the entire project.

Machiavelli's contemporary Francesco Guicciardini said of the scheme in his history of Italy: 'This undertaking began with the greatest of expectations and was pursued with even greater expenses, but it turned out to be in vain because, as so frequently happens in such ventures, even though the surveys are based on virtually manifest proof, experience will prove them to be failures, the truest examples of the distance between plan and action.'[13]

The gonfalonier's brother, Francesco Soderini, wrote a consoling letter to Machiavelli in which he declared: 'Notable man and very dear *compare*. It gave us great pain that so great an error should have been made in those waters that it seems impossible to us that it should not have been through the fault of the engineers who went so far wrong. Perhaps it also pleases God thus, for some better end unknown to us.'[14]

Machiavelli did not record his feelings about the failure of the plan to divert the Arno, but he learned a great deal from the military fiasco played out during 1504, and he clearly had this on his mind when he later wrote in *The Discourses*: 'There is no easier way to make a republic where the people has authority come to ruin than to put it into mighty enterprises, for where the people is of any moment, they are always accepted; nor will there be any remedy for whoever is of another opinion. But if the ruin of the city arises from this, there arises also, and more often, the particular ruin of the citizens who are posted to such enterprises . . .'[15]

The project's collapse was regrettable, not simply because it cost the Florentine government a fortune and ended a proposal that may well have settled the Pisa question once and for all, but also because it was a great loss to the future economic power of Florence. Leonardo, always a man with grand schemes to pursue, had seen the diversion of the Arno as merely the first step in a magnificent plan to build a canal through Prato and under Mount Serravalle. Officially his plan had been an attempt to help end the conflict between Florence and Pisa without further bloodshed, but even before the soldiers began to dig, he had started to describe what in his fantasies would have been an industrial corridor along the banks of the Arno between the two cities. He visualised mills and what we would call factories, which could produce silk, paper, pottery and all manner of things, in industrial processes powered by water from the river. Transportation would be facilitated by barge along the river and a series of locks on the main tributaries of the Arno would allow small boats to navigate into the hills and the smaller towns around the main river valley.

All this Leonardo imagined almost three centuries before the Industrial Revolution. To him it was a thoroughly practical scheme that would greatly increase the standard of living of people in the region. It would, he believed, 'increase the value of the land; the cities of Prato, Pistoia, and Pisa, as well as Florence would gain thereby an annual income of two hundred thousand ducats'.[16] Elsewhere he wrote: 'If one were to divert the course of the Arno from top to bottom, all those who wished to would find a treasure in every plot of land.'[17]

As the Republic was preoccupied with Pisa and the fiasco of the Arno's diversion, the petty rulers of small city states surrounding Florence were being encouraged and financed by the Venetians (and possibly the Pope) to make incursions into Florentine territory. The leader of this group was Bartolomeo d'Aviano, a condottiere who commanded a small mercenary army augmented by a ragtag collection of malcontents and thugs, all funded directly by the Venetians.

Florentine intelligence became aware of d'Aviano's intentions during the late autumn of 1504. They also learned that some of the rulers of small states close to Florence were planning to exploit the weak position in which the Republic had found itself now that the French were otherwise occupied. To find out more about this potential danger, through the winter and into the spring of 1505 Machiavelli travelled from city to city in the Romagna and Tuscany.

He met again Jacopo d'Appiano at Piombino, with whom he had
had dealings on his very first foreign mission for the chancery back
in 1499. He travelled to Perugia to bring into line a wayward
Giampaolo Baglioni, lord of the city, and then he moved on to
thwart the plans of Pandolfo Petrucci, Lord of Siena, who was
trying to extort lands from Florence as payment for inside
information on his aggressive neighbours.

Machiavelli succeeded in exposing some of the intentions of
these petty leaders, but, spurred on by Venice, d'Aviano remained a
genuine threat who could not be talked down by Machiavelli or the
Signoria. He had formed a loose alliance of warlords and local
leaders who had quickly grasped how frail Florence had become,
caught as it was between the two great powers, France and Spain.
To them it offered a perfect opportunity to take advantage of the situation.

The matter came to a head on 17 August 1505 at San Vincenzo,
a coastal town about a hundred miles from Florence, when
d'Aviano's troops were met by a Florentine mercenary army led by
the condottiere Ercole Bentivoglio. The mercenaries employed by
the Republic overwhelmed the weaker force led by d'Aviano and
slaughtered or took captive almost the entire rebel army.

The Florentines were elated by this news and Machiavelli shared
their relief, but with this victory his plans for a Florentine army had
hit their lowest point. Why, the reasoning went, should the city go
to the trouble of creating its own standing army when a mercenary
force such as the one led by Bentivoglio could win such resounding
victories? It seemed like a fair point, but then the Florentine rulers
demonstrated perfectly the limitations of this view and gave
Machiavelli the chance he needed. In a rush of misguided confidence the Republic overstretched itself. Turning yet again to Pisa,
Piero Soderini ordered the triumphant army, newly returned to
Florence, to make all haste for Pisa. Once there, they surrounded
the city and on 6 September they attacked.

At first the battle went well. Huge holes were punched in the city walls, and even though the plucky Pisans were putting up a fight, Bentivoglio was able to send confident messages back to Florence as he made ready for the infantry to make a final push.

Nevertheless, victory once more slipped through the Florentines' fingers. Just as had happened five years earlier, when the Republic had faced the same enemy and used the very same method of a mercenary force, the hired infantry, who fought simply for gold and had no real interest in the issues, collapsed before the resistance of the Pisans. Fighting for their lives and for the welfare of their families, the defenders had nothing to lose and resisted with their last breath forcing the mercenaries to flee into the countryside.

This came as a shocking blow to those who had, only weeks before, celebrated the victory at San Vincenzo. From being a proposal completely out of step with fashionable thinking, Machiavelli's vision of an independent Florentine militia suddenly acquired new vitality. This latest military fiasco before the walls of their old enemy Pisa was an almost unbearable humiliation for Florence. The new confidence that had come from success at San Vincenzo vaporised and Soderini, fearful for his own position, gauged the moment was right to switch sides again. In private he admitted to Machiavelli that if the Florentines were simply presented with their own army and could see that there was no danger to themselves from such a force, they would not push to revoke the decision or to dismantle it. Giving full support to his Secretary, he went over the heads of the diehard opponents of the scheme, eschewed the slow machinations involved in pushing Machiavelli's proposal through the Great Council and immediately acquired the money and approval directly from the Ten of War.

Machiavelli set to work straight away. He had been evaluating the mechanics of his plan for so long that he needed no time to think. He knew that he could not create the army in the city itself, as this would be too provocative and dangerous. And although an alternative was to base the militia in one of the cities under Florentine control, this, he reasoned, was at least as dangerous because it could be used against the Republic by an aggressor, of whom there was no shortage. A third option was to recruit from the countryside around Florence, and this he adopted, basing his operations in two small towns to the north of the city, Mugello and Casentino.

Having already worked out how to build the infrastructure for such an undertaking, Machiavelli had, by New Year's Day 1506, begun recruiting from towns and villages beyond Florence. In his capacity as Secretary to the Ten of War, he placed himself in control of every step of the process. He talked to those who had volunteered and selected those suitable for training. Writing to the Ten, he declared half-mockingly: 'I commend myself to your Lordships and to these north winds, that teach me to go about on foot.'[18]

Yet, in spite of his enthusiasm, Machiavelli soon realised that he had neither the time nor the skills to train the soldiers himself. He required a man of experience, and late in January he made the controversial decision to hire Don Michelotto (also known as Miguel de Corella and Michele Coreglia), who had been Cesare Borgia's right-hand man, known to some as 'Valentino's stranger'.

There could not have been a more inflammatory choice, and Machiavelli was well aware of it. Nevertheless, he had good reasons for deciding on Don Michelotto. He was a man of great military experience and a first-class soldier. To get his way, Machiavelli first persuaded Soderini of the wisdom of the decision and the gonfalonier then took on a resistant Great Council. By early February the motion had been passed and Don Michelotto had become the most unlikely employee of the Florentine government.

Machiavelli had had years to work out every detail of how he wanted his militia to operate. He decided that they needed to meet for training between ten and sixteen times each year, and he based the organisation of the force on models he had seen successfully employed by Cesare Borgia and the military leaders of Rome, Spain and France. He also borrowed liberally from the strategies and organisation of the Venetians, whom he considered experts in both military training and planning.

He designed the livery, a white doublet, red-and-white stockings and an iron breastplate, and he chose the Marzocco, the Florentine lion, as the emblem of the new militia. He even deliberated over the form of the army's banner, reasoning that it should be of one colour, uncluttered and bold.

Soon his friends and those who had stood by him all along were offering their praise. An associate named Leonardo Bartolini wrote from Rome to congratulate him. 'Concerning the new militia,' he said, 'I am very glad that it is turning out as well as you indicated to me in the past. If it is helped along as it is due, I judge that it will turn out to be a wonderful thing.'[19]

In March Francesco Soderini, then in Rome, wrote to Machiavelli:

Your letter gave us all the more pleasure for its being lengthy, because we learned clearly how your new military idea, which corresponds to our hope for the welfare and the dignity of our country, is progressing. It should not be thought that other nations in these times are superior to our foot soldiers, except because they have kept their discipline, which has been banished for a long time now from Italy. You must get no small satisfaction from the fact that such a worthy thing should have been given its beginnings by your hands. Please persevere and bring it to the desired end.[20]

On 15 February, a carnival day, Machiavelli was ready to make a public display of his new force. Realising the power of pageant and of piquing the patriotism of his fellow citizens, he decided to have his troops march through the city in an effort specifically designed to stir up civic pride. An eyewitness to the spectacle, the writer Luca Landucci, recorded the event:

> There was a muster in the Piazza della Signoria of four hundred recruits whom the gonfalonier had assembled. These soldiers had each a white waistcoat, a pair of stockings (half red and half white), a white cap, shoes and an iron breastplate, and lances, and some of them had muskets. These were called battalions: they were given a constable who would lead them, and teach them how to use their arms. They were soldiers, but stopped at their own houses, being obliged to appear when needed, and it was ordered that many thousand should be made in this way all through the country, so that we should not need to have foreigners. This was thought the finest thing that had ever been arranged for Florence.[21]

As Machiavelli watched his soldiers march by in formation, he could not have helped but feel proud. This was one of the highlights of his career, a moment when his analysis of the situation had borne fruit. Ever the patriot, ever motivated by what he sincerely believed to be the best thing for his country, he revelled in what was undoubtedly a glorious moment.

6

Travels with a Papal Warlord

In many respects Julius II was a most unlikely pope. He had received a traditional Franciscan education and had risen through the ranks of the Church, but in his soul he was a soldier. Born Giuliano della Rovere in 1443, he came, like Machiavelli, from a noble but impoverished family, and had spent much of his ecclesiastical career gathering riches to himself through benefices, so that, during the thirty-two years between becoming a cardinal and ascending to the papacy, he accumulated great power and influence in the Vatican.

Like many popes, Julius was a greedy, oversexed, self-obsessed and violent man, and there is little evidence to show that he was ever genuinely devout. He viewed himself, and was considered by observers, to be a far better military strategist and campaigner than spiritual leader, and he saw his role first and foremost as protector of the papal state, a warlord whose primary concern was the condition of his material dominions.

Posterity has gained much from Julius's materialism. He was a great patron of the arts who commissioned works by Bramante, Raphael and most famously Michelangelo. It was Julius who financed the painting of the Sistine Chapel and commissioned many of Michelangelo's most beautiful sculptures. (He appears to have had little time for Michelangelo's greatest rival, Leonardo da Vinci, and commissioned nothing from him.)

But the dark side of Julius's worldly ambition established a prolonged period of political chaos in Italy and led Machiavelli to take the view that his tenure in the Vatican was one of the most destructive in the long, messy history of the papacy.

Giuliano had waited many years to gain the tiara. He had been a key player during the papacy of his uncle, Francesco della Rovere, Pope Sixtus IV, head of the Church from 1471 until 1484, and he was one of the real powers behind the throne during the papacy of Innocent VIII, whom he had placed in the Vatican by bribing enough cardinals to win the day.

During his rise to power Giuliano had to deal with many enemies, men whose own careers had been thwarted by his thrusting ambition, as well as those who were his bitter rivals. The most dangerous and the most able of this second group had been Cardinal Rodrigo Borgia, who ascended to the papal throne in 1492, beating Giuliano in the conclave that followed the death of Innocent VIII.

The two men despised each other. When Rodrigo became Pope Alexander VI, Giuliano knew he could not stay in Rome for long and spent a decade in France, Spain and Italian states far from papal reach, where he worked ceaselessly to counteract the moves made by Alexander's son, Cesare, as well as scheming tirelessly to bring down the Pope himself. In 1493, little more than a year after Rodrigo's coronation, Giuliano almost succeeded in destroying the Borgias by persuading the French king, Charles VIII, to take the Vatican by force. The plan was thwarted when the Pope learned of his rival's manoeuvres and managed to bribe Charles to change his mind.

When Alexander VI died in 1503, Giuliano wasted no time in making his presence felt in Rome. Within days of the news reaching him, he had broken his self-imposed exile and taken his place in the conclave to elect the next pope. But again his plans were blocked when his fellow cardinals chose the ailing Francesco Piccolomini, who died within days of his ascension. During the following extraordinary conclave, Giuliano knew that if he wished to succeed in what would surely be his last effort to become pope, he would have to use all his resources to bribe and coerce. Skilfully balancing the desires of the most powerful cardinals, including Cesare Borgia, he simply promised his way to the throne.

Giuliano della Rovere understood well the maxim that says history is written by the winners, and once he had become pope he began to break most of the promises that had won him the papacy. In making his promises he had lied to the Venetian cardinals, to whom he had promised concessions over the Romagna; he had lied gleefully to Cesare Borgia, who had so uncharacteristically trusted him; and he had lied to the majority of cardinals, who had been promised a new constitution. This constitution included the edicts that Alexander's successor and all future pontiffs must 1) continue to wage war on the Turks, 2) restore papal discipline, and 3) ensure that no war should be undertaken without two-thirds of the cardinals agreeing to the move in a strictly monitored session of the Sacred College.

Julius the warrior could never agree to be controlled by his cardinals in this way and within a year of his ascension to the papacy he was going his own way and starting to formulate his own rules. Uppermost in his mind was the problem of the Romagna, the region of Italy that had witnessed years of upheaval and violence, a region perceived by the Vatican as papal, by the Venetians as theirs, and only recently ravaged by the campaigns of Cesare Borgia.

To the cardinals of the College who had wished to see the cities of the Romagna back in the hands of their rightful rulers, Julius had promised satisfaction, but instead one of his first decisions as pope was to organise an army to retake the region, kick out the Venetians, who had taken advantage of the power vacuum after the fall of Cesare Borgia, and snatch the lands from the petty warlords whom he perceived as acting against the interests of the Vatican.

Perhaps more than anyone, Machiavelli was aware of the dangerous character of the new pope. He had tarried in Rome soon after the election of Julius in order to gain a clearer vision of the new man at the helm. He realised he was capable, he knew his mind was filled with military matters rather than spiritual devotions and he could see that Julius II was greedy for territory, greater power and influence. By 1506, when the Pope at last began to mobilise and take practical steps to broaden his portfolio in Italy, Machiavelli found himself not at all surprised by new orders from the Signoria, who wanted him to travel with Julius in his usual twin roles of emissary and spy.

This commission had also been prompted by a letter the Pope had recently sent to the Florentines in which he had outlined what help he required of them in his effort to, as he put it, 'rid Italy of tyrants'. The tyrants he had in mind were Giovanni Bentivoglio, the ruler of Bologna, and Giampaolo Baglioni, the ruler of Perugia, and he wanted Florence to pay for the services of one of its most accomplished mercenaries, Marcantonio Colonna, and his troops, to undertake the task of ousting Bentivoglio and Baglioni.

The Signoria was understandably less than enthusiastic about this idea. Its members did not share Julius's obsession with the Romagna, believing (probably naïvely) that allowing the petty rulers to hold sway over their compact little states would stop unrest. Consequently, they were disinclined to reach into their pockets just to please the Pope. Furthermore, they needed Colonna and his men to spearhead yet another bid to capture Pisa.

Machiavelli left Florence on the night of 25 August and rode with all haste to meet the Pope's entourage at the tiny town of Nepi, a day's journey from Rome. On the way he had time to consider the volatile political situation and he certainly would not have missed the irony of Julius calling for the end of tyrants in the Romagna. It would be foolhardy, he realised, to underestimate the dangers presented by the moves of this pope. Julius was not to be trusted; he was a temporal ruler with significant power and a man who had the potential to cause Florence a great deal of trouble.

On the evening Machiavelli arrived in Nepi the Pope was said to be too busy to agree to an audience with the Florentine emissary, but the following day Machiavelli was invited to meet Julius and explain the Florentine position on his request for military assistance. Instructed to deliver words so as to 'praise his [the Pope's] good and holy intent' and to play for as much time as possible, he had to use all his tact in order to make it clear that the Republic would not be able to help the pontiff in his cause.[1]

A seasoned negotiator and politician, Julius saw through the words of the Florentine government at once. According to Machiavelli's report, he listened 'attentively and cheerfully' before responding with his astute analysis of the situation.[2] The Florentines, he decided, were scared of the enterprise for three distinct but related reasons. First, he believed the Florentine government did not have faith in the idea that the Pope could guarantee French support as he claimed he could. Second, they did not believe he was as committed to the plan as he asserted he was, and third, they considered that he would fail to remove the tyrants and that they would then be ill disposed towards Florence and cause the Republic problems for years to come.

In an effort to allay these fears the Pope showed Machiavelli letters from Louis XII detailing his support should Julius need it, and he assured the emissary that papal determination for the success of his scheme could not be stronger. As an argument against the third point – that the Republic might have just fear of a tyrant who remained in his kingdom after an attempt to remove him – he declared that the targets of his campaign would have absolutely no chance of remaining in the territories after he was finished with them.

The Pope's arguments and evidence of support appeared to be sound, but there were other reasons for the unease of the Signoria. The ruler of Bologna, Giovanni Bentivoglio was a friend of the Republic. He had maintained strong diplomatic ties with Florence, whereas Baglioni had been drawn in by Cesare Borgia during his campaigns through the region. The Republic could not betray Bentivoglio, as such a move would anger many of their neighbours who were also his allies.

Following the instructions from his superiors, Machiavelli, the master of diplomacy, stalled for time and prevaricated. The Pope, who was also a seasoned campaigner on the battlefields and in Rome's papal court and councils, expected little else. But he was a determined man and he was in a hurry. Before the first meeting was ended the Pope made his position perfectly clear. If Florence would not help him, he would instead turn to what he declared to Machiavelli would be very much his second choice, Venice.

For Machiavelli and the Republic this legation was crucial, but for the Pope there were bigger, more pressing concerns. While the Signoria pondered, Julius rode on at the head of his army. In his armour he was for all the world the image of the crusading mouthpiece of God. Marching north-eastwards, through the towns of Viterbo, Orvieto, Castel della Pieve and Castiglione del Lago, he arrived at the gates of Perugia on 13 September 1506 in no mood for compromise.

For all his faults, Julius was a brave man, as well as an astute military campaigner and politician. He knew his own power and his status in Renaissance Europe. The tyrannical Giampaolo Baglioni, formerly a henchman of the Borgias and an accomplished murderer, did nothing to stop the Pope entering his city at the head of a small troop of soldiers. Once within the walls, the Pope advised him to surrender to the papal forces or face death in a bloody battle he would inevitably lose.

Machiavelli, who was with the Pope in Perugia and so an

eyewitness to the proceedings, was initially staggered by the apparent chutzpah of the pontiff. Writing to the Ten of War immediately before Julius rode into the city, he declared: 'If he [Baglioni] does no harm to the man who has come to take away his state, it will only be out of kindness and humanity. How this affair will end I cannot tell.'[3]

But Machiavelli was quite wrong, his reasoning deeply flawed, and he regretted this statement soon after writing it. Perhaps he had been so shocked by the actions of the Pope or had simply reacted impulsively, for he soon came to the more accurate assessment that the actions of the Perugian leader had nothing to do with kindness or even astute political reasoning. Baglioni was simply a coward and a bully who crumbled when faced with a determined, stronger individual.[4]

This episode taught Machiavelli a very valuable lesson and revealed a crucial concept in the building of his political world view. Religion, and in particular the Catholic Church, he came to realise, carried an innate power that was extremely difficult to resist. Even a man such as Baglioni had been raised as a Catholic. In awe of the Lord, he was therefore in awe of his earthly representative. For this reason Cesare Borgia's fellow exterminator could not bring himself to do physical harm to a pope.

Emboldened further, the already excessively confident Julius watched Baglioni take voluntary exile. The Pope tarried for over a week at the site of his conquest before leaping on his horse to lead his troops out of Perugia and on to his next target, Bologna, where Bentivoglio, friend of the Florentine Republic, was head of state.

That week, to further encourage Julius, the French sent word that their troops would soon be joining him in the Romagna. Louis had waited to see which way the wind was blowing and after hearing of the Pope's unequivocal triumph at Perugia he had jumped off the fence. Meanwhile the Florentine government was still prevaricating and the Pope was growing increasingly impatient with the Signoria. After delivering a speech to a group of nervous and harassed ambassadors sent to Perugia from Bentivoglio in Bologna in which he declared, 'I have forces to make all Italy tremble let alone Bologna,' Julius gave Florence a final warning.[5] The Republic would be given the time it took for a messenger riding flat out to reach Florence and return with a decision before he turned to the Venetians for their participation in his campaign.

The Signoria had no choice but to comply. When Julius received the news that Colonna and his men were being diverted from their mission to Pisa and that the funds for their support of his campaign had been approved by the government, he was delighted. Writing to the Ten of War, Machiavelli told them how well the news had been received and by return post he was instructed to travel ahead of the Pope so that he could prepare towns along the route proposed for His Holiness and the papal troops.

The Republic had made the unambiguous decision to side with the far stronger and more powerful force involved in what many believed would become a bloody fight over Bologna. But in fact the Florentine forces were never used. Having no appetite for a fight with the Pope and his army, Bentivoglio fled his city, leaving it in the hands of Julius and his allies. On 11 November Julius rode into Bologna to declare its return to papal control.

Machiavelli had been deeply impressed by the Pope's actions and even before the pontiff had ousted Bentivoglio he had made a careful analysis of how Julius had achieved his ends. Having scrutinised the Pope's every move for over a month, Machiavelli concluded that he had employed factors that could initiate and sustain what he was later to define in *The Prince* as 'ecclesiastical principalities':

It now remains to discuss ecclesiastical principalities; and here the difficulties which have to be faced occur before a ruler is established, in that such principalities are won by prowess or by fortune but are kept without the help of either. They are maintained, in fact, by religious institutions, of such a powerful kind that, no matter how the ruler acts and lives, they safeguard their government. Ecclesiastical princes alone possess states, and do not defend them; subjects, and do not govern them. And although their states are not defended they are not taken away from them; and their subjects, being without government, do not worry about it and neither can nor hope to overthrow it in favour of another. But they are sustained by higher powers which the human mind cannot comprehend. I shall not argue about them, they are exalted and maintained by God, and so only a rash and presumptuous man would take it upon himself to discuss them.[6]

In other words religious leaders, absolute in their power, can do almost anything they like and get away with it. The very thing they represent, rather than their own individual power or charisma, makes enemies flee before them and allows them to rule without occupation. They lead vicariously, employing the fear of God that has been instilled in their subjects.

However, Machiavelli realised that there was more to Julius's easy victory at Perugia than ecclesiastical power. In a long letter to his friend Giovan Battista Soderini, the gonfalonier's nephew, he explained what he had learned. He begins the document, commonly known today as the *Ghiribizzi* (*Fantasies* or *Speculations*), by stating that the Pope's success would have surprised him 'but for the fact that my fate has shown me so many and such varied things that I am forced rarely to be surprised or to admit that I have not savoured – either through reading or through experience – the actions of men and their ways of doing things'. He goes on to outline these:

I believe that just as Nature has created men with different faces so she has created them with different intellects and imaginations. As a result, each man behaves according to his own intellect and imagination. And because times change and the pattern of events differs, one man's hopes may turn as he prayed they would. The man who matches his way of doing things with the conditions of the times is successful; the man whose actions are at odds with the times and the pattern of events is unsuccessful. Hence, it can well be that two men can achieve the same goal by acting differently: because each one of them matches his actions to what he encounters and because there are as many patterns of events as there are regions and governments. But because times and affairs often change – both in general and in particular – and because men change neither their imaginations nor their ways of doing things accordingly, it turns out that a man has good fortune at one time and bad fortune at another. And truly, anyone wise enough to adapt to and understand the times and the pattern of events would always have good fortune or would always keep himself from bad fortune; and it would come to be true that the wise man could control the stars and the Fates. But such wise men do not exist: in the first place, men are short-sighted; in the second place, they are unable to master their own natures; thus it follows that Fortune is fickle, controlling men and keeping them under her yoke.[7]

So, to Machiavelli, it was apparent that the taking of Perugia had come down to the fact that Julius's position as God's earthly representative bestowed on him greater power than any other temporal commander. But he also realised that the times were right for Julius and wrong for Baglioni. In addition to these conclusions, Machiavelli also saw Baglioni as a rather pathetic figure, a man whom he considered 'incapable of the greatness' necessary to win a confrontation and to overcome the power welded by Julius.[8]

As usual, while he was away Machiavelli was kept abreast of news in Florence by his trusted assistant Biagio Buonaccorsi. He had fretted about the state of his newly founded militia and was concerned, as always, with the security of his position at the Palazzo Vecchio. Indeed, as Biagio noted, he worried about these things far more than he gave thought to his wife, his small children and his close friends. He need not have worried about the militia, for it was doing well under the command of Don Michelotto. 'Matters are going the way you want with the foot soldiers,' Biagio reported.

While he was away he had unexpectedly witnessed a parade of the Pope's soldiers when they had been camped at Cesena shortly after the peaceful taking of Perugia. Unimpressed, he had written to the Ten of War: 'If you could see these soldiers of the Duke of Urbino and those of Nanni Your Lordships would not be ashamed of your own conscripts or think of them of little worth.'[9]

Along with reports on matters of state, Biagio's letter was full of gossip and he could not resist his tendency to complain: 'Thus I had them pay those four constables for whom you left me a bill. As if I did not have enough to do, this springs up again: you had not been gone two days when I was going around the palace with three of them tagging along.'[10]

As the weeks slide by and he is required to take care of more and more of Machiavelli's minor duties and domestic chores, Biagio explodes: 'Go and retch.' And then, angered about the fact that Niccolò had not written to a friend as he had promised he would, he rages: 'Write once and for all whether you gave the letter from Alessandro to San Giorgio or whether you ever saw him again after the first notice you gave attention to him. But you are a latrine cover and anyone who wants can pick you up with a stick.'[11] Even so, he always signed off his letters with the affectionate 'Brother Bi'. (A fascinating detail is that, for one of the trivial jobs Biagio was asked to perform, sending a small sum of money to a colleague of Machiavelli's, the Secretary's assistant employed a young artist by the name of Michelangelo who happened to be travelling to Volterra, where Machiavelli was then staying in the train of Julius en route to Perugia.) Machiavelli took Biagio's outbursts in good spirit and often gave back at least what he was given. In many ways this banter was a form of light relief for him, an exchange far removed from other pressing personal concerns.

Although the creation of the militia was a dream made real for Machiavelli, some of the Florentine elite, the *ottimati*, remained opposed to it. Foremost among these was his former mentor, Piero de' Medici's son-in-law Alamanno Salviati, who had been one of those most crucial to the Secretary's appointment.

Only a few years earlier, in 1502, Salviati and Machiavelli had been on the very best of terms. Writing to quell the Secretary's concerns about the prospects of his re-election while he was away in Imola, Salviati had assured him: 'Your conduct has been and is such that people will come begging you [to accept office] rather than you having to beg them.'[12] But from about 1505 onwards their formerly close relationship began to deteriorate and eventually to dissolve completely.

Salviati had been one of the *ottimati* opposed to the promotion of Piero Soderini to the position of gonfalonier for life, and indeed the Salviatis had not been on friendly terms with the Soderini family for the best part of a generation. So, as the gonfalonier and Machiavelli became increasingly dependent on each other, Salviati's relationship with the Secretary cooled correspondingly. During the first three years of Soderini's leadership, the gonfalonier and Machiavelli had already clashed with Salviati over two major political issues.

The first of these was the plan to divert the Arno, an effort that became an expensive embarrassment for the Signoria. The second was the creation of the militia, a scheme that was pushed through the legislative process and had been, in Salviati's opinion, foisted on the Florentine people.

Machiavelli, always the highly astute observer and analyst, almost certainly knew of Salviati's growing animosity, especially after the creation of his militia, and he could not have failed to have been aware of the man's resentment as he forged a close alliance with Soderini. In 1504 Machiavelli had published his first serious work, a government report called the *First Decennial* (*Il decennale primo*) which was a history of the decade in Florence from 1494 to 1504. The work, which was dedicated to Salviati, was greatly admired, but it is quite likely that Machiavelli dedicated it to his former tutor specifically to curry favour and perhaps to salvage the remains of their crumbling friendship. Salviati, though, saw right through it and was repelled by what he considered a cynical move on Machiavelli's part. His reaction weakened their relationship even more.

However, the rift between Machiavelli and Salviati was only in part created by political differences. Another source of conflict was more personal and rooted in a clash of characters. By 1506 Machiavelli was gaining something of a reputation as a libertine. When he was in Florence he frequented the establishment of a well-known prostitute called La Riccia and when he was away he wrote letters to his friends boasting of his sexual exploits. In a particularly grotesque letter written during a visit to Verona, he described being cajoled into an encounter with a hideously ugly prostitute in a seedy brothel:

> . . .once inside, I made out in the gloom a woman cowering in the corner affecting modesty with a towel over her head and face . . . to make a long story short, alone there with her in the dark, I fucked her one. Although I found her thighs flabby and her cunt damp – and her breath stank a bit – nevertheless, helplessly horny, I went to her with it. Once I had done it, and feeling like taking a look at the merchandise, I took a piece of burning wood from the hearth in the room and lit a lamp that was above it; but the light was hardly lit before it almost fell out of my hands. Ugh! I nearly dropped dead on the spot, that woman was so ugly. The first thing I noticed about her was a tuft of hair, part white, part black – in other words, sort of whitish; although

the crown of her head was bald (thanks to the baldness one could make out a few lice promenading about), still a few, thin wisps of hair came down to her brow with their ends. In the centre of her tiny, wrinkled head she had a fiery scar that made her seem as if she had been branded at the marketplace; at the end of each eyebrow toward her eyes there was a nosegay of nits; one eye looked up, the other down – and one was larger than the other; her tear ducts were full of rheum and she had no eyelashes. She had a turned-up nose stuck low down on her head and one of her nostrils was sliced open and full of snot. Her mouth resembled Lorenzo de' Medici's, but it was twisted to one side, and from that side drool was oozing, because, since she was toothless, she could not hold back her saliva. Her upper lip supported a longish but skimpy moustache. She had a long, pointy chin that twisted upward a bit; a slightly hairy dewlap dangled down to her Adam's apple. As I stood there absolutely bewildered and stupefied staring at this monster, she became aware of it and tried to say, 'What's the matter sir?' but she could not get it out because she stuttered. As soon as she opened her mouth, she exuded such a stench on her breath that my eyes and nose – twin portals to the most delicate of the senses – felt assaulted by this stench and my stomach became so indignant that it was unable to tolerate this outrage; it started to rebel, then it did rebel – so that I threw up all over her. Having thus repaid her in kind, I departed. I shall stake my berth in heaven that as long as I am in Lombardy I'll be damned if I think I shall get horny again.[13]

As well as having a taste for whores of all types, Machiavelli appears to have kept a mistress in every city to which he travelled. This habit had started as far back as his first visit to the court of King Louis in 1499, when, before he had married Marietta, he had a torrid affair with a well-known courtesan named Jeanne, whom he called Janna.

Machiavelli was no better and no worse a husband than others of the time. It is also true that he was a romantic, a poet and a free spirit. This is clear to see in the pages of letters he exchanged with his friends. An example is a letter he wrote in response to a note from Francesco Vettori, who had been drawn into an illicit affair with a woman living near him in Rome. Machiavelli advised him:

> I am obliged to tell you how I have handled love myself. As a matter of fact, I have let love do as it pleases and I have followed it through hill and dale, woods and plains. I have discovered that it has granted me more charms than if I had tormented it. So then, take off the saddlepacks, remove the bridle, close your eyes and say: 'Go ahead, Love, be my guide, my leader . . . So, master, be happy, do not be dismayed, face Fortune squarely, and follow whatever course both the revolving heavens and the conditions sent you by the times and by mankind lay at your doorstep.[14]

Nor does Machiavelli seem to have shown any inclination to hide his sexual appetite. This attitude is very much in keeping with his world view and the strong rebellious streak in his character. There was always something of the romantic about him, even as he performed the most mundane duties of his profession and followed convention and tradition. His official letters were frequently laced with lateral connections and unorthodox observations, and when he came to write fiction he filled his work with these same unconventional strands. One example is the beginning of his comedy *Mandragola*, where he announces:

> *Because life is brief*
> *and many are the pains*
> *which, living and struggling, everyone sustains,*
> *let us follow our desires,*

passing and consuming the years,
because whoever deprives himself of pleasure,
to live with anguish and with worries,
doesn't know the tricks,
of the world, or by what ills,
and by what strange happenings,
all mortals are almost overwhelmed.[15]

Such liberalism was the aspect of Machiavelli's mind that lifted his reasoning and analysis above the prosaic. He was a radical thinker and tried his utmost to live according to his beliefs. This was just as obvious in his attitude towards religion. He was not merely sceptical about Christianity, not merely without faith, but, in many regards, anti-Christian, a man who dismissed the mythology of orthodox religion on intellectual grounds. Most importantly, he could spare no time for the Christian notion that there was some kind of virtue in suppressing perfectly natural physical desires. The philosophical framework around which he was to construct his political theories, and in particular the doctrines expressed in *The Prince*, placed the power and freedom of the individual above all things. Machiavelli despised the idea of church or state controlling the will of the individual. In this respect he was a true revolutionary, a genuine philosophical radical.

Machiavelli was fortunate to live in Italy during a period when, compared with the generations before and after his, there was a degree of religious tolerance. If he had expressed his views a few decades later, during the Counter-reformation, he would have risked the stake. His opinions would have also disturbed the Establishment of the fourteenth and fifteenth centuries. Even so, as much as he may have escaped the censure of the Church, his views did upset people, and one of those most offended was Salviati, a man both prudish and pious.

Salviati and his supporters tried their utmost to create trouble for

Machiavelli by exploiting his well-known libertine attitudes. Perhaps their most vicious attack came through the use of the Otto di Guardia, the office of the magistrate for criminal justice, to which the public could make anonymous accusations against other citizens. In May 1510 this office received the following complaint: 'Lords of the Eight, you are hereby informed that Nicholò [sic], son of Bernardo Machiavelli, screws Lucretia, known as La Riccia, in the ass. Interrogate her and you will learn the truth.'

Such accusations were very common and almost always offered as an element of a personal petty vendetta. Most were ignored as subjective and without foundation, but an accusation against a public figure such as Machiavelli had the potential to cause him problems. Sodomy was a crime that came under the remit of a special office called the Ufficiali di Notte e Conservatori dei Monasteri and it was punished with fines. However, sodomy was tolerated in spite of the law, and there was obviously nothing accusers could use to support their claims or else they would have supplied incriminating evidence. In this case the magistrate seems to have taken the claim with a pinch of salt as nothing more was ever said about it and Machiavelli was never investigated for anything relating to the crime of sexual perversion.

Although they found his colourful reports of sexual exploits in foreign parts entertaining, Machiavelli's friends tried to warn him to be more discreet. Writing to him as he followed Julius around Umbria and the Romagna, Giovan Battista Soderini advised him: 'So, it might not be a good idea to fool around too much.'[16]

This comment had been prompted by nasty rumours and gossip circulating within the small community of politicians in Florence and initiated by Salviati and his friends. Within a month of Soderini's letter Biagio Buonaccorsi was writing to Machiavelli with his own warnings:

I do not want to neglect to tell you, although I could put it off until your return, that, through someone who was present there, and more than one, when Alamanno was in Bibbona, dining with Ridolfi, where there were a lot of young people speaking of you, he said: 'I never entrusted anything at all to that rascal since I have been one of the Ten,' going on in this vein or better. Note this, if you were not really totally clear about his opinion. Make sure you are here before the reconfirmations. I could write you a lot of other things, but will tell you more fully when we are face to face.'[17]

The use of the word 'rascal' is a strange one in this context. It might be argued that Salviati was merely referring to Machiavelli's political scheming but two things suggest that it was a more personal attack. First, he could not justifiably criticise Machiavelli's work or his actions in public because he had done nothing wrong; Salviati and the Secretary simply differed in their political views. More importantly, though, the very word used at an informal gathering, said over a few glasses of wine perhaps, strongly implies that Salviati was referring to what he considered a flaw in the character of the Florentine Secretary.

Machiavelli may well have not cared too much for what Salviati thought of his morals, but the last line of Biagio's letter must have made him pause. 'Make sure you are here before the reconfirmations,' his friend had warned. Biagio was referring to the regular election of key bureaucrats in the government, including the Secretary to the Second Chancery and Secretary to the Ten of War. Machiavelli had always been concerned about these elections, particularly when he was away conducting work for the Republic. Those of 1506 may have been a source of worry for him, even though his bond with Soderini was exceptionally strong.

His close relationship with the gonfalonier must have given him some reassurance, but he was well aware of the fickle nature of politics. He liked Soderini but considered him a plodder and indecisive. Furthermore, although the man had been given the grand title of gonfalonier for life, Machiavelli was quite aware that this would mean nothing if the present regime collapsed. Because of this, he was extremely unhappy about the falling out with Salviati and never stopped trying to heal the rift between them. In this effort he ultimately failed, and his close alliance with Soderini was to become a major factor in the destruction of his political career.

In 1506, though, such problems seemed a distant possibility and Machiavelli was approaching, but still not quite at, his career peak. Within weeks of his return to Florence he had published a detailed document, *Discorso dell'ordinare lo Stato di Firenze alle Armi* (*Discourse on the Military Organisation of the State of Florence*), in which he described how best to run a militia and how to place it under government control through the establishment of a specialised committee for war and military affairs.

During this period the Signoria was considering proposals for the establishment of just such a department and there is no coincidence in the fact that Machiavelli published his analysis of the idea at precisely the moment politicians were searching for an appropriate template. By 6 December the new government division had been established, with the title Nove Ufficiali dell'ordinanza e Milizia Fiorentina, the Nine Officers of the Florentine Ordnance and Militia, or simply the Nine, and with Machiavelli as its Secretary.

No record of what Salviati thought of this new appointment has survived, but others were delighted by the news. 'We do not believe that in Florence anything as worthy and well-founded as this has been done for some long time,' enthused Machiavelli's most ardent supporter, Francesco Soderini.[18] And there is little doubt that he was offering words his brother, the gonfalonier, would have written if he had been able to.

Machiavelli was now the Secretary for three major government departments, the Second Chancery, the Ten of War and the Nine for Ordnance and the Militia. His star was still rising, just as it had done without interruption for the past eight years. However, one thing had changed: Machiavelli now had powerful enemies and in order to survive he would have to be constantly looking over his shoulder.

7

The Rough with the Smooth

For Machiavelli the years 1507–10 brought a mixture of his most important political successes and an increasingly dangerous collection of problems. By the summer of 1507 he was thirty-eight, had been married to Marietta for almost six years and had fathered three children. He had soared through the Florentine civil service to become Secretary to three important government departments simultaneously. He was considered a close associate of the gonfalonier, Piero Soderini, and he had reliable, trustworthy friends who loved him, men such as Biagio Buonaccorsi and Luigi Guicciardini (a friend from early days, not to be confused with Francesco Guicciardini). Also, at around this time he was becoming recognised as one of the most erudite political theorists in Italy, a man who had garnered words of praise from tyrants and sages alike.

But by this time Niccolò Machiavelli was leading a double life, and this Janus existence became uncomfortably exposed during his most prosperous years in the Florentine government. One face of Machiavelli was the loyal dedicated patriot who excelled at his job. The other was a man who loved to explore the seamier side of life; a man who mixed with prostitutes and poets, actors and occultists.

Machiavelli's life was a collection of opposites. He was both civil servant and poet, government official and artist, orthodox diplomat and lateral thinker, caring husband and libertine. Surprisingly for a man who was such a good analyst and judge of the zeitgeist, he grew steadily incautious, seeming not to care too much who learned of his unusual interests. Perhaps this complacency stemmed from the certainty of Soderini's patronage and from the fact that he knew he did his job exceptionally well, earning himself the respect of many. But Florence was a small city and men like Machiavelli, who survived by their wits and abilities rather than with the advantage of wealth, could ill afford to make enemies. He was aware of this and was genuinely depressed over the clash with his former patron.

Salviati had first turned against the Secretary over the way his plan for a militia had been forced through government by the gonfalonier, but he did little to damage Machiavelli, merely establishing rumours and slurring him rather ineffectually. However, as Machiavelli's militia became popular and the younger man was appointed Secretary to the Nine, Salviati's anger grew. Soon he was successfully turning other aristocratic Florentine families against Machiavelli, painting him as a jumped-up bureaucrat who had swindled his way into a position far beyond his station. And in June 1507 Machiavelli received his first knock-back precipitated by Salviati's ill will and political influence. After deciding to send a legation to the Holy Roman Emperor, the Signoria, for the first time in almost a decade, passed over Machiavelli as its first choice as Florentine emissary to a foreign court.

The Holy Roman Empire had little to do with anything genuinely holy and was only an empire in the very loosest sense. It was an affiliation of small states that had been brought together in the tenth century and encompassed parts of what are today north-eastern France, Germany, Belgium and Luxemburg. More a figurehead than a traditional imperial ruler, the emperor was elected and wielded only limited power. To push through major political or military decisions, he needed to consult an Imperial Diet, a gathering of the heads of the empire's states.

In 1507 the Holy Roman Emperor, Maximilian I of Habsburg, was forty-eight years old. He had married Mary, the only daughter of Charles the Bold, Duke of Burgundy, and through this marriage he had gained the Netherlands. Elected emperor in 1486, he spent his life in political intrigue and military campaigning, but was neither charismatic nor particularly successful as a strategist. His attempts to expand the influence of the empire and to compete with the other great powers of Europe, France and Spain, achieved little, and he acquired the not entirely justified reputation of being a buffoon. In *The Prince* Machiavelli wrote of him:

> Bishop Luca, in the service of Maximilian, the present emperor, said of his majesty that he never consulted anybody and never did things as he wanted to; this happened because he did the opposite of what I said above [never to employ too many different advisers]. The emperor is a secretive man, he does not tell anyone of his plans, and he accepts no advice. But as soon as he puts his plans into effect, and they come to be known, they meet with opposition from those around him; and then he is only too easily diverted from his purpose. The result is that whatever he does one day is undone the next, what he wants or plans to do is never clear, and no reliance can be placed on his deliberations.[1]

However, as incompetent as many of his military efforts were, Maximilian never lacked self-confidence, and when, in the spring of 1507, he convened the Diet of Constance and called on the honour of the German state and that of the power brokers of the union to attempt to revive the image of the Holy Roman Empire, he succeeded in gathering together a large army and the resources to interfere for a time in pan-European politics. Faced with such support, even those who perceived Maximilian as a bungler were forced to take notice.

In Florence the government realised that Maximilian's interference in Italian politics could, once again, destabilise the tenuous balance of power in the peninsula. Maximilian, they realised, was foolhardy and sufficiently power-hungry to really believe he could succeed where others, in particular the French, had failed, and sweep through the whole of Italy, absorbing it into the empire.

Such a proposition alarmed everyone. The French were immediately aware that even if Maximilian made only partial headway through Italy, their position would be threatened most and their influence disturbed. For his part the belligerent Julius II saw Maximilian as a deadly threat because he believed, with some reason, that the Holy Roman Emperor wished to unite his role with that of Head of the Church to become the true master of Europe. Meanwhile the leaders of the smaller powers, among them Florence, reached the conclusion that they would be trapped, as always, by the clash of Titans and that their fortunes would only be damaged by any moves that might initiate war. Not surprisingly, during the early summer of 1507, immediately after the Diet of Constance was convened, emissaries from across Italy decended on Maximilian's court.

The contemporary commentator Francesco Guicciardini reported the sudden excitement: 'When Florence learned that the king of France deemed these movements [the machinations of Maximilian] significant and ordered major preparations be made and that the Pope and the Venetians had emissaries in Germany, many Florentines concluded that this was a matter of great moment and hence proposed that it would be good to send someone too. Through the intervention of Piero Soderini, who wanted someone whom he could trust, Machiavelli was chosen.'

However, this time things did not go according to plan for Machiavelli or his patron. Alamanno Salviati decided that this new legation offered a perfect opportunity for him to interfere in the gonfalonier's affairs. He succeeded in persuading a large enough group within the Great Council to oppose Soderini's decision and to put forward their own candidate as emissary, a young nobleman who, Salviati claimed, should be given a chance to shine through for the Republic. 'But just as he [Machiavelli] was preparing to depart . . .,' Guicciardini tells us, 'many well-thought-of men began clamouring that other people should be sent because there were many decent young men well-suited for going to Germany, and it would be good that they might become experienced.'[2]

Of course, Salviati cared little for Francesco Vettori, the young man who was chosen to go in place of Machiavelli. Furthermore, he knew that the Florentine Secretary was capable of doing a perfectly good job in Germany; he merely wanted to cause trouble for Soderini and his favourite.

Although Machiavelli's pride must have been knocked, in many respects this move was more of a blow to Soderini than it was to his Secretary. Machiavelli would have been too astute to show any grievance in public, but his friends felt he needed support and wrote to him with reassuring words. 'My good, and not unfortunate, Machiavelli . . .,' began a letter from his friend Alessandro Nasi, a Florentine commissioner then on business in Cascina, 'I am glad that you have shat out the imperial commission, since you are entirely purged. I believe it is a very good thing, particularly for you, to be in Florence rather than in Germany, as we shall discuss when we are together again.'[3]

Ironically, it soon became clear to the Signoria that the problem of Maximilian was too big to be resolved with the simple appointment of an inexperienced emissary like Vettori. The young man was soon writing from the German court concerning the war preparations of the emperor and throwing some of the Florentines into a panic. Salviati himself appeared to be the most disturbed, perhaps because he was receiving secret private messages from his man at

Maximilian's court as well as news from the official reports sent to the Signoria. And when, in August, the government heard that the Pope was sending a high-ranking official to attend the emperor, and then soon afterwards, the news that Maximilian wanted no less than half a million ducats from Florence to ensure its protection from his armies, the Great Council quickly agreed that Machiavelli should be sent in all haste to help Vettori.

Machiavelli's mission to the German court was a bleak affair. He was fascinated with the Teutonic lifestyle, but cared little for the frugality and the harsh, rough manners of the people he met; all so different from the aesthetic and quality of life he was used to in Italy. Admittedly he was there through a freezing winter and never saw spring flowers on the slopes of Swiss mountains or the vibrancy of German villages wreathed in June sunshine, but this knowledge did little to mitigate his time at the court.

But if it was unpleasant it was also highly educational. In Savoy and then Geneva, where Machiavelli spent Christmas 1507, he learned much that added to his wealth of knowledge on military matters. In particular he witnessed how an entirely different culture organised its armies. He later wrote of this in *The Prince*. 'The cities of Germany enjoy unrestricted freedom . . .,' he observed:

> they control only limited territory, and obey the emperor only when they want to. They fear neither him nor any neighbouring power, because they are so fortified that everyone knows it would be a protracted, difficult operation to reduce them. This is because they all have excellent moats and walls, they have adequate artillery; they always lay in public stocks of drinks, food and fuel to last a year. Over and above this, every German city, making provision for the common people without public loss, always keeps a year's supply of wherewithal for them to work at those trades which give them their livelihood and are sinews of the city itself. Military exercises always enjoy a high

rence about the time of Machiavelli's childhood. *(Alinari Archives/Bridgeman, Florence)*

sare Borgia, the great
tyrannical leader
achiavelli used as the
model for his prince.
(Scala, Florence)

Pope Alexander VI, Cesare Borgia's father, who was one of the most corrupt popes in the long murky history of the Church. *(Alinari Archives-Anderson Archive, Florence)*

The court of Lorenzo de' Medici by the Victorian painter Amos Cassioli. *(Scala, Flor*

Sant'Andrea in Percussina, Tuscany. Machiavelli stayed here during his period of exile, 1513–27; and it is here that he wrote *The Prince*. *(AKG)*

Machiavelli during the time he was Florentine Secretary. *(Scala, Florence)*

A painting of Machiavelli a few years before his death at the age of fifty-eight.

(Scala, Florence – courtesy of the Ministero Beni et Att. Culturali)

Machiavelli as he was visualised in the seventeenth century. *(Roger-Viollet/Alinari)*

MACHIAVEL.

The Prince. (AKG)

NICOLAI
MACHIAVELLI
PRINCEPS.

EX
SYLVESTRI TELII
FVLGINATIS TRADVCTIONE
diligenter emendata.

Adiecta sunt eiusdem argumenti, Aliorum quorundam
contra Machiauelum scripta de potestate &
esficio Principum, & contra tyrannos.

BASILEAE
Ex officina Petri Pernæ.
M D XXC.

Lorenzo de' Medici as a Greek hero. Highly romanticised, this is a far from
accurate portrayal but succeeds in representing Lorenzo's lofty status.

(Alinari Archives/Bridgeman, Florence)

A self-portrait of Leonardo da Vinci as an old man around 1517.
(Scala, Florence)

The Bargello, Florence, the prison in which Machiavelli was interned during February 1513. *(Fratelli Alinari Museum of the History of Photography/ Malandrini Collection, Florence)*

ball played in the streets of Florence during the late fifteenth century. *(Scala, Florence)*

A stage production in early sixteenth-century Italy. Scenes from Machiavelli's play *Mandragola* and *Clizia* would have looked something like t[his] *(Alinari Archives/Mannelli Archive Florence)*

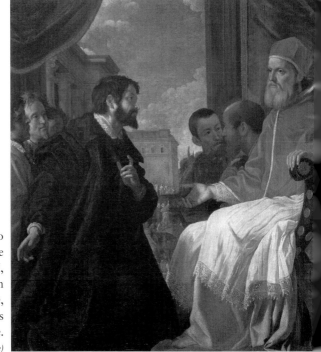

Michelangelo appearing before Pope Julius II, his great patron and an obsessive, highly ambitious warrior-pope. *(Scala, Florence)*

standing, and they have many laws and institutions providing
for them.[4]

Early in 1508 Machiavelli arrived in Bolzano, where
Maximilian had established his court for the interim, and in spite of
the fraught circumstances that had taken him to help Vettori, he
soon formed a strong and lasting bond with the young ambassador.
From the start the two immediately found much in common and
worked extremely well together. Vettori appears to have been happy
to let Machiavelli write accounts of the meetings with Maximilian
and merely signed them before they were dispatched to Florence,
and at the same time Machiavelli was gracious and co-operative,
considering the fact that officially he was the junior partner.

The Signoria was not at all interested in paying any form of
tribute to Maximilian but it was realistic enough to concede that it
had little room for manoeuvre. The Florentine militia was too small
and too inexperienced to be of any use against the powerful forces
the emperor had gathered together, and so, as ever, the Republic
was reliant on French support, which Soderini was confident he
could call upon. Salviati wanted to appease the emperor as fully and
as quickly as possible, but the gonfalonier managed to persuade his
government to offer, as a reply to Maximilian's demands, a gesture
payment of just thirty thousand ducats.

Machiavelli knew this offer would be considered as almost an
insult, but he could not persuade his superiors to reconsider. And so
began another of the political and diplomatic tussles with which the
Secretary was familiar. The Florentine government played for time
and waited for French reassurance; Machiavelli (with Vettori in
tow, taking notes) was playing a game of appeasement and prevar-
ication as he was instructed to do; and the aggressor, this time an
egotistic and bombastic emperor, was trying to speed things up
and gradually back-pedalling.

The talks dragged on into the spring of 1508 as the emissaries

followed the court around the Tyrol, spending some time in
Innsbruck before moving on to Bolzano and Trento. Vettori, who
had declared in a letter to the Ten of War that he felt 'as though they
were on some lost island', slid into a depression and fell ill, leaving
Machiavelli to negotiate alone.[5] But by March it was clear that the
emperor's plans were coming undone. The French had not inter-
vened, although they had made it clear they would not desert
Florence, and after Maximilian's forces had some short-lived success in pushing back the Venetians, they were humiliated by a series
of defeats that handed the enemy more land than they had begun
with.

The Florentines were encouraged by this development and it
gave strength to their negotiating stance, although they remained
cautious. Some members of the Signoria had been doubtful that
Maximilian would ever attack Italy anyway and that it was merely
a matter of sabre rattling or an elaborate attempt at extortion. But
the Florentines were in no position to take this risk, for the
Republic was a small power caught in the middle, vulnerable and
weak. Apart from stalling for time in the belief that greater powers
would defuse the situation, all they could do was hope that French
promises would hold true and that they might be able to play off
one major power against another.

By late spring Maximilian's own incompetence and
Machiavelli's cleverness had beaten down the price for leaving the
Republic in peace to forty thousand ducats spread over four pay-
ments, and he had managed to defer the first payment while the
Signoria waited to see if fortune would turn their way. With the
negotiations over, on 16 June, after riding at breakneck speed from
Bolzano via Bologna, Machiavelli returned to Florence, never more
pleased to see his home.

Maximilian had been embarrassed by the Venetians and
thwarted by the French, but it was clear he was not about to give up
his ambitions in Italy. He was incensed by the defeat of his forces by

a much smaller Venetian army and infuriated that Venice had not only held on to the territory it had already possessed but had increased its dominions at his expense. At the same time, some within the Signoria began to argue that the Florentine policy of appeasement with hard-earned cash was both humiliating and wasteful. Why, some demanded to know, had they suffered the political controversy and gone to the expense of establishing a militia if it was never to be used? To make matters worse, during a lull in the clash with Maximilian the Florentines did their usual trick of returning their attention to Pisa, and this time supporters and opponents of Machiavelli's militia began to call for its use against their old enemy.

By 1508 Pisa had been under siege for more than a decade. Indeed it had framed Machiavelli's time at the Second Chancery and some of his earliest work for the government had been to help resolve the problem of Pisa. One of the reasons the Secretary had been so keen to create the militia in the first place was to use it one day to break the siege and to return the errant city to Florentine possession. This new interest in Pisa, coming not from him but from influential figures within the Signoria, gave Machiavelli just the opportunity he needed to show off his militia and to prove its effectiveness.

He did not disappoint. Throughout the autumn of 1508 he travelled the countryside around Florence raising levies to finance the new Pisa campaign, and he recruited and supervised the training of those who had reported to their battalions ready for their first tour of duty. On 21 August the soldiers marched to Pisa and set up camp, planning to see out the winter outside the besieged city. By the middle of January 1509 Machiavelli was stationed with one thousand of his troops at Mulina di Cuosa, where they marched on to the mouth of the Fiumemorto. The Arno was closed to shipping, as were all the region's canals, the bridges were manned and guarded, and the siege was now total.

Machiavelli was always in the very thick of it. He had built up a rapport with his men and they admired him enormously. When the Ten of War asked him to join Niccolò Capponi (the militia commander who had recently replaced Don Michelotto) at a safer camp, Machiavelli replied: 'I know that encampment would be less dangerous and less strenuous, but had I not wanted danger and hard work, I would not have left Florence. So, may it please Your Lordships, let me stay here in these camps and work with the commissioners on the events that may occur; here I can be of some good use; there I should be of no good use at all and I would die of despair.'[6]

Here we see Machiavelli's patriotism and courage at full tilt. We must remember that he was not himself a military man. He had no training in arms and the only things he knew about soldiering were what he had taught himself and what he picked up from men like his commanders, Don Michelotto and Capponi. Machiavelli had spent most of his life pen-pushing and sitting around a negotiating table, yet here we find him arguing to stay on the front line among the filth, the disease and the ever-present risk of violent death. The Ten had to admit: '[You] hover everywhere throughout the armies . . . and we have placed on your shoulders the responsibility for all this.'[7] It was Machiavelli's patriotism that had directed him to the idea of the militia and it was this same patriotism that now compelled him to face real danger and argue against orders. The Ten knew what sort of a man he was, but others, enemies of the gonfalonier, wanted someone there they knew would be working in their interests, and so Salviati and another high-ranking government official, Antonio da Filicaia, were sent to Pisa as commissioners to oversee operations.

Machiavelli and Salviati clashed immediately. Salviati had been angered by the fact that the soldiers showed far greater respect for the Florentine Secretary than they did for such an important man as himself, and, almost as indiscreet at times as Machiavelli, in a burst of anger he had insulted him behind his back. Machiavelli learned of the incident and wrote an angry letter of complaint to Salviati, who instantly denied the charges, declaring, with barely disguised bitterness: 'Although they [the soldiers] wish to recognise your authority, you are not always present everywhere to command them. I approve that they love and esteem you because, being with you everyday, they will be the more obedient and know what they have to do.'[8]

Through the spring and into early summer, the Florentine forces attacked the walls of the city repeatedly and clashed with divisions of the Pisan army in the villages and small towns beyond the walls. The siege held firm and this, along with the demoralising effect of repeated attacks, eventually broke the spirit of the defenders, so that by early June they were ready to surrender. Machiavelli then played a key role in ensuring that Pisa was handed over to the Republic without further bloodshed or any form of undisciplined behaviour by his troops.

When it was all over Agostino Vespucci wrote to him, declaring:

Honoured Niccolò . . . Here it is not possible to express how much delight, how much jubilation and joy, all the people here have taken in the news of the recovery of that city of Pisa: in some measure every man has gone mad with exultation; there are bonfires all over the city, although it is not yet three in the afternoon; just think what they will do this evening after nightfall. I repeat to you once again that the only thing that might be lacking is for the heavens to show some delight as well, since it is not possible for men, both great and small, to show any more of it.[9]

A few days later the Florentine commissioner, Filippo Casavecchia, congratulated the Secretary in a letter: 'I wish you a thousand benefits from the outstanding acquisition of that noble city. For truly it can be said that your person was the cause of it to a very great extent.'[10]

Senior politicians in Florence knew all too well that the triumphant recapture of Pisa was all due to Machiavelli. Where condottieri such as Paolo Vitelli and Ercole Bentivoglio and engineers with ingenious schemes to divert the Arno had failed, Machiavelli, with his well-trained home-grown troops, had succeeded. But not everyone was pleased by this achievement. Machiavelli's friends and political allies praised him loudly, but his enemies, who could say nothing against the Secretary in terms of his effort, his ability or his patriotism, merely grew angrier. This was particularly ironic because, for all his efforts in winning the war for his homeland, Machiavelli had received very little genuine official recognition. The gonfalonier and his friends offered flattering words, but it was the two commissioners, Salviati and da Filicaia, arriving in Pisa just as the war was won, who presided over the surrender ceremony and received the garlands. It was they, and not Machiavelli, who, along with Capponi, had their names carved into the marble of a memorial placed at the site of the battle.

Machiavelli's friends had tried their utmost to persuade him to patch things up with Salviati, and, in spite of the fact that he had done nothing to deliberately antagonise his enemies (other than do things of which they did not approve), he did make a genuine effort at appeasement. In September he wrote a carefully worded letter to Salviati in which, with consummate skill, he detailed the political situation facing Florence and all of Italy as he saw it. Concentrating on the specific point of whether or not Maximilian would soon take the city of Padua, he described the possible manoeuvres of the major players and the bit performers, discussed the political permutations ahead and the possible outcomes, and with modesty offered suggestions for the ways in which Florence could best benefit from the tempestuous currents of political life in Italy. He offered this letter as 'a little gift' and it was clearly intended to help smooth the turbulent waters between them.

Salviati, though, was damaged by what he believed to have been

Machiavelli's betrayal. To him, not only had the Secretary turned against those who had given him the initial impetus, but his sexual manners were inappropriate for a trusted official. As a consequence, all Machiavelli received in return for his efforts in writing the letter was another slap in the face.

On the surface Salviati's reply appears to have been a perfectly measured letter, a little condescending perhaps, but then the author was one of the most respected and wealthy people in Europe, and Machiavelli was, for all his incisive intelligence and diplomatic brilliance, a man of humble means and no more than middle rank. However, on closer analysis it becomes apparent that Salviati's response positively drips with sarcasm and thinly disguised bile and that his comments reflected the feelings for Machiavelli held by Salviati's powerful clique.[11]

He began the letter by saying: 'Jesus. My dearest Niccolò. I have your letter which was very dear to me, especially since I see I am in your heart because you often remember me, for which I am most obliged' and went on to declare: 'I believe that our duty is rather to God and pray Him to let whatever is best befall rather than to hope to form some other judgement; although I do not know whether this conclusion is one that will satisfy you much, not because I believe that you are lacking in faith, but I am sure that you do not have much left.'

This introduction could be interpreted as friendly small talk, but we should remember that by the time he wrote this the commissioner despised Machiavelli, so the real sense must be: 'Thank you for writing, you are obviously concerned about the public awareness of how I feel about you and you are trying to pacify me with this wordy tribute.'

Salviati's following passage contains a more obvious attack. Pious and repelled by Machiavelli's quite recognisable anti-Christian attitudes, he is saying: 'To hell with your analysis. Who do you think you are? The fate of Man and of nations is in the hands of the Lord, not the people who make up the nations, nor even the leaders of men. But then of course, you don't believe in the One True God, do you, Machiavelli?'

But if these sleights were not obvious enough, Salviati saved his most unsubtle attack as a parting salvo. 'I shall be pleased if I have satisfied you . . .,' he stated in reference to his response to Machiavelli's lengthy discourse, 'and if I should have left anything out I shall let my teacher make up for it . . . God keep you.'[12] In other words, if my response to your lesson is not enough, you, oh illustrious teacher, know what I have missed and will excuse me for it.

We have no record of Machiavelli's response to the letter, if there was one. He would have read between the lines and seen all too clearly how Salviati had snubbed him again. Perhaps he simply accepted the fact that their relationship had moved beyond redemption and that he was compelled to make do. There never was a reconciliation between the two men, for very soon after this exchange Salviati died from malaria while camped with the army in the swamps around Pisa.

At about the time Machiavelli wrote his letter and received Salviati's reply the Secretary was preparing to make another foreign journey. After a brief respite, the exhausting vaudeville of Italian politics was preparing for another performance. Maximilian was pressing the Florentines for the first payment of their tribute, promised a year earlier, and he was mobilising his forces again, a move that was once more stirring up anxieties across Europe. Machiavelli set off for Mantua in early October and from there he rode on to join the court of the Holy Roman Emperor in Verona.

During the early summer of 1509 Maximilian had succeeded in persuading the King of Aragon, Louis XII and Julius II to form a league with him (the League of Cambrai) against the Venetians, who were presiding over their new conquests and mocking the ineffectual emperor. Largely through the use of French arms, the combined forces of France, Aragon, the empire and the Vatican overwhelmed the Venetians in a series of battles that drove them from Lombardy. This prompted Machiavelli to write in *The Prince* that 'in one day's battle [that fought between the French and the Venetians at Ghiaradadda] Venice lost what she had very laboriously acquired over the course of eight hundred years'.[13]

But this was not the end of the matter. Immediately after these victories in Lombardy, the Pope and the kings of France and Aragon decided to speedily withdraw so that they could concentrate on their own schemes and concerns. Believing quite rightly that the foreign forces Maximilian had called on once would not come to his aid a second time, within weeks the embittered Venetians had returned to recapture their lost dominions.

For Maximilian pride gave way to rashness. Acting without support, he immediately sent a large army across the border into Lombardy to strike at the advancing Venetians, but he was once more embarrassed. His forces outnumbered the condottieri of Venice, but were no match for their skill and their superior tactics, equipment and experience of fighting in the region. His army was shredded.

After handing over the Florentine tribute, Machiavelli had followed the emperor around Lombardy as his troops first advanced to engage the Venetians and then fell back, defeated. The Signoria was justly concerned that the emperor, stung and red-faced from the humiliation meted out by the Venetians, might lash out at the Republic. As events would confirm, Maximilian was impulsive, and by not trusting him an inch the Florentines were acting wisely. It therefore fell to Machiavelli to perform in his usual double role of diplomat and spy at Maximilian's court in Verona.

In a report to the Signoria of his earlier visit to the Imperial court in Germany, *Rapporto delle cose dell'Alemagna* (*Report on the State of Germany*), Machiavelli had offered a detailed portrait of the emperor, describing him as a 'man of countless virtues' and suggesting that if he was able to toughen his own character he could be a 'most perfect man'. But, because Maximilian was in thrall to the dozens of petty kings and local leaders of nations that made up the mosaic of the Holy Roman Empire, he could rarely make the decisions he wanted to. Bound as he was by internal politics, all his plans were agreed by committee. For this reason alone, Machiavelli believed, he remained 'a mediocre prince'.[14]

The events of late 1509 illustrate this point very well. Maximilian was furious over the failure of the schemes he had initiated with the Diet of Constance. He was now almost powerless, reliant on the decisions of greater forces, in particular the French and the Pope. Having lost their support, in December 1509, he was forced to return home humiliated, his plans in tatters.

Even then, Machiavelli was not convinced that the threat from Maximilian's empire had passed entirely. During the weeks he had spent in Verona, bored and with time on his hands, he had begun to sense a shift within the power structure of Italy. It was not something widely perceived, and indeed, with his finely tuned understanding of these things, he may well have been the only one to realise it was beginning to happen. The seemingly minor clashes with Venice in Lombardy had spawned far more significant events to follow in their wake. In particular, Machiavelli concluded, the most power-crazed commander in Europe, Julius, the spiritual leader of the Holy Roman Catholic Church, was preparing to take advantage of Maximilian's failings.

Still pondering this matter, and with his mission in Verona now over, Machiavelli headed back to Florence, where he planned to put his thoughts to paper and present his fears to his superiors. But then, on 29 December, as he was preparing to complete the final leg of his journey home, stopping briefly at Bologna a few days after missing yet another Christmas with his family, he received a disturbing letter from Biagio Buonaccorsi that stopped him in his tracks.

Addressed to 'Niccolò Machiavelli, An Honoured Brother . . .

Wherever He May Be,' the letter began: 'Honoured Niccolò. I have been stirred to write to you the present letter because the matter that will be narrated below is of such great importance that it could not be greater. Do not make fun of it and do not neglect it, and do not depart from what I shall tell you for anything in the world, because it will be one of the most powerful remedies for avoiding your ruin and that of others.'

Biagio continued:

Tomorrow will be eight days since a masked man with two witnesses went to the house of the notary of the conservators [Ufficiali di Notte e Conservatori dei Monasteri] and in their presence gave him a notification, protesting to him if he did not give it, etc. It stated that since you were born of a father etc., you can in no way exercise the office that you hold, etc. Although the matter was taken care of in the past and the law is as favourable as can be, nevertheless the nature of the times and a great number who have arisen to gossip about this matter and to shout about it everywhere and to threaten that if something is not done, etc., make it such that the matter is not going very well and needs a good deal of help and scrupulous care. From the time that our friends informed me of this until now, I have spared no effort night and day concerning this, so that I have softened up the minds of some people quite a bit. Where the law was being stretched in a thousand ways and given sinister interpretations by those seeking to act against you, etc., it has been laid to rest a bit. Nevertheless, your adversaries are numerous and will stop at nothing. The case is public everywhere, even in the whore-houses.

In conclusion, a genuinely shaken Biagio implored his friend to stay wherever the letter found him. 'I have been urged at this point by someone who loves you, and is a person you consider highly . . .,'

he declared, 'to write you for you to stay where you are and do not
return here for anything, because the matter is quietening down and
no doubt will come to a better end if you are not here than if you
are.'[15]

The incident cited by Biagio was in truth a rather lame attempt
by Salviati's friends and supporters to bring discredit to
Machiavelli's name. It came about because in Florence at this time
there existed a strange system that allowed citizens to proclaim
their feelings about anything they wanted by posting their grievance
in writing in specially designed boxes called *tamburi* (drums) or
buchi della Verità (mouths of Truth) dotted around the city. Citizens
could say what they liked about anything or anybody. Today this
innovation is seen as a by-product of the humanist ideology of the
time and an element of the embryonic democratic arrangement
Florence was beginning to move towards; but it was, without question, also open to abuse.

In 1476 someone had anonymously used the *tamburi* to accuse
Leonardo da Vinci of sodomy and this had led to a trial from which
the artist had emerged innocent. In Machiavelli's case we may
safely assume that any claims that he was an atheist or had loose
morals were too nebulous to gain legal attention and that his opponents did not want to engage in a lengthy legal battle that might go
against them. But, finding nothing wrong with the Secretary's performance in his job, they seized on the law which stated that if a
man became a tax debtor, his sons could not hold any form of official position in the government. Bernardo Machiavelli had been
just such a debtor. However, as Biagio makes clear, this matter had
been resolved long before. In 1509 the claim had absolutely no
legal foundation. Presumably Machiavelli had covered his father's
debt before being offered the post at the Second Chancery more
than a decade earlier, and there was no case to bring against him.
This melodramatic incident was fabricated entirely to cause
Machiavelli the greatest embarrassment.

And if this was the purpose behind the effort, it succeeded. As Biagio had stated, news of the incident spread quickly throughout the city and it became, for a short time at least, a hot topic. Machiavelli was in no real danger, principally because there was nothing in law with which to convict him, but also because he had the support of the gonfalonier, who was almost certainly the 'someone who loves you' that Biagio mentions in his letter.

This unexpected and vicious personal attack on Machiavelli's good name was understandably alarming, and it disturbed him. But, although he took it seriously, he allowed it to delay his journey by only a couple of days. Arriving in Florence on 2 January, he returned to work at the chancery immediately and did his best to dispel a gloomy atmosphere that had descended in the wake of his enemies' actions. If nothing else, he had now learned that they were growing bolder and had no qualms about trying to belittle him or finding ways to discredit him and to convince the impartial or the disinterested that the Florentine Secretary was an unsuitable figure for the important office he held.

But, at the same time as he was facing such personal trials, Machiavelli was growing concerned about the bigger picture. He had continued to analyse what he had seen in Lombardy and he was combining these observations with the daily news emerging from France and elsewhere in Europe. Back in Florence, he began to gather intelligence from Florentine spies such as Agostino Vespucci and he blended this information with his own observations of Pope Julius II. However, even the master political theorist Machiavelli could not have guessed how the schemes of a papal warlord and his own weakening presence on the political scene might conspire to completely devastate his life.

8

Trapped

Machiavelli despised Julius II long before the Pope's political moves had any adverse impact on his life and career. This hatred was partly inspired by the pontiff's odious character, but Machiavelli always viewed with distaste the way contemporary popes saw themselves as military leaders as well as spiritual guides; he was anti-Christian and opposed to the notion that a pontiff could both exercise temporal power and have influence over the political life of nations. When a French general boasted to Machiavelli that any military clash with the papal forces would constitute 'an excursion to Rome rather than a war', he retorted: 'This would indeed be a desirable thing because these priests should be made to swallow a bitter pill in this world.'[1]

However, what Machiavelli disliked most was the Pope's methods and his motivations. Above all else, he had admired Cesare Borgia for his coolness; he perceived the man as the ultimate captain, the archetypal power broker and prince. Before his fall, one almost certainly precipitated by mental illness, Duke Valentino had been merciless, calculating and exceedingly clever. Julius was all of these, but his actions were overshadowed by personal instability. He was impatient, undisciplined and flew into terrible rages that drove him to make extremely bad decisions, all of which led Machiavelli to realise that really the only truly important asset Julius possessed was his position as spiritual leader. This alone elevated him to the status of, as the historian Guicciardini put it, 'the fatal instrument of the ills of Italy'.[2] Without this otherworldly gift, he would have been almost completely ineffectual.

Machiavelli was clear about this when he wrote of the pontiff: 'Pope Julius II was impetuous in everything; and he found the time and circumstances so favourable to his way of proceeding that he always met with success . . . The brevity of his pontifical life did not let him experience the contrary. If there had come a time when it was necessary for him to act with circumspection he would have come to grief: he would never have acted other than in character.'[3]

By 1510 Julius's rages were legendary and many in Rome and beyond were reaching the conclusion that his volatility clouded his vision. During 1509 and 1510, as the relationship between France and Rome grew steadily more tense, the Duke of Savoy sent an envoy to the Pope with a message offering the duke's assistance as a negotiator. The unfortunate man was imprisoned and tortured before being returned to his master. Not long before, no less a figure than the poet Ariosto, in his role as Ferrarese ambassador, was threatened with execution merely because he delivered a note from his master containing news that Julius did not want to hear.

In Rome Machiavelli's friend Francesco Vettori, who witnessed the Pope's intemperate behaviour almost daily, reported on his pontifical decisions and his personality traits. In one missive he told Machiavelli:

Let's get to the pontiff . . . he picks a war with the king of France, and it cannot be seen up to now that he has anyone on his side but the Venetians, half-ruined and desperate, and he begins in such a way as to insult the king so that peace cannot come about very soon, because first he seizes Monsignor

D'Auch [a French cardinal whom Julius had arrested and thrown into the infamous dungeons of the Castel Sant'Angelo], whom the king showed he esteemed highly, like a thief. Then he seeks with words and deeds to make Genoa rebel against him, and before sending a fleet or anything else he says in public that Genoa will revolt, which is as much as if he said to the king, 'Guard it'. Then, when he does not succeed the first time, he says that he wants to attempt a second time. He attacks the possessions of the Duke of Ferrara in Romagna, and because they are badly guarded, he seizes part of them. There remained the fortress of Lugo, which was being bombarded: perhaps six hundred French cavalry issued forth from Ferrara, and at their mere cry all the Pope's troops took to flight and left their artillery, and the French took back all the towns that they had already taken from Ferrara. In conclusion, I do not understand this pope.[4]

Indeed it seems that few men really did understand this pope, but at least other heads of state in Europe were made wary of him. The gonfalonier, Piero Soderini, almost certainly inspired by Machiavelli's good sense and words of advice, declared of Julius II: 'Although a pope as a friend is not worth much, as an enemy he can do much harm.'[5] Such a philosophy at first encouraged the Florentines to try appeasement. In early July 1510 the government took the risky decision to allow Marcantonio Colonna, a condottiere who had recently worked for them, to aid the Pope in taking Genoa and then to pass through Florentine territory when his forces returned south towards Rome.

On the surface there were aspects of Julius's thinking the Florentines could have supported. The Pope was determined to see Italy freed entirely from French influence and was quoted as saying that his duty was to: 'Deliver Italy from servitude and out of the hands of the French.'[6] His aggression was fuelled by the fact that, in May 1509, the Cardinal of Rouen, Georges d'Amboise, had died. The cleric had been one of Louis XII's most trusted and capable advisers and a man who had played a crucial diplomatic role in the relationship between the monarch and the Pope.

The Florentines certainly had no love for the French and viewed them as vultures feeding off the weaknesses of others. Louis, his advisers and ministers were entirely self-serving and had exploited Florentine military weakness for decades. Furthermore, Florentines, like all Italians, resented the presence of any foreign occupier, and when the Venetians had been pummelled by the alliance created by Maximilian twelve months earlier, many Italian states had grown wary of the fact that France had acquired so much territory in Italy. Moreover, they distrusted the power of Rome and the brooding presence of Spain, whose interest in Italy was growing steadily. And, behind it all, there was the realistic fear that France could align itself with another powerful foreign state to conquer all of Italy. They would then divide the spoils and effectively destroy the country.

Florence was placed in a particularly delicate position. It could not become an ally of the Pope because it was dependent on France. Louis's forces would have crushed it if there had been the slightest hint from the Republic that it was going to turn away. Beyond this, Julius did not approve of Soderini, so as long as he was head of the Florentines any union with Rome was impossible.

But at the same time, by not coming out openly against Julius and indeed helping him with his campaign, the Signoria was beginning to irritate Louis. In an effort to appease both sides, Soderini continued to offer the hand of friendship to Julius, but sent Machiavelli to the French court to reassure their king that Florence was still his close ally.

Machiavelli arrived at Blois on 17 July, and that night he received a letter of instruction from Soderini in which he declared rather desperately: 'You must tell the king that I have no other wishes in life than three things: the honour of God, the well-being of my homeland, and the prosperity and honour of His Majesty the King of France.'[7]

The Secretary's mission was a complex and delicate one and as the weeks passed it grew steadily more crucial to the well-being of Florence. Once again Machiavelli was treated like a second-class citizen by his own government, for the Signoria did not provide its emissary with enough money to pay for dispatch riders to take his gravely important messages to Italy, nor did it supply adequate funds for him to make his way through the social scene at the French court.

By the late summer of 1510 it was becoming increasingly difficult for many Italian states to refuse to take sides. First, Julius called on his compatriots to fulfil their Christian duty and support him as a moral imperative. When this failed he applied strong-arm tactics, threats, interdicts that effectively excommunicated the entire populations of cities, a move designed to incite civil disobedience. At Blois the foreign politicians, advisers and generals found the French court in a dark mood. 'All here are disappointed by the Pope . . .,' Machiavelli reported to the Ten of War, 'who seems to be trying to ruin Christendom and to lay the foundations for the destruction of Italy.'[8]

Within this climate of escalating tension and violence, the French wanted Florence to make an open declaration against the Pope and to pledge their support for France in the approaching war. They also wanted the Florentine government to send its own troops and pay for hired armies to fight alongside the French. This was unpopular with the Signoria for two reasons. First, it would be expensive, but the second and more significant reason to oppose it came from the fear that by committing its forces to the French it would leave Florence vulnerable to attack.

It took Machiavelli two months to fight his way to a position where he could put his case to the French court. More respected diplomats with greater political clout were ahead of him in the pecking order, but finally, during the last week of August, he had his moment and addressed the French council of war.

The speech was one of Machiavelli's most important and he delivered it with a display of skill and eloquence that impressed the gathered generals and advisers. The essence of what he had to say, a policy dictated by the Signoria (but with which he entirely agreed) was that Florence was a faithful and supportive ally and could be trusted to stand shoulder to shoulder with the French, but that it would be entirely wrong for the Republic to move its limited military forces south to confront the Pope. The reason for this was clear: it would leave the Republic wide open to attack and occupation, which was not only a terrifying prospect for every Florentine citizen but would also prove disastrous for French ambitions.

Even as the Signoria, through Machiavelli, was attempting to remain on good terms with the French, it continued to play a two-faced game, doing all it could to defuse the Pope's increasingly bitter feelings towards the Florentine government. But by this stage the politicians of the Republic should have realised that there would be no appeasing Julius. He was fundamentally opposed to Soderini's government, and, in common with his predecessor, Alexander VI, he wished to reinstate the Medici as rulers of Florence because he believed he could control them and make the city a dominion of Rome.

But, as the final months of 1510 slipped by and the inevitable war between France and the Pope grew ever more likely, the gonfalonier and his supporters continued to do what they always did: to sit on the fence and bide their time, believing that it would be unwise to openly declare for France and yet finding it impossible to side with the Vatican. It was a short-sighted and limp-wristed policy that could only lead to disaster.

Unimpressed with Florentine intransigence, the Pope was, by the summer of 1511, coming to the conclusion that the Signoria was a collective of traitors and collaborators. This opinion was strengthened when the Florentine government gave its support to Louis for the creation of a Universal Ecclesiastical Council (effectively a Catholic administration to rival the Holy College), with Pisa to be used as a venue for this new controversial council. Realising that by offering the French this support it had inadvertently crossed the line from neutral observer to ally of the French, in September the Florentine government panicked and ordered Machiavelli (who was then struggling to be noticed at Blois) to try to persuade Louis to reconsider his plans for a rebel council.

That summer a pan-Italian war was in the air. Many city states had mobilised their troops and hastily ratified treaties while Florence made it clear to potentially rebellious states within its dominions that it would show no mercy in quashing any insurrection. All roads from the south were carefully monitored by scouts and the new militia was placed on the highest alert. Machiavelli had spent the previous winter recruiting several thousand more infantrymen from the countryside around Florence and the militia had been granted funds and resources to establish a light cavalry to further bolster the city's defences.

Machiavelli's mission to the French court ended up being only a partial success. He failed utterly in his attempt to persuade Louis to cancel his plans for the council of rebel cardinals. The Florentine offer of a compromise in which the council could be moved to another location also failed. But he did succeed in persuading the French king to delay the first meeting of the council for three months by convincing him that this reprieve would allow Florence time to strengthen its forces and therefore better help the French.

It was a clever move and genuine, but in the end it was not necessary. Although Louis had been filled with enthusiasm for his Universal Ecclesiastical Council, the idea captured the imagination of only a handful of French and Spanish rebel cardinals, of whom Bernardino Carvajal, the Cardinal of Jerusalem, was the most important. These clerics, although fired up by Louis's bombast, were motivated solely by selfish intentions that fooled no one.

However, this small, enthusiastic band was determined. After doing all he could at Blois, Machiavelli was sent to meet the cardinals to dissuade them from continuing with their mission. He disliked these men intensely. To him they were even more odious than the vile pope who presided over the faith. Each of the cardinals was only interested in deposing Julius so that he might increase his own chances of succession to the papal throne. Each of them was using his ecclesiastical power to increase his earthly status. Machiavelli hated the principles on which these men had founded their power and he loathed even more the hypocrisy that lent them influence.

Furthermore, the cardinals were extremely difficult men to negotiate with. They knew they held a position of influence and they understood clearly that Florence had placed itself in a very awkward position by allowing the planned council to gather at Pisa in the first place. And yet Machiavelli's abilities as a persuader and negotiator were such that he succeeded in gaining an agreement that they would delay their mission by breaking their journey at the small town of Pontremoli. Here they were gradually made aware of the lack of enthusiasm for their mission and the fact that Louis had, by now, lost interest in the idea. After two months they finally agreed to change their plans and set off for Milan, a comfortable distance from the Republic. There the council met just once, in November 1511, and promptly dissolved in the face of almost unanimous apathy.

By this time what has been dubbed the 'spiritual war' instigated by Louis's use of rebel cardinals had been overtaken by the 'material war'. This had moved on to a new, frenetic level when, in October 1511, Julius succeeded in creating what became known as the Holy League. Under the banner of God the Pope had secured an alliance between Rome, Venice, Ferrara and Aragon. In

November the League was joined by Maximilian's Holy Roman Empire and the armies of Henry VIII of England, to create a formidable force that seemed certain to outmatch the French, who were fighting away from home with their resources spread perilously thin.

At first, however, the war went in favour of the French. Led by the charismatic Gaston de Foix, they captured the town of Brescia and ousted the forces of the League before going on to crush a united force of Spanish and papal soldiers at the Battle of Ravenna in April 1512.

But this was the high-water mark for French ambitions in Italy. Foix was killed at Ravenna. Within a few weeks the Swiss had entered the war on the side of the League and Maximilian had managed to persuade an army of German mercenaries who had been fighting for the French to switch sides. In rapid succession the Swiss took Milan and papal forces claimed Bologna, Piacenza and Parma. The final blow came when the Genoese revolted against their French occupiers, and by 3 May the war was effectively over, the French were expelled from the Peninsula and the victorious Pope stood unopposed and all-powerful.

Julius celebrated with a Lateran Council, ostensibly a pious affair but really an exercise in political crowing. As Guicciardini so perceptively declared: 'There were lovely and sacred ceremonies that would touch the cockles of the heart if one believed that the true thoughts and purposes of those who staged these events were consonant with the words they spoke.'[9]

Not surprisingly, the defeat of the French generated widespread alarm in Florence. Throughout the winter and spring Machiavelli had been busy with his militia, recruiting in the Romagna and helping to organise the new cavalry force. On 19 February this new force had been paraded in the city, prompting the diarist Luca Landucci to report: 'Three hundred bowmen and musketeers were levied here, all from our district. They were mustered in the Piazza della Signoria.'[10] In March Machiavelli was given instructions to start preparing a second cavalry group, but within weeks such ideas had become completely redundant. The fate of Florence was no longer in the hands of the Florentines; it would be decided by the leaders of the Holy League, who in June, a few weeks after Julius's Lateran Council, gathered in secret in Mantua to divide the spoils and to redraw the political map of Italy.

The Pope was now in no mood for clemency or compromise. He immediately placed an interdict on Florence forbidding the administering of the sacraments at any church in the city. The Lateran Council agreed that the Medici should be returned to power either with the willing acceptance of Soderini or by force of arms if necessary; and to press the issue, a Spanish army of some ten thousand men was moved quickly into Tuscany.

'When it was decided at a meeting in Mantua to restore the Medici in Florence . . .,' Machiavelli wrote soon after the event, 'people in Florence greatly feared that the Spanish army would come into Tuscany. Nevertheless, since no one could be sure on this score, because matters had been handled in secret during the meeting, and since many people were unwilling to believe that the Pope would permit the Spanish army to stir that region up . . . we waited with our minds irresolute, without making any other kinds of preparations until certainty about it all might come.'[11]

Once more and for one last time, the gonfalonier prevaricated. Whatever Machiavelli said in this account to excuse them, faced with a clear unquestionable threat, the members of the Signoria acted like rabbits caught in the headlights' glare. By 27 August the Spanish under the command of their Viceroy, Ramón de Cardona, had established themselves at Campi, just a few miles from Florence, and in desperation Soderini wrote, through Biagio Buonaccorsi, to Machiavelli, who was then stationed with his militia on the border between Florence and Bologna. 'Honoured Niccolò. You know who wants me to inform you to make haste there in working out some arrangement, because he does not at all like this enemy camp coming to Campi this evening to lodge there, and he is surprised at it. Farewell. Do what good you can so that time is not wasted in discussion.'[12]

In this extraordinary letter the head of the Florentine state reveals just what a sorry mess the government had found itself in and also just how much he personally relied on Machiavelli, especially during times of crisis. Quite what the besieged gonfalonier thought the envoy could do to help him and the Signoria is impossible to judge.

Before he had had a chance to receive a reply from his Secretary, Soderini ordered two thousand of Machiavelli's militia to go to the fort of Firenzuola, but then, perhaps at Machiavelli's suggestion, he changed his mind and decided to pull back to Prato, some ten miles north of the city, and established a defensive front. This the government believed would be a strong enough force to buy it time to negotiate with the Spanish and the Pope.

On 28 August Soderini called an extraordinary meeting of the Great Council to propose that he step down and the city allow the Medici (who were waiting impatiently behind the Spanish lines a few miles away) to return as private citizens. The first proposal was rejected but the second passed. Within hours news of these decisions reached Prato, and so, needing no further motive, Cardona's forces attacked.

To everyone's surprise this first attack was resisted successfully and the Spanish were forced to regroup. For a brief moment some believed there could be a chance of salvation for the Republic. Florentine intelligence had discovered that the Spanish army gathered before the walls of Prato was exhausted and its supply lines had been overstretched. Its first attack on the garrison had been a half-hearted attempt, and with his army in such a sorry state Cardona would have much preferred to come to a negotiated settlement with Soderini than to have brought things to a fight. But the successful resistance of the militia at Prato, together with the confidence boost he had gained from the support of the Great Council, gave Soderini a renewed sense of hope and a grim, misguided determination.

Meeting unexpected resistance from the Florentine militia, Cardona took the bold and unconventional step of letting the Florentines know that his men were starving and that on their behalf he was willing to negotiate a peaceful settlement in exchange for bread. An envoy was sent to the Signoria, where the Great Council met to discuss the proposition. It was at this precise moment that Soderini made the worst decision of his life. Emboldened, the gonfalonier and many of his closest advisers (excepting Machiavelli, who was with the militia) decided to act, not out of goodwill or to show any inclination to forge a compromise, but to take Cardona's offer as a sign of weakness and to throw it back in the Spaniard's face.

It was a decision that cost the lives of more than four thousand men, women and children, it ended Soderini's rule and it threw Florence into utter chaos. On 30 August the Spanish army, half-crazed with hunger, armed to the teeth and outnumbering a peasant army five to one, stormed the fortress at Prato, slaughtering every living thing in its way. The soldiers raped and murdered hundreds of women who were holed up behind the inner defences and then they razed the fortress. Machiavelli reported:

> The Spanish, having broken through some of the walls, began to force the defenders back and to terrify them. So that, after slight resistance, they all fled and the Spaniards took possession of the city [Prato], put it to the sack, and massacred the city's population in a pitiable spectacle of calamity . . . better than four thousand died; the remainder were captured and, through various means, were obliged to pay ransom. Nor did they spare the virgins cloistered in holy sites, which were filled with acts of rape and pillage.[13]

In *The Discourses*, written a few years after these terrible events, Machiavelli described the lesson he had learned from the decisions made by the Signoria on that fateful day:

> Rulers of states, when attacked, cannot make a greater mistake than to refuse to come to terms when the forces attacking them are a good deal stronger than their own, especially if the overtures are made by the enemy: for the terms will never be so hard but that in them some benefit will accrue to those who accept them, so that in a way they will share the victory . . . It should have sufficed the people of Florence that the Spanish army had yielded to any of their demands instead of fulfilling all their own, for this would have been a considerable victory. For what the Spanish army wanted was to change the form of government in Florence, to put an end to its attachment to France, and to levy a tribute. If of these three things the Spaniard had gained the last two, and the people of Florence had gained the first, that is the retention of their form of government, each would have acquired a certain honour and a certain satisfaction.[14]

It was an ignominious end to Soderini's leadership of the Republic of Florence. News of the slaughter in Prato quickly reached the city and caused widespread panic. By eight o'clock on the evening of 30 August Ramón de Cardona had ordered the Signoria to make an immediate decision. Either the gonfalonier step down or the Spanish army would launch a devastating attack on the city of Florence itself.

This time the gonfalonier and his advisers knew they could follow only one course of action: Soderini could not be allowed to risk the lives of his people again. With great haste a representative of the Signoria was dispatched to the Spanish camp to inform Cardona that the Florentine government would comply with their terms without condition. Before a reply could be sent Machiavelli and Francesco Vettori drafted Soderini's resignation and organised his escape into exile. In the dead of night the gonfalonier was spirited away to Siena, protected by a heavily armed guard.

Machiavelli had never held Soderini in great esteem, and although the gonfalonier had been his lifeline to power, he had little respect for his approach to leadership. The way Soderini had handled the final crisis of his tenure filled Machiavelli with disgust, and in *The Discourses* he comments witheringly: 'Piero Soderini thought that by patience and goodness he could quell the desire of "Brutus's sons" [that is, any violently radical opponent] to return to another form of government, but in this he was mistaken. Though being a prudent man, he recognised the need for action, and thought the type of ambitious men who were against him gave him ground for getting rid of them, yet he could never make up his mind to do this.'[15]

Soderini stood at the opposite end of the leadership spectrum to a man like Cesare Borgia. Indecisive and weak, he intellectualised and resisted when he should have yielded, and he gave way when a show of strength was called for. To Machiavelli the erstwhile gonfalonier for life of the Republic of Florence was a perfect example of how the selection of a leader based almost solely on the criterion of nobility often leads to instability and failure. Quite simply, Soderini had shown that he was not the right sort of man to lead a country, a fact Machiavelli expressed with untainted brutality when, on the death of the former gonfalonier in 1522, he wrote:

> *That night when Soderini died,*
> *his spirit went to the mouth of Hell;*
> *Pluto roared, 'Why to Hell? Silly spirit,*
> *Go to Limbo with all the other babies.'*

As far as Machiavelli was concerned, hell was the rightful place only for strong and successful politicians, and his former leader, Piero Soderini, did not make the grade.

During the first days of September 1512 the Republic, which Machiavelli had served for fourteen years, faced a complete political overhaul and he knew that his own future was now cast into uncertainty. He had been closer to the gonfalonier and his policies than to any other politician in Florence, and while the old regime continued on its meandering way he had been safe. Now, however, the crutches that had supported his political life were falling: first the French and then the gonfalonier and the old order had gone, leaving Machiavelli exposed and vulnerable.

Florence began to change very quickly. The Medici, returning from a long exile, seemed to sense accurately the mood of the people and did not make any immediate play for power. Instead they set up a puppet leader in the form of the austere Giambattista Ridolfi, who had been Savonarola's right-hand man during the late 1490s. He was established as gonfalonier for a term of one year only and was always perceived as a transitional figurehead. An assembly of the people (*parlamento*) was called and many of the mechanisms of the Florentine government that had served Soderini and his Signoria were abolished or changed radically. Overnight the Nine Officers of the Florentine Ordnance and Militia were disbanded, and so too was Machiavelli's militia. The Great Council was dismantled and the position of gonfalonier for life was no more.

'On the sixteenth of this month [September],' Machiavelli reported in a letter written within days of these tumultuous events:

the Signoria assembled many citizens at the Palazzo [Vecchio], and with them was the magnificent Giuliano [de' Medici], and they were discussing governmental reform when there chanced to be an uproar heard in the Piazza, so that Ramazzotti [a condottiere in the service of the Medici] with his soldiers and some other men seized the Palazzo crying, '*Palle, palle*' [the traditional rallying call of the Medici]. The entire city was suddenly up in arms, and that name was echoing everywhere throughout the city, so that the Signoria was compelled to summon the populace to an assembly which we call a parliament, where a law was proclaimed that reinstated the Magnificent Medici in all the honours and dignitaries of their ancestors.[16]

The new government was run by a parliament of fifty wealthy citizens, all Medici supporters, and the two brothers now at the head of the family, the thirty-six-year-old Cardinal Giovanni de' Medici and his younger brother, Giuliano, were effectively rulers of the Republic. (Piero de' Medici, sometimes known as Piero the Unfortunate, had died in 1503.) Wily and astute, they knew that after the chaos and the slaughter of 30 August they would be wise to do all they could to brighten the mood of their fellow Florentines. To do this they put on lavish carnivals and pageants. Oxen and horses covered with the skins of exotic animals were paraded before floats decked out in gold cloth. Men at arms in burnished armour and a float with an emperor dressed in a toga accompanied by dozens of handmaidens passed through the piazza, while men dressed as griffins and demons frolicked among the crowd.

Through all the political changes Machiavelli was virtually ignored. He turned up at his office in the chancery each morning and continued with the more mundane elements of his work, the administration of government that continues even while all around is in a state of ideological flux. Then, in late September, prompted by the fact that the Medici were now once more at the helm of government and had secured popular support, he wrote a 'letter of advice' to Cardinal Giovanni de' Medici. In this he stated that it would be in the best interests of the Medici to act with clemency and moderation towards those who had confiscated the family's lands when they were exiled in 1494.

The letter was ignored; and so, a few weeks later, Machiavelli wrote another longer and more detailed screed to the Medici. In this treatise, now known as *Ai palleschi (To the Mediceana)* or *Memorandum to Medici Supporters*, he pulled no punches. He criticised many of the followers of the Medici and declared that it would be extremely unwise to go too far with reform too quickly and that to cast aspersions on the old regime would do the new one little credit. 'I therefore believe that it is necessary for your house to win friends over to your side and not to turn them away . . .,' he suggested, before adding: 'I repeat that I should like to make friends for your house, not enemies.'[17]

This time Machiavelli did receive a response. On 7 November 1512 he was 'dismissed, deprived and totally removed' from all his duties.[18] He must surely have expected such a reaction, but such expectation did little to temper his shock. He had served his country faithfully and had never openly opposed the Medici, but to them he was perceived as a fallen angel, a man they had supported in the past, who in fact owed his job to them, but a man who had been a close ally of one of their enemies. As Soderini and the Medici had helped to make Machiavelli's career, so, too, they destroyed it.

And so began Machiavelli's rapid fall from power. Having taken away from him the job he loved, the Medici decided to make an example of him and initiated a succession of cruel moves. On 10 November he was sentenced by the Signoria to stay within Florentine territory for twelve months and forced to pay one thousand gold florins as a bond. The following week the former Secretary was banned from entering the Palazzo Vecchio.

For a man whose life had revolved around his job and the travels he enjoyed so much, these were painful rulings, and there is little doubt they were calculated to cause him anguish. These sanctions not only humiliated and belittled the former Secretary, but also served to separate him from any political means by which he might have stirred up trouble for the Medici.

Not content with inflicting this punishment, the Signoria, late in November, called for an investigation into Machiavelli's accounts and accused him of embezzling funds during his time as Secretary to the Second Chancery. The investigation required the Medici to break their own ruling so that Machiavelli could attend a series of hearings at the Palazzo Vecchio. There, for four weeks, he was questioned and cross-examined by some of his former underlings, men who had worked with him for over a decade. These included Niccolò Michelozzi, a dedicated Medici man and a one-time assistant, who chaired each meeting and led the judicial inquiry. In spite of strenuous efforts the investigators could find nothing at all to incriminate Machiavelli and ended up paying him a small sum to redress an underpayment he had made to himself a few years earlier.

The year 1512 ended in misery for the Machiavellis. Niccolò, Marietta and the children retired to the small family estate of Sant'Andrea, near San Casciano. In Florence the rehabilitation of the Medici was now almost complete, while in Rome Cardinal Giovanni de' Medici was acquiring new friends and gaining influence in papal politics. The rise of the Medici seemed almost unstoppable.

But the new rulers had many enemies in Florence, and they were justly wary of potential conspiracies against their regime. In early 1513 one such conspiracy was initiated by four anti-Medici activists, Pietro Paolo Boscoli, Agostino Capponi, Niccolò Valori and Giovanni Folchi, but luckily for Giuliano and Giovanni, the enthusiasm demonstrated by this group was matched by their incompetence. In a wonderful display of ineptitude one of the conspirators, most likely Boscoli, lost a document listing all those the group believed would join them if there was an uprising against the Medici brothers. For no other reason than the fact that he had been a very well known victim of the new regime, Machiavelli's name had found its way on to this list.

The document reached the hands of the authorities and all those named in it were arrested by the Otto di Guardia. The public declaration to bring Machiavelli into custody read: 'Whoever knew or sheltered, or knew who sheltered Niccolò, son of Bernardo Machiavelli, must denounce him within the hour under pain of being called a rebel and forfeiting his possessions.'[19]

Machiavelli was almost certainly at his country estate and there was some delay before he heard of the warrant for his arrest, but he quickly handed himself in. On the evening of 8 February he was thrown into Florence's Bargello prison to await trial.

The cell was freezing cold and almost airless. He was half-starved, allowed no visitors and forced to share his tiny cell with the rats that scurried around throughout the day and night. It was undoubtedly the lowest point of his life and a far cry from the world he had occupied only a few short months earlier. Most agonising of all was the fact that he had little notion of why he had been imprisoned. He had barely known the conspirators and had no idea his name was on the lost document. But if the Medici hated him as much as it seemed and they could find the smallest scrap of evidence to show that he had been involved in a plot against them, he was as good as dead.

Then the torture began. Machiavelli was subjected to the strappado: his arms were tied behind his back, he was winched up to the ceiling, released suddenly and then brought up just before reaching the floor. He was subjected to this barbarism a total of six times, but he neither incriminated himself nor confessed to things he had not done. And yet, for all his courage, he could have had no idea whether or not the real conspirators were lying and giving his name as an accomplice in order to help their own case. It was only later that he learned Boscoli and Capponi had indeed mentioned his name, but the most incriminating thing they could say about him was that he had made disparaging remarks about the ideology of the Medici.

Two weeks after their arrest, and after repeated torture, the two leaders of the conspiracy, Boscoli and Capponi, were sentenced to be executed. Just before dawn on 23 February Machiavelli was awoken in his cell by the clanking of chains and the sound of hymns sung by the friars and brothers of the Compagnia dei Neri (a charitable organisation dedicated to the welfare of condemned prisoners) as the two men were led to the block.

Hearing these sounds, Machiavelli felt little remorse for the condemned. Instead his overriding emotions were anger and self-pity and he decided to express his feelings in a sonnet he composed in prison for the only man he believed could save him, Giuliano de' Medici.

It may seem odd to imagine Machiavelli writing a sonnet in jail and planning to send it to the head of the Florentine state in order to beg for a reprieve, but this would be to miss an essential aspect of his character. He was, after all, a poet, a natural writer. More importantly, as a young man he had known Giuliano de' Medici and had been recognised as a published poet at the Medici court during the early 1490s. He must have believed that he could capture Giuliano's imagination and make him remember him from his childhood, make him realise his many talents and conclude that holding him in the Bargello was an absurdity. The sonnet begins:

> *'Giuliano, I have a pair of shackles on my legs*
> *and six drops of the strappado on my back;*
> *my other misfortunes I shall not tell,*
> *since that is the way they treat poets.*
> *These walls are full of lice so big and fat*
> *they seem like butterflies,*
> *and there never was such a stench in Roncesvalles*
> *or in Sardinia amid those groves,*
> *as in this fine dwelling of mine.*
> *With a noise that sounds like Jove*
> *and all Etna were hurling thunderbolts to earth,*

one prisoner is chained up and another unbound,
padlocks, keys and bolts rattle together,
and another cries: 'Too high from the ground!'
What worries me most is that, as I slept, near dawn
I began to hear 'We pray for you'.
Now let them go.
I pray if only your mercy may turn towards me
and surpass the fame of your father and your grandfather.'[20]

It was, of course, a begging letter, but one written with wit and style. Of all the lines in this sonnet, those that have generated most comment come towards the end: 'I began to hear "We pray for you". Now let them go.' Here Machiavelli refers to his experience of hearing Boscoli and Capponi being led away to their execution, and it was this aspect of his ordeal that prompted him to write to Giuliano in the first place. Many commentators have claimed that this is a callous remark, but it is merely an expression of fact. The men had sealed their own fate by their foolish actions. It was they who had placed Machiavelli in the terrible situation he now faced; why should he have felt anything other than contempt for them?

Not surprisingly, Giuliano de' Medici did not deign to reply to the sonnet and indeed he may never have received it. But Machiavelli remained undaunted. He had little other recourse but to try again, so he wrote a second, even more self-mocking sonnet. In this he imagined a muse visiting him in jail and berating him: 'You are not Niccolò, but Dazzo [a contemporary Florentine poet of little talent but great popular acclaim], for you have your legs and heels tied together and are chained up like a lunatic.'[21]

If Giuliano received this second sonnet it must surely have amused him, but there is no evidence that it influenced Machiavelli's fate. On 21 February, two days before the execution of Boscoli and Capponi, the sixty-nine-year-old Julius had died suddenly. On 6 March the cardinals went into conclave and on the

11th a new pope was elected. He took the name Leo X, but until then he had been known as Cardinal Giovanni de' Medici, one of the rulers of Florence and the brother of Giuliano de' Medici.

Florence had rarely witnessed anything like the celebrations that greeted this news. Businesses throughout the city closed and it seemed as though every section of society was energised and excited by the election of a Florentine pope. Traders and bankers realised quickly that this turn of events would boost business enormously; the pious gave thanks for this new union of the ecclesiastical and the secular, and the Medici could feel a sense of security and confidence the family had not known since the time of Lorenzo. Suddenly Giuliano and Giovanni were beloved in both Florence and Rome.

Machiavelli also had good reason to rejoice. As part of the celebrations in Florence, all prisoners, except the two surviving conspirators, Valori and Folchi, were released. On 12 March Machiavelli was one of the first to be led from the doors of the Bargello a free man.

One of the first things he did on arriving back at his country estate was to write to his friend Francesco Vettori, the Florentine ambassador to the Vatican, who had been using his limited influence in Rome to secure Machiavelli's early release. Vettori had completely failed in his efforts, but Machiavelli knew that he was one of the few people who might open doors for him in the future and he wanted to express his appreciation of the efforts Vettori had made and to show him how he had come through his ordeal with fortitude. 'As for turning my face towards *Fortuna*,' he wrote, 'I should like you to get this pleasure from these troubles of mine, that I have borne them so straightforwardly that I am proud of myself for it and consider myself more of a man than I believed I was. And if these new masters of ours see fit not to leave me lying on the ground, I shall be happy and believe that I shall act in such a way that they too will have reason to be proud of me.'[22]

For Machiavelli this episode had been one of the pivotal

experiences of his life. In jail he had faced pain and imminent death with stoicism. He felt justly proud that he had borne up so well under terrible suffering. But, even more importantly for his own state of mind and his future, he had discovered great solace in writing. He probably never considered the sonnets to Giuliano de' Medici to be anything other than desperate attempts to gain his freedom, but he had poured his heart and soul into them. At the lowest point of his life he had turned to the written word. He had always felt a great love for literature and he had been admired by those who had read his letters and his essays. As Soderini's speechwriter he had placed appropriate words before the powerful of the world and sometimes they had been heeded. Now he had discovered the soul-preserving quality of creativity. It was one of the few things he could depend on in this ever-changing, untrustworthy world, and soon it would become essential to his very survival.

9

Exile

Physical torture was one thing, the prospect of a pointless, valueless future quite another. But that was exactly what Machiavelli appeared to be facing when he left jail in March 1513. He was without a job, he had very little money and he had many dependants; he was distrusted by his masters, the rulers of Florence, he had few friends of influence and he was approaching his forty-fourth birthday, an age respected for experience but not any easy stage of life at which to begin afresh.

It appears that for a short time after his release Machiavelli celebrated his freedom and consoled himself with the company of his friends, mostly men who had also lost their jobs and were out of favour with the city's rulers. These friends included the ever-faithful Biagio Buonaccorsi, who had, not long before this, suffered the loss of his beloved wife. Also among this band were Filippo Casavecchia (who would later become the first person to read *The Prince*), Tommaso del Bene, a former employee at the chancery and the shopkeeper and renowned libertine Donato del Corno. 'The whole gang sends you regards,' Machiavelli told their mutual friend Francesco Vettori, who was still in Rome. 'Every day we visit the house of some girl to recover our vigour.'[1]

But soon Machiavelli needed to get out of Florence, to stand back and to observe, to leave behind for a while the sneers and the aggression of his detractors. The obvious bolt hole was the rather sad little country home at Sant'Andrea, just seven miles from Florence. It was close enough to the city for the towers clustered along the Arno to be visible from hilltops near the farmhouse, but far enough away to allow Machiavelli to feel completely detached from unsavoury memories. In a sense he was in exile, but for a time at least, a part of him deliberately wanted isolation; for if he could not be a part of things, as he had been for the past fifteen years, then he preferred to be physically removed from the source of his pain. He wanted to be 'far from every human face'.[2]

It was a change of lifestyle that did not come at all easily to Machiavelli. During the past decade and a half he had spent less time at home than he had away from Florence working at the courts of the powerful. He cared for his family, but being a good husband and father did not come naturally to him. He was too self-absorbed, too focused on his thoughts to be easily domesticated. On the one hand he was preoccupied with the big issues of the day, and on the other he was enamoured with manly pursuits, drinking, whoring and gambling. He had huge inner resources, but they were best directed to dealing with the great affairs of the world, so that he found it almost impossible to concern himself with the business of everyday life.

In a letter written some nine months into his self-imposed exile and shortly before returning with his family to Florence for an extended period, he described in detail the routine he had managed to establish in his new life:

I am living on my farm, and since my last disasters, I have not spent a total of twenty days in Florence. Until now, I have been catching thrushes with my own hands. I would get up before daybreak, prepare the birdlime, and go out with such a bundle of

birdcages on my back that I look like Geta when he came back
from the harbour with Amphitryon's books [an allusion to a
popular story of the time]. I would catch at least two, at most six
thrushes. And thus I passed the entire month of November.
Eventually this diversion, albeit contemptible and foreign to me,
petered out – to my regret. I shall tell you about my life. I get up
in the morning with the sun and go into one of my woods that I
am having cut down; there I spend a couple of hours inspecting
the work of the previous day and kill some time with the woodsmen who always have some dispute on their hands either among
themselves or with their neighbours . . . Upon leaving the
woods, I go to a spring, from there, to one of the places where I
hang my bird nets. I have a book under my arm: Dante,
Petrarch, or one of the minor poets like Tibullus, Ovid, or some
such. I read about their amorous passions and their loves,
remember my own, and these reflections make me happy for a
while. Then I make my way along the road towards the inn, I
chat with passers-by, I ask news of their regions, I learn about
various matters, I observe mankind: the variety of its tastes, the
diversity of its fancies. By then it is time to eat; with my household I eat what food this poor farm and my minuscule patrimony
yield. When I have finished eating, I return to the inn, where
there usually are the innkeeper, a butcher, a miller and a couple
of kilnworkers. I slum around with them for the rest of the day
playing *cricca* and backgammon: these games lead to thousands
of squabbles and endless ambushes and vituperations. More
often than not we are wrangling over a penny; be that as it may,
people can hear us yelling even in San Casciano. Thus having
been cooped up among these lice, I get the mould out of my
brain and let out the malice of my fate, content to be ridden over
roughshod in this fashion if only to discover whether or not my
fate is ashamed of treating me so.

When evening comes, I return home and enter my study; on

the threshold I take off my workday clothes, covered with mud and dirt, and put on the garments of court and palace. Fitted out appropriately, I step inside the venerable courts of the ancients, where, solicitously received by them, I nourish myself on that food that alone is mine and for which I was born; where I am unashamed to converse with them and to question them about the motives for their actions, and they, out of their human kindness, answer me. And for four hours at a time I feel no boredom, I forget all my troubles, I do not dread poverty, and I am not afraid by death. I absorb myself into them completely. And because Dante says that no one understands anything unless he retains what he has understood, I have jotted down what I have profited from in their conversation and composed a short study, *De principatibus*, in which I delve as deeply as I can into the ideas concerning this topic, discussing the definition of a princedom, the categories of princedoms, how they are acquired, how they are retained, and why they are lost.[3]

Machiavelli makes his account so clear we can easily imagine him living out this new alien existence, a way of life that was, as he says, so 'contemptible and foreign' to him. We can picture him acting as the good diplomat in the disputes between the woodsmen, involving himself in settling these matters in the very same way he had once dealt with counts and dukes, princes and popes. Most striking is his description of the way he wrote *The Prince*, getting dressed up in finery otherwise mothballed now he no longer needed anything but rough and shabby clothes suited to life catching thrushes on his farm. And yet to us, modern observers of Machiavelli's life, even his own description of such things seems somehow so strange as to be almost unimaginable. How could Machiavelli, the man now so famous and so misunderstood, the man whose ideas have influenced so many during the five centuries since he wrote his famous books, simply have pottered around on his farm? How could he have dealt with the sudden and shocking change of lifestyle he now experienced, swapping the company of kings for tavern games and petty arguments with his workmen?

The simple answer is that Niccolò Machiavelli had no choice. He could do nothing but accept *fortuna* and to use the ephemeral concerns that filled his days as a counterweight to his nights. 'Slumming with the lice' grounded him as he set to work on what would one day be considered a literary masterpiece.

And as Machiavelli returned in his mind to the courts of kings and the venerable ancients, the real affairs of state moved on as though he had never existed. When he returned to the microcosm of his country home, the macrocosm of European politics did not skip a beat. News of events in Florence and beyond came his way through visiting friends and from letters, particularly those exchanged throughout this time with Francesco Vettori. It is not difficult to imagine Biagio Buonaccorsi, who had been sacked from his position at the same time as his former boss, dropping by, and other old associates, those unafraid of being tarnished by association, also remained loyal. From these sources, as well as from the 'passers-by' with whom he tells us he chatted, Machiavelli kept abreast of political affairs.

The Medici, he learned, had very quickly become a locus of power in Europe. This power revolved around four key members of the family. In Rome Giovanni de' Medici had been crowned Pope Leo X in March 1513 and in Florence Giuliano de' Medici had for a short time acted as a caretaker ruler. By August the nephew of the brothers, twenty-one-year-old Lorenzo di Piero de' Medici was appointed governor of Florence by his elder uncle, Giovanni. Lorenzo, who became Duke of Urbino after the Pope took the duchy away from its rightful owner, Francesco della Rovere, was a keen military man who had little time for anything but the acquisition of lands and status and he was already acquiring a reputation as a callous warrior in the same mould as Cesare Borgia.

Giuliano was the very opposite of his nephew. Later given the title Duke of Nemours, he was a man not at all well suited to high-level politics. He was somewhat effeminate, famously homosexual and more interested in the Arts than affairs of state. Even so, he demanded a role in the Medici power structure. Preferring a lucrative position with little responsibility but a degree of grand-iloquence, he was given the titles Patrician of Rome and Captain of the Ecclesiastical Military Forces.

The fourth member of this elite group was the cousin of Giuliano and Giovanni, Giulio de' Medici, who was, at thirty-five, the eldest of the four. A cleric, Giulio was, within weeks of Giovanni's ascension to the papal throne, made Archbishop of Florence and then became a cardinal four months later, in September. He was later to follow his cousin to the papacy, becoming Pope Clement VII in 1523.

At the hub of this new political structure was the Pope, which meant that the affairs of Florence were now almost exclusively controlled from Rome. Indeed Florence virtually lost its independence or any form of separate political identity. Instead it had become a part of a wider network of papal and ecclesiastical concerns. This was a self-serving move by Leo, but it was also entirely appropriate because, for a time at least, it insulated Florentine interests from foreign states that were eager to gain a foothold in Italy.

Early in 1513 Louis XII, who had been most damaged by the actions of Leo's predecessor, Julius, and the Holy League, succeeded in forming a tenuous alliance with Venice. In June, at the Battle of Novara, the joint forces of France and Venice tried to reclaim Milan but were soundly defeated by the armies of the Pope and mercenaries employed by the former rulers of Milan, the Sforza family. This led to the reinstatement of Massimiliano Sforza, son of the former duke, Ludovico Sforza, and Beatrice d'Este.

Retreating from Italy in disarray, Louis's troops arrived home too late to help fight another war. This had been precipitated by an unexpected attack launched by Henry VIII of England, who in July had joined forces with another ally from the Holy League, Emperor Maximilian I, entered France and taken Picardy. In August the English and Imperial armies went on to crush the demoralised French at Guinegate, near Calais. This clash became known as the 'Battle of the Spurs' because of the hasty flight of the French cavalry.

For Machiavelli the most valuable source of political news and contemporary affairs came from Francesco Vettori, with whom he had been friends since the machinations of Alamanno Salviati took them to Maximilian's court in 1507. On 30 December 1512, shortly before Machiavelli had become embroiled in the conspiracy against the Medici, Vettori (along with two others, Jacopo Salviati and Matteo Strozzi) had been appointed as one of the three permanent Florentine ambassadors to Rome. This posting lasted almost three years and during that time Machiavelli and Vettori corresponded regularly, filling their letters with finely detailed argument and political analysis.

The exchange began with a letter from Machiavelli written immediately after his release from the Bargello and the dozens of letters that followed chart his time at Sant'Andrea, his writing of *The Prince* and *The Discourses* and his many failed attempts to secure a job in the new Medici-ruled Florence. These are fascinating but odd letters crammed with insightful observation, argument and counter-argument. But, between the lofty monologues, a sort of sparring match between two intellectuals, there is gossip and light-hearted chat about love, sex and the social scene in Rome. As well as providing Machiavelli with information about the latest political manoeuvres of the key players in Europe, this exchange also kept politics alive for him. Meanwhile Vettori, who had enormous respect for his friend's knowledge and judgement, used the letters as a way of keeping his intellect sharp while he went through the motions of a largely unfulfilling life in Rome. For Machiavelli this correspondence was a lifeline, but, more than this, his words in response to Vettori's musings and questions acted as an inspiration; they were nothing less than the sparks that set alight the fire at the heart of *The Prince*.

When Machiavelli first set up home in the country soon after his release from imprisonment, he felt utterly sick of the world and wanted in particular to dissociate himself from politics. 'I have resolved to think no more about politics or to discuss them,' he told Vettori.[4] But this was soon to change, for politics was in his blood and he could no more stop thinking about it than he could choose to stop breathing.

Throughout 1513 the two men discussed the ebb and flow of European power politics and each made predictions about what would happen and how. This led Machiavelli to think back over his experiences and to rekindle his belief that, at a fundamental level, the actions of men in his time were really no different from the actions of men in the ancient past, nor indeed would they be at all different in the foreseeable future. From this came the notion of 'general rules', 'maxims' or 'proposals' for what might constitute 'ideal leadership' and the factors that led to political success and potential failure.

August 1513 was both a terrible month and the beginning of one of the most satisfying experiences of Machiavelli's life. Writing to his nephew Giovanni Vernacci on 4 August, he reported that Marietta had given birth to a baby girl who died three days later. He then goes on to say: 'Physically I feel well, but ill in every other respect.'[5] Perhaps prompted by this sad event and feelings of despair, he set about starting a new project. For several months he had been struggling with what would later become the beginning of *The Discourses*, a more general political tract than *The Prince*. As Machiavelli was considering the ways in which leaders could maintain power in their states and thinking about how a true prince would find and hold on to success, he was suddenly gripped by the idea of a short, direct treatise dealing with the concept of the 'ideal ruler'.

The Prince was written between August 1513 and January 1514. We know this primarily from comments and hints in the correspondence with Vettori. During November Machiavelli had shown some parts of the first draft to a close friend in Florence, Filippo Casavecchia, and by Christmas Eve he was ready to send a copy of his work to Rome. Vettori's initial reaction was rather lukewarm and he seemed to be somewhat bemused by it. At the end of a long chatty letter he said simply: 'I have seen the chapters of your work . . . and they please me beyond measure.'[6]

Although Machiavelli was almost certainly a little deflated by Vettori's faint praise, by this time he was so fired up by what he had written that he had already moved on from considering the content of his work to wondering what he might be able to do with it. In January, about the time he received his reply from Francesco Vettori, he was closing up the farmhouse for the winter and returning with his family to Florence. In his bag he had an almost completed manuscript of *The Prince* and part of *The Discourses*.

Machiavelli was quite aware of the fact that in writing *The Prince* he was drawing on his experiences in the courts of the great leaders of Europe. He had made this clear in his lengthy letter of December 1513 in which he described how he wrote his book. He reiterated this point later in the same letter with the comment: 'And through this study of mine, were it to be read, it would be evident that during the fifteen years I have been studying the art of the state I have neither slept nor fooled around.'[7]

But just as important as his past experiences were the very circumstances of his life during the latter part of 1513, for there can be little doubt that his literary masterpiece might never have been written if he had remained in his old job. If his career had survived the return of the Medici he would not have found the time nor, more importantly, the necessary motivation to distil his thoughts

and draw on his long political service. In this way he was following
in the footsteps of Dante, who, two centuries earlier, had created his
most enduring work, *The Divine Comedy*, while in exile from
Florence. Of his experiences Dante had written:

> *You shall leave behind all that you love*
> *most dearly, and this is the arrow*
> *that the bow of exile shoots first.*
> *You shall find out how bitter*
> *someone else's bread tastes,*
> *and how hard is the way*
> *up and down another's stairs.* [8]

It was perfectly understandable that Machiavelli now wished to
gain recognition for what he knew was a work of great power and
merit. The return to Florence of the Machiavelli family in January
1514 was prompted by the practical wish to avoid a winter in the
country, but there was also the fact that Machiavelli needed to be in
Florence to supervise the copying of his manuscript and ensure that
it reached people of influence. Besides, he missed human contact
after so long in the wilderness. He had written what he knew was a
fine piece of work, a treatise that encapsulated all he had learned
and experienced in his career at the chancery, and now he wished it
to be read.

Although Machiavelli had been thoroughly abused by the
Medici, he realised that little of real value could be achieved in
Florence without their help and he had never entirely given up the
idea that he might still be accepted by the Medici and acquire gain-
ful employment through them. So it seemed a perfectly reasonable
idea to use his treatise as a showcase for his talents, a means by
which he might influence the most important family in Italy to
employ him again. He aimed to do this in two ways. First, he hoped
that Vettori would use his influence to persuade the Pope to view

him in a better light. Second, he intended to dedicate his book to one of the Medici in the belief that this might prompt one of them to at least read his work.

Throughout 1514, as Machiavelli put the finishing touches to his treatise, worked on *The Discourses* and continued his exchange of letters with Vettori in Rome, he began to harbour genuine hopes that his fortunes would soon change. To Vettori he had declared towards the end of the previous year:

> I desire that these Medici princes should begin to employ me, even if at first it were only something menial; for if I then did not gain their favour, I should blame myself. And if they read this work of mine, they would see that the fifteen years I have spent at the study of politics, I have not wasted or gambled away; and anyone ought to be glad to use a man who has gained a great deal of experience at other people's expense. Of my fidelity there should be no doubt, for having always kept faith I should not learn to break it. A man who has been faithful and virtuous for forty-three years as I have, cannot change his nature; and my poverty is evidence of my fidelity and virtue.[9]

But Vettori could offer only limited help. First, he had no real influence at the papal court, and second, even if he had the ear of the Pope, he would have been risking his own position by praising a man who had only recently been released from jail accused of conspiring against the family of the pontiff.

The Medici were certainly aware of Machiavelli's talents and they also knew he had been a faithful and patriotic member of the previous government. But ironically, they, like all successful leaders, thought in the very terms Machiavelli espoused in his political writings. In *The Prince* he had asserted:

> It should be borne in mind that there is nothing more difficult to

handle, more doubtful of success, and more dangerous to carry through than initiating changes in a state's constitution. The innovator makes enemies of all those who prospered under the old order, and only lukewarm support is forthcoming from those who would prosper under the new. Their support is lukewarm partly from fear of their adversaries, who have existing laws on their side, and partly because men are generally incredulous, never really trusting new things unless they have tested them by experience. In consequence, whenever those who oppose the changes can do so, they attack vigorously, and the defence made by the others is only lukewarm. So both the innovator and his friends come to grief.'[10]

To look at it clinically, the Medici were wise to leave Machiavelli out in the cold. He had been a loyal and trustworthy supporter of their former foes, a government they had ousted in what had amounted to a coup immediately after the bloodletting at Prato. Beyond this, there were other reasons for the Medici to distrust him, reasons that had nothing to do with his undeniable abilities as a political analyst and diplomat. The Medici were a materialistic family, but they were also pious and hypocritical; they saw themselves as occupying the moral high ground. Machiavelli's well-known views on sex and religion did not suit their image.

This was, of course, an almost farcical injustice. Giuliano de' Medici was famous for his liking of young boys and the history of the papacy itself read as a catalogue of debauchery and corruption (which was part of the reason Machiavelli despised the Church), but the former Florentine Secretary had lost all power, all influence, all say. He had become a pawn in the games of the powerful.

But Machiavelli was nothing if not persistent. At times this determination and pushiness embarrassed Vettori, but for a long time the ambassador was unable to come out and declare unequivocally that his friend was placing too much hope in his ability to help. It was not until June 1514, well over a year after he first began trying to gain the ear of the Medici through Vettori, that Machiavelli (who by now was himself embarrassed by the situation) finally asked Vettori directly whether or not he had any chance at all of finding favour with the Pope.

Vettori seized this opportunity to get himself off the hook, and told Machiavelli that the situation was completely hopeless and that, as far as he could see, the Medici would probably never want to employ him again. His frustration boiling to the surface, Machiavelli responded:

> So, I shall stay here among my lice, without there being anyone who remembers my services or believes that I can be useful in any way. But it is impossible for me to go on like this for long, because I am rotting away in idleness, and I see that if God does not help me, I shall some day be forced to leave home and take a job as a tutor or as secretary to a governor if I cannot find anything else, or settle in some deserted spot to teach reading to children, and leave my family here to carry on as though I were dead.[11]

It was a deflating and demoralising discovery, but Machiavelli could not give up entirely, nor did he blame his friend. But then, towards the end of 1514, there came a far more crushing blow to his morale. In mid-December Vettori approached him with a puzzle which he assured him was a matter of great concern to the Pope himself. If Machiavelli could offer a theoretical solution, Vettori claimed, he would pass this on to His Holiness, and this might possibly open the door to bigger and better things. 'I know that you are a man of such talent that, although it is two years since you gave up the business, I do not believe you have forgotten your skill,' Vettori wrote. He then went on to explain the problem.

The Pope was seeking advice concerning the delicate political scene in Europe. The French, with the support of the Venetians, had renewed their efforts to regain Milan from the Sforzas. Aligned against them were the Spanish, the Swiss and the Holy Roman Empire. The Pope, Vettori said, was seeking unity in Italy, and had begun to see himself as an emulsifier, a shepherd of the faithful. But he did not know which side to support. Should he throw his weight behind the old enemy and align himself with the French? Should he remain aligned with the other members of the Holy League he had created to oppose the French? Or should he remove himself and his states from the conflicts entirely and accept neutrality?

Machiavelli could not, of course, refuse this intellectual challenge and on 10 December he composed a long and detailed analysis of the situation which he concluded by advising the Pope to form an alliance with the French. According to Vettori, this study was passed on to the Pope, who responded by saying that 'all have marvelled at their cleverness and praised the judgement of their contents'.[12] Then, a few days later, Vettori wrote and admitted to Machiavelli that the request for this analysis had not originated with him but had in the first place come directly from Leo.

Machiavelli was more excited than he had been in years and immediately wrote a lengthier and more carefully constructed essay on the situation facing the Pope and the reasons for forming an alliance with the French. In the attached letter he reminded Vettori that in spite of their exchange a few weeks earlier, he was, as ever, hopeful that he might still find some form of employment with the Medici either in Florence or elsewhere.

Over Christmas and the New Year more letters were exchanged between Vettori in Rome and Machiavelli, who had returned to Sant'Andrea for a short stay. Then, in early January 1515, Vettori's brother Paolo arrived in Florence on business and visited Machiavelli to impart words of encouragement from Francesco.

Paolo Vettori was an accomplished politician and a close associate of the Medici. He was particularly close to Giuliano de' Medici, who was then about to be made ruler of four small Italian states, Parma, Piacenza, Modena and Reggio, the first two of which had been purchased by his brother Giovanni for their important strategic positions and the other two returned to papal control in return for favours. Paolo Vettori was being groomed as Giuliano's right-hand man and both admired and liked Machiavelli.

From his conversations with Paolo Vettori, Machiavelli quickly came to the conclusion that the Pope was testing him. After all, Leo knew the former Secretary was a close friend of the Vettori brothers and that he would be a most suitable adviser to the proposed government of the new papal states. At least this is what Machiavelli convinced himself to be true, and because of it, he was buoyed up by a sense of relief and expectation.

On 31 January he wrote to Vettori telling him how he had discussed the creation of the new government with his brother Paolo, and how Giuliano de' Medici had subsequently gone over the matter in great detail with his advisers in Florence. His confidence was soaring, and with some justification. He was now simply waiting for the invitation from Rome to re-enter public life.

But the invitation never came. Instead Machiavelli learned third-hand that the Pope's scheme had been altered and that Giuliano and Paolo Vettori would not now be taking over the designated lands. Any chance of a position as adviser to the new states had withered to nothing.

This latest catastrophe for Machiavelli had little to do with any failing on the part of his friends, for the Vettoris and even Giuliano de' Medici had acted in good faith. But in spite of his declared admiration for Machiavelli's analysis of the contemporary political scene only a few weeks earlier, the Pope never had the slightest intention of employing him. When the idea of using Soderini's former Secretary in any capacity had been mooted at the Vatican, the papal secretary, Piero Ardinghelli, wrote immediately to Giuliano de' Medici with a sharp rebuttal:

Cardinal de' Medici questioned me yesterday very closely if I knew whether Your Excellency had taken into his service Niccolò Machiavelli, and as I replied that I knew nothing of it nor believed it, His Lordship said these words: 'I do not believe it either, but as there has been word of it from Florence, I would remind him that it is not to his profit nor to ours. This must be an invention of Paolo Vettori . . . write to him on my behalf that I advise him not to have anything to do with Niccolò.'[13]

It is difficult to judge whether Machiavelli perceived his misfortunes in the light of his own political theories, but his plight was probably too painful a thing to consider dispassionately as an example or a demonstration. But, however he saw his own situation, he needed to deal with his pain. He had exorcised his bitterness by writing two masterpieces, *The Prince* and *The Discourses*, but he still sought solace in other ways. Exhausted perhaps with the world of the intellect and the fruitless struggle to seek out a new career, he dissociated himself from his responsibilities, cut himself off from the currents of a respectable, predictable existence and dived headlong into a world filled with flesh and lust.

Machiavelli had always enjoyed the company of prostitutes and courtesans. When he was in Florence he had frequented the city's brothels and had many famously debauched friends such as the licentious bisexual Donato del Corno and the prostitute La Riccia. But at the same time he was a romantic who fell in and out of love easily and frequently. A few months before his latest disastrous episode with the Medici in August 1514, he met a young girl who lived close to the his country estate, and from the way he described her to Vettori, it seems he fell passionately in love with her. In letters to his friends in which Machiavelli tells of this local beauty, there is none of the bravura and machismo that accompanied his usual descriptions of amorous affairs with courtesans and flirtatious young women he encountered on his travels. Now, at forty-five, he began to write of love as if he were a fresh-faced youth.

'Fortune truly has brought me to where I may be justly able to requite you, for while in the country I have met a creature so gracious, so refined, so noble – both in nature and in circumstance – that never could either my praise or my love for her be as much as she deserves,' he reported to Vettori:

> I ought to tell you . . . how this love began, how Love ensnared me with his nets, where he spread them and what they were like; you would realise that, spread among the flowers, these were nets of gold woven by Venus, so soft and gentle that even though an insensitive heart could have severed them, nevertheless I declined to do so. For a while I revelled within them, until their tender threads hardened and locked into untieable [sic] knots. And do not think that Love employed ordinary means to capture me, because aware that they would be inadequate, he resorted to extraordinary ones about which I was ignorant and against which I declined to protect myself. Suffice it to say that although I am approaching my fiftieth year [Machiavelli often exaggerated his age during this period in his life], neither does the heat of the sun distress me, nor do rough roads wear me out, nor do the dark hours of the night terrify me. Everything seems easy to me: I adapt to her every whim, even to those that seem different from and contrary to what my own ought to be.[14]

Machiavelli never referred to his lover by her real name but always called her La Tafani. Evidence suggests that she was the younger sister of one Niccolò Tafani, an associate of Machiavelli's from a village nearby, and that the girl's husband had deserted her and left the region to begin a new life in Rome. Yet, as beautiful as this young woman may have been, it is clear from the long, tortured letters to Vettori that Machiavelli found the affair far from easy.

According to his descriptions, La Tafani teased and played with him, persuading him to write her sonnets and to buy her gifts he could ill afford.

It is impossible to say for sure whether or not the long-suffering Marietta knew of the affair. It is likely she did, but either she could do nothing to stop it or she and Niccolò had long since come to an understanding about his sexual needs. It is equally uncertain how the affair ended. In all probability La Tafani's husband returned to take her away, or else she remarried. What is unambiguous, though, is just how much Machiavelli relied on this amorous adventure to help him deal with his great misfortunes. 'Even though I may now seem to have entered into a great travail,' he told Vettori, 'I nevertheless feel so great a sweetness in it, both because of the delight that rare and gentle countenance brings me and because I have laid aside all memory of my sorrows, that not for anything in the world would I desire freedom – even if I could have it.'[15]

Yet the pleasure and the relief La Tafani brought him were fleeting. After she had gone the emptiness returned more complete than ever, so that 1516 and 1517 were perhaps the worst years of Machiavelli's life. During this time there was not the slightest indication of an improvement in his fortunes, no sign of a job from any quarter and no fresh inspiration. Bemoaning his lot to his nephew Giovanni Vernacci in a letter of 15 February 1516, he declared: 'The best I can say is that all I have left is my own good health and that of all my family. I bide my time so that I may be ready to seize good Fortune should she come; should she not come, I am ready to be patient.'[16] In September he wrote again, telling his nephew: 'I have become useless to myself and to my family and my friends, because my grievous fate has so willed it.'[17] The following summer the situation was still unchanged. 'I am forced to stay in the country by the adversities I have suffered and suffer still,' he wrote to Vernacci in June 1517. 'I am sometimes a month together forgetful of my true self.'[18]

A major contribution to Machiavelli's depression was the huge disappointment he felt over the reception of *The Prince*. He had been unable to find a publisher for the book and had paid for copies to be made. (His friend and erstwhile assistant Biagio Buonaccorsi had made fair copies of the text. One given to their friend Francesco di Bernardo Quaratesi still survives in the French Royal collection.) He then thought long and hard about targeting the book by dedicating it to an appropriate potential patron. Soon after he had completed *The Prince*, Machiavelli had decided to dedicate it to Giuliano de' Medici, but when it became clear that Giuliano was moving away from political life and losing influence in the world, he had quickly reconsidered.

The new ruler of Florence was Lorenzo di Piero de' Medici, the young nephew of the Pope. By 1516 he had shown himself to be a masterful military leader and a strong force behind Florentine politics. It seemed obvious to Machiavelli that this young man would be someone who would appreciate his words and that on reading the book he could not fail to recognise the genius behind it.

After months of string-pulling and calling in old favours, Machiavelli finally, early in 1517, got his chance to present his work to Lorenzo. Francesco Vettori had returned to Florence and was now one of the most trusted servants of the Medici. Under pressure from Machiavelli he agreed to offer his friend's work in person to the Florentine leader. However, even he could only present the book to his master; he could not make him value it. Legend has it that at the same time Vettori handed the book to Lorenzo, the ruler was presented with a pair of racing dogs. Lorenzo merely glanced at the book without comment before lavishing his undivided attention on the dogs.

Lorenzo shared his uncle's feelings towards Machiavelli. He was a proud but poorly educated man who, even if he had bothered to read *The Prince*, would have understood almost none of the book. Furthermore, he viewed Machiavelli as little more than a jumped-up plebeian who was in no position to offer 'advice' to the grand rulers of the world. In holding these views, Lorenzo exemplified the sentiments of all the Medici of this generation, and such exclusivism was another barrier to the former ambassador's prospects. Machiavelli had been elevated beyond his station by the previous generation of the family, men who had a better sense of civic duty and egalitarianism. He was misguided in believing he would get a second chance with their descendants. A further problem for him was the fact that once the Medici had chosen their favourites it was almost impossible to break into this exclusive inner circle.

(Machiavelli was not the only one to suffer in this way: his friend Leonardo da Vinci experienced similarly cold treatment from many of the Medici family and was never honoured by them in the way Michelangelo was. Some historians have suggested that it was Leonardo's overt homosexuality that had stopped the Medici from favouring him, but this view ignores the fact that Michelangelo was also homosexual. A more likely reason is that Leonardo was not really a clubbable man, and, like Machiavelli, he was irreligious, unconventional and too wayward for the sometimes straight-laced Medici.)

More than any of the misfortunes he had suffered during recent years, Lorenzo's show of ignorance and utter indifference cast Machiavelli into a deeply despondent mood. There was now little to gainsay the fact that fate, luck, *Fortuna*, whatever he chose to call it, was not on his side. Like many men of the time, he believed in fate and trusted astrology, but what distinguished Machiavelli's view from that of the majority was his conviction that one must be prepared to take advantage of change when it comes. To him, all things, whether the small and the personal or the grand and overarching, followed a cyclical pattern. There were times of ill fortune and times during which good luck shone down. What differentiated the successful man from the failure did not depend only on the way they acted during the good times, but how, in the dark, they prepared themselves for the return of the light. 'The less a man has relied on fortune the stronger he has made his position,' he wrote in *The Prince*.[19]

For Machiavelli the darkness seemed to go on for ever, one misfortune following so quickly in the wake of the last that they appeared to form an endless stream. Love and sex had offered him a temporary reprieve, a short-lived escape, and he had lived on hope and faith. Ultimately, however, none of the things he had done or tried to do during the four years since his release from prison led him back into the light. Vettori never did achieve a breakthrough for him with the Medici and Machiavelli's political writing failed utterly to open up a path towards any form of rehabilitation.

A new lease of life did finally come to Machiavelli, but only when he struck out in a completely different direction and exploited his talents as a writer rather than his abilities as a political tactician or commentator. He found this path by turning away from the nobility, who distrusted him, and forging connections with the literary fraternity of Florence. But before we consider how this led him to a new and sometimes glamorous lifestyle, we should stop to consider what Machiavelli had written in *The Prince*, the work ignored by those of his own generation but today recognised as one of the most important achievements of the Italian Renaissance.

10

The Prince

Although I consider this a work unworthy to be put before you, I am fully confident that you will be kind enough to accept it, seeing that I could not give you a more valuable gift than the means of being able in a very short space of time to grasp all that I, over so many years and with so much affliction and peril, have learned and understood . . . Nor I hope will it be considered presumptuous for a man of low and humble status to dare discuss and lay down the law about how princes should rule; because, just as men who are sketching the landscape put themselves down in the plain to study the nature of the mountainside and the highlands, and to study the low-lying land they put themselves high on the mountains, so, to comprehend fully the nature of the people, one must be a prince, and to comprehend fully the nature of princes one must be an ordinary citizen.[1]

In this way Machiavelli dedicated his treatise to the one person he saw as both a potential patron and a man who could act on the ideas he had expressed in his account, Lorenzo de' Medici. If we ignore the expected genuflecting, it is clear that Machiavelli was being sincere in at least one respect: he believed that a prince is best understood from the perspective of what he called 'an ordinary citizen'.

Machiavelli was no ordinary citizen and what he was offering Lorenzo de' Medici and posterity was the culmination of two decades of thinking about what he referred to as 'principalities' and the vast experience he had gained as Secretary to the Second Chancery. He had been mulling over a formal representation of his ideas for some years before the fall of the Soderini government, but he had always been too busy to spare the time to put pen to paper. In exile, and with the memories still fresh, he found the autumn and winter of 1513 precisely the right time to coalesce and to formulate his ideas.

The Prince is divided into twenty-six very short chapters, beginning with 'How Many Kinds of Principality There Are and the Ways in Which They Are Acquired' and ending with an 'Exhortation to Liberate Italy from the Barbarians'. In just thirty thousand words Machiavelli succeeds in explaining how principalities differ, how they may be established and, most importantly, how a prince may keep hold of his kingdom.

It is accepted universally that Machiavelli used Cesare Borgia, Duke Valentino, as the model for his ideal prince, and throughout his treatise he makes references both oblique and obvious to the man who had inspired in him the concept of the 'perfect ruler'. Quite early in the book he writes: 'I know no better precepts to give to a new prince than those derived from Cesare's actions . . . and if what he instituted was of no avail, this was not his fault but arose from the extraordinary and inordinate malice of fate.'[2] And later he remarks: 'having summed up all that the duke did, I cannot possibly censure him. Rather I think I have been right in putting him forward as an example for all of those who have acquired power through good fortune and the arms of others.'[3]

Machiavelli had known the man at the peak of his powers and at his nadir, but *The Prince* was not simply about Cesare Borgia, for he wanted his image to inspire another, a man who, he hoped would not be so vulnerable to the capricious tides of *Fortuna*. The final chapter of *The Prince* is an exhortation to the Medici, and in particular the young Lorenzo, to take up the baton and lead the Italian states to union and glory:

> So now, left lifeless, Italy is waiting to see who can be the one to heal her wounds, put an end to the sacking of Lombardy, to extortion in the Kingdom and in Tuscany, and cleanse those sores which have now been festering so long. See how Italy beseeches God to send someone to save her from those barbarous cruelties and outrages; see how eager and willing the country is to follow a banner, if only someone will raise it. And at the present time it is impossible to see in what she can place more hope than in your illustrious House, which, with its fortune and prowess, favoured by God and by the Church, of which it is now the head, can lead Italy to her salvation.[4]

In certain respects *The Prince* is not an entirely original work, but an example of the 'advice book' that was quite popular during the sixteenth century. It is also a misconception to imagine that Machiavelli was the first to create the idea of 'perfect' or idealised states and leaders. The Chinese philosopher Mencius, writing in the fourth century BC, put forward a framework for a form of government in which a model prince (utterly different from Machiavelli's) worked with the people to produce a stable society. Plato's *Republic*, the most famous and probably the most enduring testament of the ideas of Mencius's Western contemporary, also describes an idealised political and social construct. But it is important to realise that, although Mencius was hugely influential in the evolution of Chinese society, his ideals have left almost no mark on the West. Equally, no government in history has modelled itself on the tenets of Plato's proposed republic, a state governed by a highly educated and aesthetically evolved elite who can maintain rule purely through intellectual merit. (However, it is interesting to note that the Catholic Church between the Dark Ages and the late Renaissance might be seen as incorporating some of the elements of Plato's imagined state. The *Republic* has also inspired fictitious societies, perhaps most notably that created by the Nobel Laureate Hermann Hesse in his 1943 novel *The Glass Bead Game*.)

Machiavelli's writings in *The Prince* and the *Discourses* have been categorised as belonging to a tradition known as 'civil humanism', a political philosophy in which Christianity may be perceived as nothing more than an optional extra (because it plays no genuine role in the decision making of a Machiavellian ruler). It is a social template within which the citizenry plays an integral role in the smooth functioning of the state.

However, Machiavelli's most famous work differs distinctly from any written before it in two very important ways. The first of these is the way in which he combined ancient examples with events contemporaneous with his own time. Throughout *The Prince* we encounter such figures as Hannibal and Agathocles (King of Syracuse during the fourth century BC) and in one ten-page section Machiavelli compares and contrasts a set of 'successful' and 'unsuccessful' Roman emperors. Elsewhere he draws in the ideas and actions of a huge cast of characters from Renaissance Europe, many of whom he met in person and with whom he discussed matters of state.

Indeed it is Machiavelli's intimate knowledge of the people and events he describes that endows *The Prince* with great authority; without it, the reader would be left with nothing but opinion. As Florentine Secretary, Machiavelli conversed and discussed matters with the great and the good of late-fifteenth and early-sixteenth-century Europe, and so he was able to imbue his work with enormous wisdom, experience and the deep understanding of a pre-eminent political analyst.

Describing a conversation with Cesare Borgia in 1503, Machiavelli is able to write: 'If, when Alexander died, he [Borgia] had been well himself, everything would have been easy for him. And he himself said to me, the day Julius was elected, that he had thought of everything that could happen when his father died, and found a remedy for everything except that he never thought that when he did so he himself would also be at the point of death.'[5]

In another passage Machiavelli recalled an exchange with Cardinal Georges d'Amboise, the second most powerful man in France: 'When the Cardinal of Rouen said to me that the Italians did not understand war, I retorted that the French did not understand statescraft, because if they understood it, then they would not let the Church become so great.'[6] And when Machiavelli calls Pope Julius II 'impetuous' and the Holy Roman Emperor Maximilian I 'secretive' and 'unable to take advice' we may take his word for it, for he was in the courts of these men and had spoken to them, observed them and described them in written accounts he sent to the Ten of War in Florence.

The other way in which *The Prince* is very different from anything written before it is Machiavelli's tone and style. It is a book often referred to as 'the first modern political treatise'. This description is quite justified because, unlike all those before him, Machiavelli wrote about what *is*, what is *real* and not about some fabulous wished-for ideal. He addresses this issue in the book itself:

It being my intention to write a thing which shall be useful to him who apprehends it, it appears to me more appropriate to follow up the real truth of a matter than the imagination of it; for many have pictured republics and principalities which in fact have never been known or seen, because how one lives is so far distant from how one ought to live, that he who neglects what is done for what ought to be done, sooner effects his ruin than his preservation; for a man who wishes to act entirely up to his professions of virtue soon meets with what destroys him among so much that is evil.[7]

Plato and other ancient political writers attempted to describe an idealised state, a desirable state, not one that was based on experience or any realistic expectation of men. It was a theme Machiavelli returned to over and over again in his later works. In *The Prince* he asserted that he wished to 'depart from the orders of others'.[8] In his more complete and detailed political treatise *The Discourses*, he pronounced his intention to 'enter upon a new way, as yet untrodden by anyone else'.[9] He visualised himself as a political Columbus and realised that in literature and politics there were pitfalls just as there were perils for those who explored the physical world: 'It has always been no less dangerous to discover new ways and methods than to set off in search of new seas and unknown lands,' he wrote.[10]

Unlike Plato and other antecedents, Machiavelli aimed to produce a book of generalisations, to create overarching rules, to offer instructions, formulae, all of which could be employed by real people in the real world. He had no interest in theoretical constructs that could never be more than a chimera to those living in the flesh-and-blood world of men.

In *The Prince* Machiavelli deals with six major concerns. First, a successful prince may excuse his methods if he is working for the common good of his people and his state (although Machiavelli accepted that in so doing the prince was also acting in his own best interest). Second, a prince must not allow Christianity to get in his way or to hamper his decisions. Third, princes, like all mortals, are subject to the vagaries of fortune, and in order to maintain their realm they must, during good times, prepare for the bad. Fourth, a successful prince must be both strong and cunning. To illustrate this need for duplicity Machiavelli used the examples of the fox and the lion. Fifth, a prince may only be successful by creating and maintaining strong armed forces. Finally, Machiavelli called on an

Italian dynasty to bring order to the peninsula and to unite the divided warring states of Italy.

The first four of these concerns have probably caused more controversy than the establishment of Machiavelli's other tenets because they go against the grain of what the reader of today (or of any era since *The Prince* was written) has been indoctrinated into believing, describing the way the 'virtuous' leader should behave.

In Chapter XVII of *The Prince*, 'Cruelty and Compassion: and Whether It Is Better to Be Loved than Feared, or the Reverse', Machiavelli declares:

> Cesare Borgia was considered cruel; notwithstanding, his cruelty reconciled the Romagna, unified it, and restored it to peace and loyalty. And if this be rightly considered, he will be seen to have been much more merciful than the Florentine people, who, to avoid a reputation for cruelty, permitted Pistoia to be destroyed. Therefore a prince, so long as he keeps his subjects united and loyal, ought not to mind the reproach of cruelty; because with a few examples he will be more merciful than those who, through too much mercy, allow disorders to arise, from which follow murders or robberies; for these are wont to injure the whole people, whilst those executions which originate with a prince offend the individual only.[11]

The point Machiavelli is making here is that often what most people would consider 'good' and 'virtuous' behaviour or decision making leads to greater pain for more people than actions that, in orthodox thinking, would be considered cruel, murderous or barbaric. But he does not simply state these ideas and leave them there: he illustrates his case with example after example from Roman, Greek and contemporary European history. In this way he not only gives weight to his argument, but also demonstrates one of the key strengths of *The Prince*, namely its timeless quality. And it is timeless because it describes what is, what has always been and probably what will always be, not what Christians and most other moralists believe to be the way the world should be. He returned to this idea in *The Discourses*: 'Prudent men are accustomed to say, and not by chance or without merit, that whoever wishes to see what has to be considers what has been; for all worldly things in every time have their own counterpart in ancient times. That arises because these are the work of men, who have and always had the same passions, and they must of necessity, result in the same effect.'[12]

One of the most widely expressed criticisms of Machiavelli is that he advocates evil, corruption and dishonesty. Such opinions derive from numerous passages in *The Prince* in which the author does appear to advocate the very opposite of Christian values and what men have always perceived as 'good', 'noble' and 'honourable' actions. But this misses the point of what Machiavelli was trying to express.

Machiavelli certainly had a very low opinion of his fellow human beings and the societies in which humans live. Over and over again in *The Prince* he deflates human dignity with verbal barbs and words of burnished steel. He wrote in Chapter XVII: 'One can make this generalisation about men: . . . they are ungrateful, fickle, liars and deceivers, they shun danger and are greedy for profit; while you treat them well, they are yours.'[13] Later he offers the idea that 'above all, a prince must abstain from the property of others: because men sooner forget the death of their father than the loss of their patrimony'.[14] A few pages further on he remarks that 'men will always do badly by you unless they are forced to be virtuous'.[15]

These comments have upset many readers, from the devout of the sixteenth century to modern critics, but such upset is born out of pure vanity. Machiavelli was describing the world he saw, the world we all see. Unlike many other social commentators, he simply had no qualms about putting such observations on to the page unsweetened.

It is, Machiavelli believed, precisely thanks to the ethical poverty of mankind that, for the common benefit of the people, a successful prince must be strong, unemotional and willing to go against what has always been considered right or good. But it is completely wrong to believe that he advocated mindless or unnecessary violence or the abuse of power. 'A prince should not deviate from what is good, if that is possible, but he should know how to do evil, if that is necessary,' he wrote.[16] Elsewhere he emphasises: 'It cannot be called prowess to kill fellow citizens, to betray friends, to be treacherous, pitiless, irreligious. These ways can win a prince power but not glory.' Then, writing of Agathocles, a man who demonstrated the callousness of Cesare Borgia but possessed few of what Machiavelli considered the man's positive attributes, he adds: 'Agathocles's brutal cruelty and inhumanity, his countless crimes, forbid his being honoured among eminent men. One cannot attribute to fortune or prowess what was accomplished by him without the help of either.'[17]

In connection with this, another accusation levelled against Machiavelli is that in some sense he advocated the sort of leadership exemplified in modern times by men such as Hitler, Pol Pot or Franco. This could not be further from the truth. Machiavelli was against the formation of a military establishment that ruled as a junta and he believed in the concept of the citizenry working *with* the ruler to make a better society for all. This need for strong, clinical leadership is the first major theme of *The Prince*, but naturally it is inextricably linked with the second thread in our list: Machiavelli's low regard for the contribution of Christian doctrine to the establishment and running of a successful principality.

It would be a mistake to believe that Machiavelli was actively, publicly anti-Christian. He had been raised in a household quietly split by religion. His mother had been a pious churchgoer, whereas his father was privately cynical about the Church and untrusting of the institutions that surrounded it. Machiavelli made no great show of turning away from the Church – that would have been damaging – but he had little good to say for it. He rarely attended church, but he went along with convention in having his children christened (as much to please Marietta as to dispel gossip), but privately he was not a believer, nor had he been since his childhood.

He understood that religion had its uses; religion, he knew, played a role in supporting social order and served to shame the wicked. But he also claimed that being a good Christian was not compatible with being a strong ruler. 'The fact is that a man who wants to act virtuously in every way necessarily comes to grief among so many who are not virtuous. Therefore, if a prince wants to maintain his rule he must learn how not to be virtuous, and to make use of this or not according to need.'[18] The philosopher and historian Isaiah Berlin summed up what Machiavelli meant by this when he wrote: 'A man must choose . . . one can save one's soul, or one can found or maintain or serve a great and glorious state; but not always both at once.'[19]

According to Machiavelli, the reason for this contradiction is that Christianity demands strength of a person, but strength only to suffer rather than to fight for one's beliefs. A Christian, he observed, is expected to be 'capable more of suffering than of doing something strong'.[20] He was also clear about the way Christians are conditioned to place greater importance on what he considered to be an imaginary afterlife rather than to concentrate on the here and now, the material world of ambition and earthly success. Furthermore, religion, he claimed, is a selfish creed which encourages individuals to think of their own salvation rather than placing their concern with the common good or with fulfilling their responsibilities as citizens.

For Machiavelli, a far better source of religious impulse was the pagan notion of *virtù*, which places paramount importance on the ability of the individual to tap into inner strengths. However, in expressing this view he discarded the traditional idea of *virtù*, which had been described by Cicero and later popularised by Christian philosophers who believed that in order to be 'virtuous' one should always act 'honestly' and 'honourably'. Machiavelli's *virtù* is very different. It represents the unquenchable determination and ambition of the true prince. It is an essential ingredient in the personality of any successful ruler. Possession of this quality does not ensure success, but without it a prince is doomed to failure.

This definition of *virtù* was the very opposite of its popular meaning and in placing so much emphasis on it and shunning the central tenets of Christian doctrine as being useless to a true leader, Machiavelli caused outrage. His opponents could not tolerate the idea that in Machiavelli's estimate Christian ideology was no better than any other redundant faith system, that some fifteen hundred years after they had been supplanted by Christianity, pagan ideas could explain so well the actions of men. This rejection of orthodox ethics in *The Prince* lies at the core of the arguments offered by almost all anti-Machiavellian thinkers and writers since the book appeared.

More than many men, Machiavelli was intimate with the idea of fate, or what he called *Fortuna*. When he began to write *The Prince* he was living through the worst period of his life up to that time. He was facing financial ruin and felt lost and discarded. Writing his treatise, he was doing all he could to control his own destiny, employing his range of talents and his years of experience in an effort to reverse his bad fortune. 'Time sweeps everything along and can bring good as well as evil, evil as well as good,' he wrote one evening as he sat alone contemplating the rude walls of his study, his belly filled with cheap wine from the local tavern.[21]

Machiavelli had watched closely as Cesare Borgia had risen to a pinnacle of success and then collapsed so terribly quickly. He had witnessed the rise and fall of nations and the shifting sands of European political life. He had seen men die in battle and waste away with disease, he had lost a new born baby, a sister, a mother, a father, friends and loved ones. Machiavelli perceived humans as flotsam and jetsam, our lives in the hands of fate, our fortunes unpredictable and, to a degree out of our control.

But the words 'to a degree' are of the essence here. Machiavelli knew that even kings and princes, no matter how powerful or brilliant, how ruthless and calculating, were neither immortal nor omnipotent. Kings and princes are as vulnerable as the rest of us. But a truly 'perfect' prince is aware of this and takes account of it. A true leader of men understands that the only way to combat the wiles of fate is to prepare oneself for ill fortune when it is possible to do so: during the good times.

Machiavelli was so taken with this concept that he devoted an entire chapter of *The Prince* (Chapter XXV) to discussing 'How Far Human Affairs Are Governed by Fortune, and How Fortune Can Be Opposed'. Here he concluded that fortune was not determined solely by divine intervention, but that success or failure relied on an interaction between 'luck' and 'individual action': 'I think it is probably true that fortune is the arbiter of half the things we do . . . leaving the other half or so to be controlled by ourselves.'[22]

And so, again, no need for God:

> I compare fortune to one of those raging rivers, which when in flood overflows the plains, sweeping away trees and buildings, bearing away the soil from place to place. Everything flies before it, all yield to its violence, without being able in any way to withstand it; and yet, though its nature be such, it does not follow therefore that men, when the weather becomes fair, shall not make provision, both with defences and barriers, in such a manner that, rising again, the waters may pass away by canal, and their force be neither so unrestrained nor so dangerous. So it happens with fortune . . .[23]

Man, then, is the arbiter of his own destiny. There is no need to conjure up a divine overseer, for man need only be aware of his place in the universe and to be cautious enough to prepare ahead of time. It is ironic that Machiavelli did not apply his own advice when times were good, but then he never declared himself to be a prince; he was simply a thinker, a writer who understood how men should act to become and remain princes. Lacking the benefit of exceptional resources or a privileged birthright, he was little able to control his own fate.

Machiavelli would have also failed as a prince because he did not possess the ruthlessness or many of the other attributes he deemed necessary for any leader of men. In *The Prince* he first establishes what is required of a man who would be king and then disposes of traditional morality and ethics as being incompatible with genuine lasting temporal power. But what are the special talents a Cesare Borgia must possess? Aside from being unshackled and free from morality, what turns a suitable man into a 'superman'?

To answer this question Machiavelli used the analogy of the fox and the lion. This was in itself a subversive decision given the received wisdom about the characteristics of these two animals, but Machiavelli had chosen carefully and well. The fox, he reminds us, is considered a master of deception and cunning, but it cannot fight very well. A lion may be physically strong, but it has little cunning or ability to deceive. It is only by combining the best elements of each animal that a ruler may remain in power and control his realm. 'So, as a prince is forced to know how to act like a beast, he must learn from the fox and the lion,' Machiavelli states. 'Those who simply act like lions are stupid.'[24]

The reasons for this are clear. Some situations require muscle and some require clever manipulation; those leaders only capable of reacting in one way are limited and impaired and therefore unworthy to lead. 'If all men were good . . .,' Machiavelli reiterates, 'this precept would not be good; but because men are wretched creatures who would not keep their word to you, you need not keep your word to them . . . But one must know how to colour one's actions and to be a great liar and deceiver. Men are so simple, and so much creatures of circumstance, that the deceiver will always find someone ready to be deceived.'[25]

This sums up the stance a prince should take, but there is still one missing element. The prince, whether we see him as a king, a military leader or a twenty-first-century captain of industry, must be armed in some way, and weapons may come in many forms: swords, nuclear warheads, money, shares or damaging information about a rival. (Here is another reason why Machiavelli found little success for some time after he lost his job under Soderini. He had no 'arms', he was not rich, he had a skill that was not required by the new regime and he was not of noble birth; all he had was his talent, and in the circumstances in which he found himself this was of little real use in accruing wealth, power or influence.)

Machiavelli had always placed great importance on the need for military power. A prince, he believed, could be clever, imaginative, ruthless and cunning, but without military clout he could do almost nothing. Three entire chapters of *The Prince* are devoted to military matters, and Machiavelli goes into some detail to explain the dangers of using mercenaries, the need for a citizen's army and the importance of adequate funding, training and deployment of troops. He saw military prowess as the very cornerstone of a strong government and the key to continued security within any society. 'The main foundations of every state . . . new states, as well as ancient or composite ones, are good laws and good arms; and because you cannot have good laws without good arms, and where there are good arms, good laws inevitably follow, I shall not discuss laws but give my attention to arms.'[26]

If many of the characteristics of a prince had been distilled from Machiavelli's experiences with men such as Cesare Borgia, Pope Julius II and the Medici, his insistence on the need for strong armed forces came directly from his often bitter experiences with his own government in Florence. Believing that many of the woes that had befallen his country in the years that led up to his writing of *The Prince* had stemmed from his government's lack of understanding on this matter, Machiavelli called on his imagined all-powerful prince never to make the same mistakes. 'Mercenaries and Auxiliaries are useless . . . I shall have little need to labour this point, because the present ruin of Italy has been caused by nothing else but the reliance placed on mercenary troops for so many years . . . mercenary armies bring slow, belated and feeble conquests, but sudden, startling defeat . . . and as a result they have led Italy to slavery and ignominy.'[27]

And so, with these tenets, Machiavelli set out to offer a template for the men most likely to pick up where Cesare Borgia had left off, and to complete the job he had started. Having described what it takes to be a great leader and how to maintain the realm once it is conquered, Machiavelli, in the final chapter of *The Prince*, calls on Lorenzo to take up the great challenge:

> This opportunity, therefore, ought not to be allowed to pass for letting Italy at last see her liberator appear. Nor can one express the love with which he would be received in all those provinces which have suffered so much from these foreign scourings, with what thirst for revenge, with what stubborn faith, with what devotion, with what tears. What door would be closed to him? Who would refuse obedience to him? What envy would hinder him? What Italian would refuse him homage? To all of us this barbarous dominion stinks. Let, therefore, your illustrious house take up this charge with that courage and hope with which all just enterprises are undertaken, so that under its standard our native country may be ennobled, and under its auspices may be verified the saying of Petrarch:
> *Virtù contro al Furore*
> *Prendera l'arme, e fia il combatter corto:*

Che l'antico valore

Negli italici cuor non e ancor morto.

['Virtue against fury shall advance the fight, and through it
combat soon shall put to flight; for the old Roman valour is not
dead, nor in the breasts of Italians extinguished.']

For Machiavelli, the political system and society that in all
human history had came closest to perfection was the Roman
Republic before it had degenerated into empire at the hands of
Julius Caesar (a leader he criticised relentlessly in both *The Prince*
and *The Discourses*). The Italy of Machiavelli's time, could, he
believed, have been regenerated in the form of a new republic modelled on the lines of Rome at its peak, and it was this very conviction
that drove him to write *The Prince*.

It is certainly true that Machiavelli was seeking employment
and favour with the Medici, for he needed to support himself and
his family. His treatise, he convinced himself, could not fail to
impress. But behind this practical need lay a grander design, a
greater drive, one that drew strength and inspiration from
Machiavelli's deep-rooted and enduring patriotism. Under
Soderini he had been a loyal and effective servant of Florence and
he could have again served Florence well if he had been given a
responsible job by the Medici. But, more than this, deeper than
this, he was a patriot of Italy. A few days before his death he told a
friend: 'I love my native country [*mia patria*] more than my own
soul.'[28] In Machiavelli's mind the image of Italy as a single state
burned bright and imbued his thinking as he wrote *The Prince*.

On the simplest level *The Prince* was written to explain contemporary political life, a guidebook for Lorenzo or any other suitable
leader of the time. It illustrated how a powerful family such as the
Medici could have created a unified Italy. But it transcends this
ambition. It remains one of the most potent of political studies
because it addresses timeless, human issues. In writing this book

Machiavelli demonstrated pure honesty, pure logic, and it is a work of razor-sharp, unsentimental intelligence, for as Machiavelli stresses again and again, sentimentality and power cannot coexist.

In this we find perhaps the greatest irony of *The Prince*. Through the centuries critics have lambasted Machiavelli for his belief that a ruler need not be honest, need not be moral, yet Machiavelli's writing demonstrates remarkable honesty and purity. This is a point that has often been overlooked in the scramble to criticise what he had to say. For, whatever one may think of the political vision expressed in *The Prince*, it is impossible to deny its power or its clarity. Amid the barbs and the brutal stripping away of niceties, alongside the constant and absolute denial of wishful thinking, Machiavelli offered an analysis of reality as he saw it; a steely, acerbic analysis certainly, but a human vision untarnished by whimsy, faith or charity.

11

Rehabilitation

By 1517 Machiavelli was making the best of a bad lot and he was ready to find a new direction. Empowered by his achievement with *The Prince*, he began to turn his energies towards literature.

Among his earliest works is a collection of poems and sonnets which includes *L'Asino* (*The Ass*), a piece he started in 1517 but never completed. It was modelled on *The Golden Ass* (also known as *Metamorphoses*), by the second-century Roman rhetorician and poet Apuleius. Machiavelli went on to write a novella, *Belfagor arcidiavolo*, known in English as *The Devil Who Took a Wife*. He probably wrote this in 1517, but it was not published until some thirty years later, ten years after his death.

Writing *The Ass* was a form of therapy for Machiavelli. Although he had every reason to feel sorry for himself, he knew that the reader would find it unappealing to be presented with the author's woes. What he did instead was to mock himself. Portraying himself as the ass, the central character, he wrote: 'And our ass, who has trodden so many of the stairs of this world to observe the mind of every mortal man . . . heaven itself could not prevent him from braying.' In other words, I am Machiavelli, I've been there, and I've learned the ways of the world. No one can stop me describing the world. You (the Florentine nobility and most especially the Medici) may ignore me but you will have my thoughts anyway. And again, referring to the ass euphemistically, he exclaimed: 'Among all people ancient and modern . . . no man has suffered greater ingratitude nor greater labours.'[1]

Part of the inspiration for these first attempts at fiction came from Machiavelli's pain and a need to express himself, but he was also hugely encouraged by a new set of friends with whom he spent a lot of time when he was in Florence. This group of like-minded individuals gathered at the Rucellai Gardens, on the outskirts of the city. Sometimes called 'the beautiful garden' by Florentines, the gardens had been created by Bernardo Rucellai towards the end of the 1490s. Bernardo came from a family of humanists and he established the site as a place in which philosophers and writers could gather in debate. Antique statues stood along the many gravel paths and exotic trees had been imported and planted throughout the gardens. Machiavelli described the spot where his friends met as the 'shadiest and most secret part of his garden'. Here the gathered intellectuals sat on benches or on the grass, 'in that place as green as green'.[2]

Bernardo Rucellai died in 1514 and by the time Machiavelli joined the group at the gardens it was led by Cosimo Rucellai, Bernardo's nephew, who from about 1516 became one of his closest friends. Among the others who joined them were the philosopher Francesco da Diacceto and the historian Filippo de' Nerli, whom Machiavelli had known for some years. Another historian, Jacopo Nardi, was a key member, as were the writers Antonio Brucioli and Anton Francesco degli Albizzi, the poet Luigi Alamanni di Piero and the political thinker Zanobi Buondelmonti. Of these the three closest to Machiavelli were Alamanni di Piero, Buondelmonti and Cosimo Rucellai.

The group consisted almost entirely of wealthy young men from noble families. They held humanist, liberal views, they were not fond of the style of leadership adopted by the new ruler, the Duke of Urbino (Lorenzo de' Medici) and they were all exceptionally bright and ambitious. Influential and rich, they were young men who would one day play major roles in running Florence. By contrast, Machiavelli was penniless and unemployed but he could draw on enormous experience. He was immensely knowledgeable, a gifted poet and political analyst, a superb conversationalist, gregarious and possessed of a fine sense of humour. It was quite natural that before long he began to perceive himself as playing the role of a teacher for the younger men of the Rucellai Gardens, and they in turn were impressed and influenced by his political ideas.

Slowly Machiavelli began to see that by becoming involved with the gatherings he was finding a quietly subversive way of influencing political life again. He was never a man for revolution or rebellion and considered those who had tried and failed to usurp by force and amateurish intrigue extremely foolish, but he loved the idea of being an intellectual whose ideas could be channelled into developing the political education of young men who possessed latent power. Such a vision, coupled with the insistence of his new young friends, pushed him to complete *The Discourses* and later led him to write *The Art of War*, the third volume in what, with *The Prince* and *The Discourses*, is effectively a trilogy.

Machiavelli had almost certainly started *The Discourses* before breaking off to write *The Prince* and he had returned to it early in 1514. Spurred on by discussions in the Rucellai Gardens, he agreed to deliver a set of lectures to his friends in which he refined the ideas expressed in the earlier drafts of the book, and later, around 1518, he produced a final version of *The Discourses*, although this was not published until after his death.

The Discourses may be considered the work of Machiavelli's most closely linked to *The Prince*. But whereas *The Prince* deals with the behaviour of leaders and is a guidebook for the aspiring ruler, in *The Discourses* Machiavelli concerns himself with the ordinary people and their role in the running and maintenance of a successful society. It is a longer, more detailed book and a controversial work entirely different from any political treatise that preceded it (apart from *The Prince*). *The Discourses* deals with many of the themes that had preoccupied him throughout his career: the methodology of good government, the need for a strong military force, the role of religion and the relationship between the various elements of government. Machiavelli again uses the technique of drawing on examples taken from the Classical tradition and combining them with contemporary political experience. Because *The Discourses* is based on his analysis of *The First Ten Books of Titus Livy*, throughout the work he refers to the Roman paradigm and reaches the inevitable conclusion that the very best form of government for any state is that of a republic. (Livy lived during the first century BC and is considered the most important historian of the Roman era.)

By the time Machiavelli reworked *The Discourses* he had embraced his new role as educator. 'It is the duty of a good man to teach others the good . . .,' he wrote, 'which, because of the malignity of the times and of fortune, you could not achieve, so that when many are capable of it, one of them more loved by heaven may be able to achieve it.'³ In other words he considered it to be his duty to impart his learning and experience because if many understood what he was trying to convey, one at least may have the good fortune and be properly prepared to act on what he had learned.

At the same time Machiavelli had quickly realised what a great debt he owed his friends from the Rucellai Gardens. It had been largely thanks to their enthusiasm and support that he had regained his self-confidence and self-respect. At the same time he had also begun to realise that men like Lorenzo de' Medici, who were ignorant and complacent, were not worthy of his words or his advice. Perhaps he had Lorenzo in mind when he wrote in *The Discourses*: 'Infamous and detestable are those men who are enemies of the virtues, of letters, and of every other art that brings utility and honour to the human race, as are the impious, the violent, the ignorant, the worthless, the idle, the cowardly.'[4]

So, instead of offering his book to a potential patron as tradition and commercial instincts dictated, he chose to dedicate *The Discourses* to two men he considered far more worthy, Cosimo Rucellai and Zanobi Buondelmonti, men whom he cared about rather than someone he should honour in order to gain something in return.

'To Zanobi Buondelmonti and to Cosimo Rucellai. Greetings,' the dedication begins:

I send you a present which if it is not equal to the obligations that I have toward you, it is without doubt the best that Niccolò Machiavelli has been able to offer you. Because in it I have expressed what I know and what I have learned through a long experience and a continuing study of the things of the world. And neither you nor others being able to desire more of me, I have not offered you more. You may well complain of the poverty of my endeavour since these narrations of mine are poor, and of the fallacy of my judgement when I deceive myself in many parts of my discussion. Which being so, I do not know which of us should be less obligated to the other, either I to you who have forced me to write that which by myself I would not have written, or you to me that having written I have not satisfied you. Accept this, therefore, in that manner that all things are taken from friends, where always the intention of the sender is more than the quality of the thing that is sent. And believe me I obtain satisfaction from this when I think that even if I should have been deceived on many occasions, I know I have not erred on this one in having selected you, to whom above all other of my friends I dedicate these Discourses; as much because in doing this it appears to me I have shown some gratitude for the benefits

I have received, as well because it appears to me I have departed from the common usage of those writers, who usually dedicate their works to some Prince, and blinded by ambition and avarice laud him for all his virtuous qualities when they should be censuring him for all his shameful parts. Whence I, so as not to incur this error, have selected, not those who are Princes, but those who by their infinite good qualities would merit to be such; and not to those who could load me with rank, honours, and riches, but to those who although unable to would want to do so. For men, when they want to judge rightly, should esteem those who are generous, not those who are able to be so; and likewise those who govern a Kingdom, not those who can but have not the knowledge . . . Enjoy this, therefore, whether good or bad, that you yourselves have wanted; and if you should continue in this error that these thoughts of mine are acceptable, I shall not fail to continue the rest of the history according as I promised you in the beginning. Farewell.

Most telling in this dedication is Machiavelli's insistence on highlighting the difference between those whom fortune has unjustly benefited, men who 'can govern but have not the knowledge', and those worthy men, such as his friends, who really do 'know how to govern a kingdom' but do not. The identity of those to whom Machiavelli was referring would have been obvious to any educated reader of the time, and it was a daring thing to write. He was effectively saying to the Medici and all the others who had shunned him: 'Well, if you choose to ignore me, if you prefer a hunting dog to the offerings of my experience and intelligence, you probably will not read this either, so go to hell.'

The third book in Machiavelli's trilogy of political and military analysis, *The Art of War* (*Dell'arte della guerra*), was the only book of his to be published during his lifetime. Probably begun in 1518, it was inspired by his friends from the Rucellai Gardens and developed in lectures he delivered as well as through long hours of discussion. It was published in 1521 and quickly became accepted as a masterful treatise on all aspects of war and its political ramifications.

Some have criticised Machiavelli's treatise for the fact that he makes no mention of firearms, which had been introduced in Europe shortly before the book was written. However, this misses the essential point of what he was trying to do with this work. *The Art of War* follows the same paradigm as *The Prince* and *The Discourses* in that it was conceived as a book of instruction, a description of generalised ideas to be applied to a wide range of scenarios. Based on a fictional dialogue between some of Machiavelli's friends from the Rucellai Gardens and the captain of the papal armies, Fabrizio Colonna, it expounds on what Machiavelli conceived as the best way to form and maintain a strong military force. It is a book that may be understood and utilised by military men from any nation and from any age. The historian Pasquale Villari wrote of *The Art of War*: 'It is a portent not only of its own age, but also considered absolutely.'[5]

But Machiavelli was not content to simply teach, nor was he interested in only writing about politics and military matters. There was another side to his creativity, the purely poetic aspect of his character, the part that led him to fall in love so easily, the part that made him decide to send a sonnet from his prison cell to the Medici ruler. It was a powerful force, the older part of the man, the original creative spirit that had infused all his writing, on whatever subject. It was this impulse that led him to compose a comic play called *Mandragola* (*The Mandrake*):

The writing of *Mandragola* was another therapeutic exercise. Machiavelli was laughing to stop the tears and he wanted to make others laugh at his vision of the world and its absurdities. But it was also a weapon, a dagger with which he could subtly attack those who had kept him down. Declaring that he would 'reward with a flask of wine anyone who did not laugh at his play', he went on: 'And if this subject for being lighter, is not worthy of a man who wishes to appear wise and grave, pray excuse him because he is trying with these vain thoughts to relieve his misfortune, as he has nowhere else to turn; for he has been prevented from showing other virtue with different works, his labours having received no reward.'[6]

Like everything else Machiavelli wrote, *Mandragola* is, for the era in which it was composed, a thoroughly modern creation, and like his 'serious' works, as he called them, it had little connection with the literary tradition of his time. In his style and delivery Machiavelli was a radical through and through. He composed in Tuscan and felt strongly that the vernacular, not Latin, should be the language of Italian literature. In this he shared with his friend Leonardo da Vinci a deep aversion towards the traditional dependence on Latin. He was also keen to express his philosophies using the vehicle of a lightweight comedy, a novel, a popular play or a sonnet, and so in *Mandragola* he succeeded in attacking the Church, the wealthy but poorly educated snobs of Florence, the sanctity of marriage and the social imperatives of chastity and honour.

The plot is simple and subversive. On returning to his native city, a young Florentine, Callimaco Guadagno, a libertine who has been studying abroad for some years, learns of an exceptionally beautiful young woman, Lucrezia, who is married to a much older, wealthy, but supposedly impotent gentleman, Messer Nicia. Callimaco sees the woman and instantly falls in love with her so that now his one desire is to sleep with her as soon as possible. However, Lucrezia is virtuous and faithful. So, with the help of his cunning friend Ligurio, Callimaco hatches a plan to ensnare the woman he desires. They quickly discover that the old man is desperate to have a child and they use this to get Callimaco into Lucrezia's bedchamber.

Ligurio has the trust of Nicia and tells him that in order to get Lucrezia pregnant they must trick a young man into drinking some mandrake root and then to make love to Lucrezia. His wife will conceive but the mandrake will kill the young man the same night. Nicia agrees, but his wife still needs persuading. Callimaco and Ligurio then bribe a priest, Friar Timoteo, to talk the young woman into the plan.

Callimaco is, of course, not poisoned and has his way with Lucrezia. Machiavelli concludes the tale not with any moral retribution or payback for what the conventional audience would see as Callimaco's immorality. Instead Nicia agrees to let the young man live with him and Lucrezia in a *ménage à trois*. Machiavelli ends the play with another sharp dig at the Church. In a final scene we see the helpful Friar Timoteo taking another payment from a family who want approval for an abortion.

The play was certainly read before the gathered friends of Machiavelli's humanist literary group during the spring or summer of 1518 and it was first performed for the public in Florence that summer. It became an instant hit and the following year it was performed before Leo X in Rome. Amazingly, the Pope thoroughly enjoyed it and it did much to help heighten Machiavelli's profile among the Medici. Leo, who had rather simple, childish tastes and little interest in high art or matters of intellect, evidently enjoyed the risqué, almost smutty dimension to the story while ignoring (or not noticing) the obvious anti-clerical and anti-Medici subtext.

For Machiavelli such a response came as an unexpected but very welcome surprise, and it marked the first tiny reversal in the attitude of the Medici towards him. By this time he had been out in the cold for some six years. It had been the most productive period of his life, a period during which he had been forced to mine his creativity and free the expression of his soul, unencumbered by the responsibilities of his job as Secretary to the Second Chancery. Between 1513 and 1517 he produced all the works for which he is most famous and laid the foundations for a system of political thought and a military philosophy that have already lasted half a millennium. It was a time of great suffering and despair for Machiavelli, but this darkness acted as a catalyst for the making of his name.

By 1519 things were beginning to look up a little. New vistas were unfolding and new opportunities offering themselves. And, even if Machiavelli had not been so good at following his own rules, nor a man with the resources of a prince, he was at least wise enough to have realised the importance of preparation. When Soderini had fallen from power, Machiavelli had been swept up by ill fortune and had been unprepared. Now, as bad fortune was superseded by good, he was ready to grasp opportunities and make the most of what came his way.

In 1519 two deaths affected Machiavelli greatly. Most traumatic for him was the loss of the man who had become perhaps his closest friend, the founder of the group who met at the Rucellai Gardens, Cosimo Rucellai. Machiavelli owed much to him; he had been revitalised by his interest, advised by him and he appreciated his criticisms. Rucellai had helped him more than anyone else during the desperate years after Machiavelli's fall from power, encouraging him to write and teach. The group continued to meet at the same venue, for this collection of intellectuals were never short of rich patrons and energetic organisers, but from 1519 the spirit of the gatherings changed.

The other death, that of Lorenzo di Piero de' Medici on 4 May 1519, a few months short of his twenty-seventh birthday, had no emotional impact whatsoever for Machiavelli. However, it did play a significant role in altering his life for the better. Lorenzo had been a great disappointment to Machiavelli, not simply because he had done nothing to further his career and had snubbed him over *The Prince*, but because he had been a failure to himself and a disappointment to the city he had governed for almost six years. Lorenzo had abused his position, grown steadily more self-obsessed and corrupt and had succeeded in turning most Florentines against him.

For Machiavelli, Lorenzo's premature death loosened some of the binds that held him and it allowed him fresh hope. It also threatened Medici control in Florence, prompting Pope Leo X to hastily dispatch his cousin, Cardinal Giulio de' Medici, who quickly stamped his authority on the government. Giulio was everything Lorenzo had failed to be: wise, measured, intellectual, a patron of the Arts and a man whose own political vision had more in keeping with those of Machiavelli and his friends than many of his own family. Of all the Medici (except perhaps Giuliano, who had died in 1516) he was the best disposed towards the former Secretary.

Timing is everything, and Machiavelli realised this fact more than most men. Back in the dark, hopeless days immediately after he had been imprisoned he must have known that he was entrenched in a period of re-evaluation and slow, painful change. And that change had been dramatic. He may have once perceived himself as a politician, but by 1519 he was a member of the Florentine literati, a playwright, a political analyst and a poet. He had been out of politics for seven years, and although he may still have found it difficult to accept the fact, literature could offer him a better chance of re-entering public life than any political status he may once have had.

The chance of rehabilitation came in March 1520, when one of his closest friends, Lorenzo Strozzi, a member of one of the most wealthy and powerful families in Italy, arranged a brief meeting between Machiavelli and the new ruler of Florence, Giulio de' Medici. According to witnesses, this first meeting went very well. However, recent bitter experience had made Machiavelli and his friends acutely aware of the frailty of such encounters. All of them were wary of relying on a single meeting and were suspicious of the mood of the man who really held the reins of power, Pope Leo X.

They did not want a repeat of the unfortunate events of early 1514, so another of Machiavelli's close friends, Battista della Palla, then in Rome and very much in favour with the Pope, did his best to brighten Machiavelli's image at the papal court. Della Palla described to Leo the gatherings in the Rucellai Gardens and spiced up his account by painting pictures of cultured men discussing lofty matters among the marble and the flowers, almost as if it were some Classical tableau. He then went on to tell the Pope how Machiavelli was a leading light of the group and how he had enthralled them with his learning. He then reminded him of Machiavelli's hilarious play *Mandragola*, which Leo and his court had enjoyed so much.

This time it worked. In a letter to his brother Lorenzo, Filippo Strozzi, then in Rome, wrote: 'I am very glad you took Machiavelli to see the Medici, for if he can get the master's confidence, he is a man who must rise.'[7] A few weeks later, during the early summer of 1520, Machiavelli was offered a few small commissions in which he was asked to resolve minor disputes and wrangles. Some of these came from business contacts, but he was also contracted by Cardinal Giulio de' Medici to visit the city of Lucca to resolve a few rather trivial matters for Florence. One concerned an argument over the working of the mint. The other required him to settle a dispute over some Pisan students who had defied the authorities and escaped the city. These were rather demeaning jobs for the man who had once been the most important emissary of the Florentine Republic, but Machiavelli saw them for what they were, tests, minor offerings to smooth the way for what he hoped would be something more worthwhile.

It is hard to judge exactly what Machiavelli was hoping for at this stage of his life. He had loved his old job and for some seven years now he had missed the thrill of travel and responsibility. He thrived on finding the resolution to a conflict, he was forthright and extrovert, a man who loved an audience. He relished power and was aroused by working with powerful people even if he had no special influence himself. But the world had moved on, and so had he. The Medici had their own loyal emissaries, their own civil servants who had gained considerable experience in their positions. Furthermore, Machiavelli had never been trusted by the Medici, and could no longer hope for a position in which he had any influence or to play a significant role in the political life of the city. In 1520, when he renewed contact with the rulers of Florence, he was fifty-one; and even during the sixteenth century seven years was an eternity in the world of politics.

He was poor, but he had survived as an outcast for the best part of a decade. He had grown to accept loss and had moved on intellectually and emotionally. Perhaps now he considered himself a writer more than a political spokesman or emissary. The young men of the Rucellai Gardens had given him an audience and now that audience had been multiplied a hundredfold with his successful play. His treatise *The Art of War* was at the printers, ready for publication, and even if the political theories he expressed in *The Prince* and *The Discourses* were widely misunderstood, they were at least being discussed and disseminated among the intellectual community. Taking all these factors into consideration, it was clear the way forward for him was to embrace the challenge of being a writer, an historian and a political theorist. The Medici and their advisers obviously thought this too, because in July 1520 Machiavelli was invited to meet Cardinal Giulio de' Medici again, this time to discuss the possibility of a commission to write a history of Florence.

The proposal was perfect for Machiavelli and he was immediately inspired by the idea. It came with only a relatively small financial reward, but for any intellectual it would have been a great honour. The contract was for two years, the second approved only after a review of the work-in-progress. Officially the commission came from the Studio Fiorentino and a body called the Officials of the University negotiated the agreement, but the Medici funded it and had the final say over the author chosen for the task. Machiavelli was asked to outline the basic form of the contract himself and to Francesco del Nero, an associate and lawyer dealing with the commission, he wrote: 'He [the author] is to be hired for . . . years at a salary of . . . per year with the condition that he must be, and is to be, held to write the annals or else the history of the things done by the state and city of Florence, from whatever time may seem to him most appropriate, and in whatever language – either Latin or Tuscan – may seem best to him.'[8]

Machiavelli was to be paid an annual salary of one hundred *fiorini di studio* (studio florins). The studio florin was 'devalued currency' worth only four lire, whereas the gold florin was worth seven. This meant that Machiavelli's salary was approximately fifty-seven florins, less than a third of his annual salary during his first year as Florentine Secretary more than two decades earlier. He may have been justified in thinking himself worth far more than this, but the chance of writing a history of Florence was a golden opportunity and one he did not consider turning down for a single moment. His history would be the latest in a line of accounts which in the past had been written by esteemed and powerful men, including at least three former First Chancellors of the Signoria.

Machiavelli began right away. For most of a year he worked at the farmhouse in Sant'Andrea, just as he had done when writing *The Prince*. And just as he had done in 1513 and 1514, he travelled into Florence for human contact and to dust off the cobwebs of scholarship. But this time things were very different. He was still poor, he was still not regarded as highly as he deserved to be by the most powerful people in Europe, but he had work to do, work that had been asked of him, work that was also deeply satisfying. When he returned to Florence for a day or two, or for a week, he almost certainly maintained his habit of visiting whorehouses and gambling dens and drinking dives, for he loved these things. But the man who was writing a history of Florence was in many respects a different man from the one who had drowned his sorrows as he finished *The Prince*. Machiavelli was at least tolerated by the Medici and he had powerful and devoted friends. In 1520 he also had hope and a purpose in life, and with these came renewed self-confidence and self-belief.

A perfect indication of just how much Machiavelli's life changed during 1520 may be seen by his reaction to an astonishing piece of news, a letter, and an invitation. In April 1521 the former gonfalonier, Piero Soderini, wrote to him offering him the position of Secretary to his tiny province on the Adriatic coast, the Republic of Ragusa (close to the modern port of Dubrovnik). The post came with a handsome salary, a comfortable residence and the sort of responsibility for which the former diplomat had long yearned.

Flattered, Machiavelli nevertheless turned down the offer. But Soderini was not so easily put off and we must wonder if he had ulterior motives in trying to get Machiavelli away from Florence just as the Medici were growing interested in him again. He quickly improved his offer, but still Machiavelli refused to budge.

Then, a few weeks later, Soderini offered him a second job. This time it was proposed on behalf of the powerful Roman nobleman Prospero Colonna, a cousin of the condottiere Fabrizio Colonna, to whom Machiavelli had dedicated *The Art of War*. The job was to take on the role of adviser to the nobleman at a salary of two hundred gold ducats plus expenses. It was an amazing offer. Two hundred gold ducats was equivalent to many times the salary Machiavelli had enjoyed at the height of his success in the Florentine government. The position would offer him comfort and excitement as well as security for his family. He could move his wife and children to Rome and he could wash his hands of the pain and the heartache of the past. But although he must have been sorely tempted, Machiavelli turned down this offer too and remained in Florence to complete his book.

His decision was prompted by what he considered a matter of

honour. He had agreed to write a history of Florence. It would be a noble and important undertaking and it would etch his name in history. He also believed that by making it clear that he would continue to work for the Medici in spite of strong incentives to do otherwise, his loyalty would be rewarded. Machiavelli knew that he could live out his days in the comfort of Colonna's palace and perhaps a part of him felt that he deserved this reward, but he was now driven by greater ambitions. If the offer had come a year earlier, perhaps his decision would have been entirely different. Now, though, he was feeling strong and confident. He had acquired a new impetus, a fresh sense of enthusiasm, and he believed he knew the best course to follow. In this he was only partly right, for the road through his final years was littered with gold and pyrites – plaudits and honour, as well as misfortune and pain.

12

The Final Years

Machiavelli was now a professional writer, supported by the Medici and academia. His *Art of War*, published in 1521 by the Florentine Filippo di Giunta, was extremely well received by military analysts and political commentators. One of the first to receive a copy was the well-connected Cardinal Giovanni Salviati, who was proud to be 'the first in Rome to see such a fine work'.[1]

At the same time Machiavelli was working on his *Florentine Histories*, although this was bringing him problems as well as intellectual satisfaction. The most difficult aspect of the work was the need to gratify his sponsors, the Medici, while at the same time writing a history that was truthful and accurate. This meant that at times Machiavelli was forced to massage the truth, putting at risk his intellectual integrity. To his friend the powerful nobleman and papal governor Francesco Guicciardini, with whom he began an often revealing and intimate correspondence in 1521, he confessed:

As for the lies of these citizens of Carpi [he had just returned from a visit to a community of priests in the town], I can beat all of them out, because it has been a while since I have become a doctor of this art – and good enough not to require Francesco

Martelli [a contemporary storyteller] as an errand boy; so, for
some time now I have never said what I believe or never believed
what I said; and if indeed I do sometimes tell the truth, I hide it
behind so many lies that it is hard to find.[2]

It was indeed ironic that Machiavelli, a committed republican,
should be writing a history of his city commissioned by the Medici,
but he could hardly have turned down the invitation to write the
book; and with his usual cleverness he did find a way to accommo-
date his employers' vanity and his integrity. By 1524, as he was
approaching the end of his task, he could tell Guicciardini:

Here in the country I have been applying myself, and continue
to do so, to writing the history, and I would pay ten *soldi* – but no
more – to have you by my side so that I might show you where
I am, because since I am about to come to certain details, I
would need to learn from you whether or not I am being too
offensive in my exaggerating or understating of the facts.
Nevertheless, I shall continue to seek advice from myself, and I
shall try to do my best to arrange it so that – still telling the
truth – no one will have anything to complain about.[3]

As Machiavelli wrote these words, in the world beyond his country retreat the politicians, kings and pontiffs were engaged in their
usual games and shaping the events that would fill the pages of
future histories. The balance of power in Europe, always a delicate
thing, had been destabilised in recent years by two deaths. In 1516
Ferdinand II (also known as Ferdinand the Catholic) who had
been King of Aragon, Castile, Sicily and León (as well as ruler of
Naples since 1504), had died. The Holy Roman Emperor
Maximilian had followed him to the grave in 1519.

That year the nineteen-year-old grandson of Ferdinand and
Maximilian and son of the late Philip I and Joanna of Castile

became Holy Roman Emperor, as Charles V, having already been crowned King Charles I of Spain three years earlier. This union of two of the major power blocs of Europe posed an intolerable threat to France, and from 1521 it sparked a series of wars that were to drag on for a generation. Italy was inexorably drawn into these wars because of a succession of incompetent popes, beginning with Leo X (Giovanni de' Medici), who tried to play the two ends off against the middle.

Leo died in December 1521 and was succeeded by Adrian Boyers of Utrecht, the Cardinal of Tortosa, who took the name Adrian VI. Cardinal Boyers had been tutor to the boy who had grown up to become King of Spain and Holy Roman Emperor, and because they shared a close bond his election should theoretically have stabilised the political situation in Italy. But instead it achieved the opposite.

Adrian's election was bad news for the Medici because it gave an unexpected boost to all those opposed to the family. Foremost among these were Piero Soderini, who could contemplate more seriously his long-held dream of returning to Florence, while his brother, Cardinal Francesco Soderini, could try to increase his influence and leverage in Rome. But if any of these active opponents of the Medici harboured hopes that 1522 might bring them triumph and a political reawakening in Italy, they were quite misguided. They were instead about to face a season of death.

The summer of 1522 was hot, and in May plague struck with more than usual venom. Florence was one of the worst affected places in Italy. The city shut down completely, many of the wealthier citizens fled to their country villas, there were no elections that year and no law enforcement, and those suspected of being ill were forced to wear a white cloth and have their homes sealed up. Machiavelli's brother Totto was one of the victims. From a letter written by the gonfalonier of justice, Roberto Pucci on 8 June, Niccolò had learned that Totto was *in extremis*. He did not manage to visit him before he died the following day, aged forty-seven.

Then, on 14 June, the man who had been Machiavelli's master for many years, the former gonfalonier for life, Piero Soderini, died in Rome, possibly also a victim of the plague. Soderini had never entirely given up hope of deposing the Medici and returning in glory to Florence, and along with his brother Francesco he had, during the final days of his life, become involved in a conspiracy to remove the Pope. Piero died a day or two after the conspiracy was discovered, but before his part in the affair had been revealed. Francesco was exposed by a rival cardinal, captured before he could flee Rome. Locked up in the Castel Sant'Angelo, he was tortured and killed.

Meanwhile, in the very week of this conspiracy in Rome, a group of rebels in Florence made a failed attempt on the life of Giulio de' Medici, and most alarmingly for Machiavelli, it was a conspiracy led by two of his closest friends from the Rucellai Gardens, Zanobi Buondelmonti and Luigi Alamanni di Piero. Although they succeeded in escaping Florence, two of their fellow conspirators, Luigi Alamanni di Tommaso and Jacopo da Diacceto, were not so lucky. They were caught, tortured until they confessed every detail of their plan and then promptly beheaded in the Piazza della Signoria.

Strangely, Machiavelli was never suspected of being involved in this conspiracy. This is surprising because he was known to be a leading light within the group of humanist intellectuals who gathered at the Rucellai Gardens. He was a famous republican, and most importantly, he had been implicated in an attempted conspiracy against the Medici only a decade earlier. He had every motive to work with the conspirators and all the opportunity he needed. The fact that the seditionists did not mention Machiavelli's name even under extreme torture means that he must have had a perfect alibi.

The year 1523 is something of a blank to Machiavelli's biographers. From this time there are only three surviving letters to Machiavelli (two from his brother-in-law Francesco del Nero and one from his close friend Francesco Vettori) and it seems most likely that he retreated to his hermit-like existence at Sant'Andrea and his continuing work on the *Florentine Histories*. The meetings at the Rucellai Gardens had ended with the failed conspiracy of the previous year; Machiavelli did no official work for the government and there is no record of him travelling beyond the environs of Florence.

While he lived in self-imposed isolation, there were great changes in Florence and Rome. In September Pope Adrian VI died, and by the middle of November 1524 the Holy College had elected Giulio de' Medici as the new pope. He took the title of Clement VII, and although he was never a corrupt man, as many popes had been, and did not suffer the faults of self-obsession or aggressiveness, he was indecisive and politically naive.

The 1520s was a time when the Church needed a strong pope because it was under attack from all sides. Martin Luther had nailed his Ninety-five Theses to the door of the Castle Church in Wittenberg in 1517. This had prompted Leo X to excommunicate him, but still the attacks on Catholicism were coming from all directions and growing steadily stronger. Intellectuals were undermining doctrine, and the ubiquitous printing press was perhaps the greatest danger because so many new books in the vernacular offered the chance of education for the masses; the last thing the clergy wanted. Books such as the humanist Erasmus's *The Praise of Folly* (1509) and *Freedom of the Will* (1524) were beginning to erode the intellectual traditions of the Church and helping to free the minds of anyone interested enough and able to read.

A more immediate danger came from politics. In a repeat of recent history Rome was once more caught between the two bullying superpowers of Europe, Spain and France. Clement tried to emulate Pope Julius II, who had attempted to act as broker, and to keep both powers at arm's length. Julius had enjoyed a modicum of success for a short time before his schemes collapsed, but Clement came from a very different mould and with staggering speed his policies led Italy into massacre and humiliation.

The solitude and scholarly quiet in which Machiavelli had submerged himself in 1523 could not have kept him contented for very long. Letters to friends show that by the first weeks of 1524 he had begun to re-emerge from Sant'Andrea and was once more socialising and making merry in Florence. It is about this time that a new figure appeared on the scene, a wealthy merchant named Jacopo Fornaciaio.

Fornaciaio was very different from many of Machiavelli's other friends and this new relationship serves to illustrate just how cosmopolitan Machiavelli was. He loved the company of fellow intellectuals, but he could socialise with almost anyone. Even his closest friends came from a wide range of backgrounds. He was on intimate terms with Francesco Guicciardini, who was the papal governor of Mantua and Reggio and was made 'President' of the Romagna in 1524. His friends from the Rucellai Gardens were almost exclusively young men from the wealthiest and most powerful families in Florence, and he had once been on very close personal terms with the Soderini brothers, themselves sons of immensely rich and influential patriarchs. Yet Machiavelli could talk freely with the lowest-born farm workers and labourers who drank in the tavern close to his country home. He had cherished the love of his social equals, men such as Biagio Buonaccorsi, and now here he was readily mixing with merchants and wealthy 'plebeians' such as Fornaciaio.

Such social networking was not unusual in sixteenth-century Florence. Many wealthy nobles mixed with well-to-do commoners and men who had succeeded in the Arts, in politics or in religious careers, and successful people from lowly backgrounds could acquire a degree of social acceptance that cut across the classes. For this reason it was not uncommon to find men like Jacopo Fornaciaio, who owned a vast home just outside Florence, hosting parties attended by some of the most illustrious figures in Tuscany, at which they would rub shoulders with successful artists, actors, writers and men such as the social magpie Machiavelli. It was at one such grand party at Fornaciaio's home in January 1524 that Machiavelli met the ravishingly beautiful actress Barbara Salutati Raffacani.

Machiavelli fell in love with Barbara very quickly and, just as he always did, he threw himself into this affair with unbridled energy. Writing to his friend Vettori a decade earlier, he had told him: 'Love tortures only those who attempt to clip his wings or to fetter him whenever he flies into their laps. Because he is a young, fickle boy, he gouges out the eyes, livers and hearts of such people. But those who rejoice at his arrival and pamper him, and then let him go whenever he wants to, gladly welcoming his return visits – these he always reveres and cherishes: under his command they triumph.'[4]

Fine words, but like so much Machiavelli wrote, his thoughts on paper did little to guide his actions. He certainly had loved freely and enjoyed liaisons with dozens, perhaps scores, of women during his lifetime, but he was never as detached from love's consequences as the voice of Il Machia suggests in his letters or in the guise of characters in his fiction. Furthermore, as he grew older, his love affairs caused him more and more pain. He had become obsessed with La Tafani, a girl less than half his age, and he had suffered as their impossible relationship dissolved. And now, as he approached his fifty-fifth birthday, he became smitten with the beautiful Barbara.

By all accounts Barbara was easy to fall in love with. Confident, talented and beautiful, she was in great demand as a performer on stage and in the bedchamber and Machiavelli was neither so foolish nor so naïve as to believe that he was her only suitor. He would have liked to have been, but all he had to offer was his reputation, his intellect and the admiration of the brightest and most liberalminded of Florentines. He was ageing, he was poor and he was from ordinary stock, in many ways no great catch for a woman of Barbara's quality.

Yet many surviving letters testify to the fact that Machiavelli did enjoy a serious and lasting relationship with Barbara. Indeed some of those who learned of the affair were shocked by his antics and tried to warn him against making such a display of what they viewed as his latest dalliance. Some even tried to intervene. An old friend, the lawyer Filippo de' Nerli, wrote to Francesco del Nero: 'Since "Machia" is a relative of yours and a friend of mine . . . I have to tell you that here in Modena everyone is talking about him and about this "family man" falling head-over-heels in love with "someone whom I should not refer to in name".'[5]

It is difficult to ascertain exactly what de' Nerli was trying to achieve with this letter. He was supposed to be a good and loyal friend; he had known Machiavelli at the chancery and had been an active member of the Rucellai Gardens group, but by directing these comments to Marietta's brother he knew he might be stirring up trouble for Niccolò. It is possible he was trying to change his old friend by forcing him into a conflict with his family, but a less ingenuous conclusion would be that he was simply jealous.

Whatever de' Nerli's motivations, Machiavelli seems to have completely ignored him. Indeed we can only assume that the long-suffering Marietta was by now so used to her husband's ways that she simply accepted them as an unalterable facet of his character, for there is no indication that de' Nerli's interference changed anything.

During the spring of 1524 Machiavelli was rarely seen in public without his new *amore*. Fornaciaio was a major figure on the Florentine social scene of the early 1520s, and he was keen to impress. He was wealthy and loved having beauties such as Barbara at his parties. He also revelled in the fact that famous and colourful figures like Machiavelli favoured him. For Machiavelli's part, social acceptance went a long way to salve his inner anguish, and it gave him a sense of belonging. It was perhaps inevitable that after knowing Barbara for only a few months she would become his muse, leading him to pen a play for her. It was also an inspiration for Fornaciaio, who spared no expense in arranging a public performance of the work in the grounds of his palatial home.

The play, *Clizia*, was first performed on 13 January 1525. Fornaciaio employed a famous stage designer named Bastiano da San Gallo to create the scenery. A large area of his garden was levelled to build a stage, and the best musicians and actors in Tuscany were called on to support Barbara in the lead role. According to one observer: 'all the leading citizens came and the most distinguished men of the government then in power'.[6] Even the new leader of Florence, Ippolito de' Medici (the illegitimate son of Giuliano), whom the Pope had just installed as head of state, was there.

Clizia's plot is even more sexually driven than that of *Mandragola*. It revolves around the character of Nicomaco, a wealthy old man who lusts after a young girl, Clizia, who has been brought up in his household as his ward. Nicomaco's son, Cleander, also loves the girl and wishes to marry her, but the old man refuses and instead insists that a young tenant of his named Pirro will marry her. This is because Nicomaco and Pirro have come to an agreement whereby the old man will be allowed to have as much sex as he likes with the young bride.

On the wedding night the old man, having swallowed a special draught from the pharmacist to help him perform, takes the place of the groom and awaits the arrival of Clizia. However, Nicomaco's astute wife, Sofronia, has paid a male servant to dress up as Clizia and take her place. In the dark of the bridal bedchamber Nicomaco tries repeatedly to have his way with whom he thinks is Clizia, only to be beaten off by the servant. Eventually he gives up and goes to sleep, whereupon the servant sodomises him. This twist would have been doubly outrageous and, to some, hysterically funny, because the concept of an older man allowing himself to be the passive partner in a homosexual encounter was repulsive to Florentines of this time.

In the final scene Clizia's father turns up unexpectedly and we discover that he is not only extremely rich but also understanding. He insists that his daughter should be allowed to marry the man she loves, Cleander, and they all live happily ever after.

The play became an instant *succès de scandale* and was talked about across Italy. De' Nerli was moved to write: 'The fame of your comedy has spread everywhere; and do not think I have had this from friends' letters, I have had it from travellers who all along the roads go proclaiming the glorious displays and fine games of Porta a San Frediano [the gate of Florence close to Fornaciaio's home]. I am sure that as the greatness of such magnificence has not been content to remain within the bounds of Tuscany, but has also come as far as here, it will cross the mountains too . . .'

If we ignore this sarcasm – Machiavelli and his close friends often exchanged letters in this tone – it is clear *Clizia* was a huge success. As with its predecessor, *Mandragola*, it was simple and shocking and appealed to audiences across the social spectrum. Indeed, during his lifetime Machiavelli was better known as a comic author than anything else. (Around the time of this first performance of *Clizia*, a production of *Mandragola* in Venice had to be stopped because the over-enthusiasm of the audience made it impossible for the actors to carry on.)

Clizia was also the most autobiographical and self-mocking work Machiavelli ever wrote. The lead character is obviously based on the actress who played her, Barbara, and Machiavelli chose the name of the old man Nicomaco to make it abundantly clear that he saw himself as the sad old lecher who tries and fails to bed the heroine. It was a play prompted by the agonies he suffered because of his doomed love for Barbara, but unlike his pathetic creation Nicomaco, Machiavelli almost certainly did succeed in fulfilling his sexual desires with the beautiful actress, although their relationship could never have developed into anything more than an affair.

A part of him revelled in the image he had of himself as a tragic lover and abused genius. For a while he adopted the habit of addressing himself in letters to friends as 'Niccolò Machiavelli, Historian, Comic Author and Tragic Author'. And he certainly knew Barbara was engaged in many other relationships simultaneously. He was probably not far off the mark in viewing himself as, in her eyes, just another admirer with whom she had shared a bed. To his friend Guicciardini he wrote: 'As for Barbara and the singers [for a new performance of his play], I believe I can bring her for fifteen *soldi* to the lira unless some other consideration holds you back. I mention this because she has certain lovers who might block the way; still, one might contrive to keep them quiet.'[7]

At the same time, when his friends were not trying to dissuade him from making a public display of his affair with Barbara they offered to help him through the heartache. 'You are used to your Barbara who strives, as does her kind, to please everyone and seeks rather to seem than to be,' Guicciardini commented in a letter of August 1525.[8]

Machiavelli almost always let his heart rule his head and was driven by a libertine disregard for form or convention, but it is evident that he did have a hold over women. Barbara never deserted him and they remained lovers until his death in June 1527, more than three years after they first met, and as late as the spring of that year she was still writing frequently to him while he was away from Florence on matters of state. Machiavelli was certainly never faithful to Barbara. He had at least one other lover while making a public show of his affair with the actress; the most important to him was a mysterious young woman named Maliscotta whom he met during a trip to Faenza in the summer of 1525.

That year marked a genuine shift in Machiavelli's fortunes. It had begun with the triumphant performance of *Clizia* in Florence, and little more than a few weeks later he had finished his *Florentine Histories* (up to the death of Lorenzo the Magnificent in 1492). Fired up and confident, he decided he should present the book to the Pope in person and so he wrote to Vettori, who had just returned to Rome and was close to Clement VII, to ask for advice. Vettori told him that the time was not right and stalled him. But then, in early March, he changed his mind. 'My dear *compare*,' he wrote:

> I could not advise you as to whether you should come with the book or not, because the times are opposed to reading and to gifts. On the other hand, the Pope on the first evening I arrived, after I had talked to him of something I had to, asked me about you on his own and inquired of me whether you had finished the *Historia* and whether I had seen it. When I said that I had seen a part of it and that you had completed up to the death of Lorenzo, and that it was something that would give satisfaction, and that you had wanted to come and bring it to him but I had dissuaded you from it on account of the times, he said to me: 'He ought to come, and I feel for certain that his books are going to give pleasure and be read willingly.' These are the very words he said to me; but I would not want you to put your trust in them for coming and then find yourself left with empty hands.[9]

Quite why Vettori had ignored the earlier suggestions of his friend and advised him to stay in Florence is not certain. The most likely explanation is that he was jealous of Machiavelli. A decade earlier Vettori had done little to help him through fear that his own good name might be besmirched by association. Now, as Machiavelli's star was rising and he was not only acquiring fame as a playwright but was once more favoured by the Medici, Vettori was probably feeling envious.

It is certainly true that during the first months of 1525 Clement VII was distracted. Having vacillated between Charles Bourbon and the French king, Francis I, who had ascended the throne in 1515, he had backed the wrong side by giving his support to the

French just before their armies were defeated at the Battle of Pavia on 24 February. On that day twelve thousand troops led by Bourbon had routed a much larger French force. (Bourbon was formerly the Constable of France. In 1523 he defected to Charles V's side, becoming one of his most trusted generals and the new hero of the Holy Roman Empire.) Thousands of French infantry died at Pavia, but for Clement the worst calamity of the battle had been the capture of Francis, who was taken to Madrid as a prisoner of war.

When news of this humiliation reached the Vatican, Clement immediately decided to switch his allegiance and started diplomatic moves to woo Charles V. Realising that such a move would generate suspicion among Charles's advisers, the Pope arranged for a diplomatic mission to Madrid, which he believed would serve to demonstrate his honest intentions and to prove that his support would be genuine. In April 1525 Clement ordered his nephew, Cardinal Giovanni Salviati, to Madrid and began to search for a suitable secretary, a man with experience and expertise who could assist the cardinal in his delicate task.

Giovanni Salviati was a great admirer of Machiavelli, and the former Secretary had gone to great pains to cultivate a relationship with him. The cardinal had been one of the first to receive a printed copy of *The Art of War* and he had been moved by Machiavelli's gesture. More importantly perhaps, Salviati's father, the elderly Jacopo, had long held Machiavelli in the highest regard. So keen was Jacopo to help him that he took it upon himself to put Niccolò's name forward as the best candidate for the role of secretary to his son. 'As a secretary, and as a man with whom you might take council,' Jacopo wrote to Giovanni on 3 May: 'Niccolò Machiavelli would please me better than anyone. I have spoken about it to His Holiness and he is undecided: I shall see if I cannot get him to make up his mind.'[10] But two weeks later Jacopo was disappointed. Writing again to his son, he told him: 'We shall have to give up with Niccolò Machiavelli, because I see that the Pope is reluctant.'[11]

Machiavelli almost certainly knew nothing of this exchange until it was all over, and quite why things went the way they did is unclear. The most likely explanation is that Clement was not yet prepared to offer Machiavelli such an important role. This was unfortunate because if Machiavelli had not listened to Vettori and had travelled to Rome earlier in 1525, it is quite possible things would have been very different. This view is supported by the fact that when, in June, Machiavelli did finally secure an audience with Clement to present his *Florentine Histories*, the Pope was so delighted with the book he gave the author an impromptu gift of 120 gold ducats.

Clement was genuinely appreciative of Machiavelli's writing, but it is also quite evident that, having had the opportunity to discuss politics and history face to face with him, he was captivated by the man's obvious charisma and his natural abilities as a political analyst. Before leaving Rome, Clement had reinstated Machiavelli as both adviser and emissary and had increased his salary to one hundred gold florins.

With the political situation utterly confused, Clement was in desperate need of advice. Francis was still imprisoned in Madrid, Charles V's German troops were amassing in the north and looking increasingly dangerous, and a pan-Italian war appeared ever more likely. It was at this moment that the Pope began to listen to Machiavelli's well-known convictions that Italy must defend itself by creating a citizens' militia, that the defences of vulnerable cities (such as Florence, directly in the line of any predicted advance from the north) should be strengthened, and that papal armies must be better organised and trained.

June 1525 marks the true beginning of a regeneration in Machiavelli's political and diplomatic career. From then until his death two years later, he wrote very little and devoted himself exclusively to one last burst of frenetic political activity, swapping theory for practice. He never did return to his *Florentine Histories*. Deemed the most entertaining and the most beautifully written (if not the most accurate) of all those of the fifteenth and sixteenth centuries, it is a book that is still read widely today and it has remained in print for almost five hundred years. *Mandragola* was performed to delighted audiences in Venice at the carnival of 1526 and elsewhere during Machiavelli's lifetime, but after *Clizia* there were no more plays. Machiavelli stopped composing sonnets and there were no more works of political analysis. Instead, reinstated as an emissary, roving diplomat and military adviser, he returned to the front line of politics and military affairs just as Italy was about to tumble into the abyss of all-out war.

At the start of 1526 the military sparring between the great powers of Europe intensified. In January Francis I signed the Treaty of Madrid, drawn up by Charles V. This offered him his freedom in exchange for compliance with four conditions. First, he was to agree to give up all claims and interest in Italy. Second, he was to marry Charles's sister, Eleanor of Austria (the widowed wife of the King of Portugal, Emmanuel the Great, who had died five years earlier). Third, he had to restore the state of Burgundy to the emperor; and finally he was to leave his two sons, Francis and Henry, in Madrid as hostages. But, in a move of purest Machiavellianism, the moment Francis reached Paris he rescinded the agreement with Charles, claiming that he had signed the treaty under duress and that it was therefore morally and practically invalid.

For Charles this was as good as a declaration of war, and Clement, who had never been entirely happy trying to appease the Holy Roman Emperor, immediately absolved Francis of his broken promise, switched sides yet again and in May 1526 formed the League of Cognac, a union of France, Rome, Venice, Milan and Florence.

This new union should have been a match for the emperor, but the strategies, plans and actions of the League were bungled from the start, and the policies agreed on by its members instead brought chaos and disaster to Italy. More than almost anyone else at the cutting edge, Machiavelli was both wary of the League and certain that the Italians were not well prepared for the inevitable war. 'However matters turn out, I believe that war in Italy is inevitable – and at hand,' he wrote to his friend Guicciardini in March 1526.[12] Both men had been following the unfolding events in Europe with a deepening sense of dismay, for they could not trust Clement to make a correct decision nor to see a plan through to its conclusion. Guicciardini had the measure of the pontiff when he wrote to Machiavelli at the end of 1525: 'I've never heard of anyone who when he saw a storm coming did not attempt to take cover, except ourselves who prefer to wait for it in the middle of the road without any protection. So, we shall not be able to say that our sovereignty has been taken away from us but that it fell shamefully from our own hands.'[13]

Clement had been double-dealing almost from the moment he had ascended to the papacy. He had employed Machiavelli because he believed he had suitably aggressive ideas for the protection of Italy. The Pope also used intelligent, observant and very able men such as Guicciardini, placing them in positions of real power. The problem did not lie with those whom he employed, but with the fact that he himself could never deliver the goods. Clement was forever wrong-footed by enemies and allies alike and he was distrusted by almost everyone because of his duplicitous behaviour. To make things far worse, he made extremely bad decisions and allowed himself to become confused by too much conflicting advice. Most damaging of all, after taking this advice, he chose the wrong course of action every single time. Not only was he facing insubordination from some of the minor participants in the League (the most disgruntled of whom was the Duke of Urbino, Francesco della Rovere, who had been exchanging harsh words with the Pope over disputed lands in Tuscany since 1524), but at the same time he was forced to comply with the wishes of the French king, who, after the humiliation of Pavia, was hungry for revenge.

To Machiavelli it must have seemed as though history was repeating itself. Instead of acting as Secretary to the vacillating and indecisive Soderini at the head of a Florentine government, he was now a servant of Pope Clement VII, who was both the head of the Church and the master of Florence. Once more his commander-in-chief was trying to deal with the French and forming ineffectual unions. Machiavelli's treasured and hard-won militia had dissolved into nothing at the hands of the Medici and Tuscany was once more left effectively undefended. Italian security was now reliant on incompetent statesmen who barely deserved their titles and continued to bicker while Europe's most powerful leader was advancing into Italy.

Machiavelli knew they had little time and did everything he could to salvage something from the mess. In April he was instructed by the Pope to inspect the walls of Florence and he wrote a report entitled *Provvisione per la Istituzione dell'Ufficio de' cinque Provveditori della Mura della Città di Firenze* (Provision for the Creation of the Office of Five Superintendents for the Walls of the City of Florence). This led the Pope to establish a new magistracy, the Curators of the Walls, to which Machiavelli was appointed secretary while his son Bernardo was made an assistant. Within weeks this new government department was gathering funds to inspect and repair all defensive walls around Florence and her dependencies.

For the first time in thirteen years Machiavelli found himself in an official governmental position, with an office in the Palazzo Vecchio. During the spring and summer of 1526, fired up and enthusiastic, he seemed to be everywhere at once, travelling throughout Lombardy and Tuscany and taking on the work of three men.

The papal forces had gathered at Piacenza, in Lombardy,

north-west of Florence, and from there Guicciardini wrote to the Florentine ambassador, Roberto Acciaiuoli: 'Machiavelli is here. He came to reorganise the militia, but, seeing how rotten it is, he has no hope or any respect from it. Since he is unable to remedy the faults of mankind, he will do nothing but laugh at them.'[14]

The ambassador replied a few days later: 'I am glad that Machiavelli gave the orders to discipline the infantry. Would to God that he might put into action what he has in mind . . . but it would seem to me better if he were to return to Florence and carry out his duty of fortifying the walls because the time when we will need them is rapidly approaching.'[15]

It is easy to detect an edge of panic in Acciaiuoli's response, but he was merely reflecting the general feeling in Florence during this dark season. Throughout the summer and into the autumn of 1526, the war raged on, with Charles's forces bearing down from the north. Towns and small city states across Lombardy and the Romagna changed hands several times in as many months, but the underlying feeling throughout Italy was that the League of Cognac was failing, that the forces of the Holy Roman Empire combined with the Spanish were steadily gaining ground.

This view had been encouraged by a pathetic attempt in July to capture Milan from the occupying Spanish forces. The army of the Duke of Urbino (who was only ever fighting this war half-heartedly), combined with a small force of Venetians, had pressed north to attack the city without waiting for French reinforcements. On the point of seizing Milan, Urbino inexplicably ordered a retreat and the entire effort ended in embarrassment and humiliation for the League.

Two months later, and with the disgrace of Milan still fresh in their minds, the League celebrated a rare victory when, after a long siege, their forces captured the city of Cremona, close to Piacenza. Machiavelli was there to witness this triumph for himself, standing before the walls of the city as French, Venetian and Florentine soldiers stormed the gates. However, the celebrations at Cremona were short-lived because, as the city fell, four hundred miles to the south the Pope was courting disaster.

As the war had gone from bad to worse, and Clement's incompetence was becoming clear for all to see, some of the more powerful cardinals and their wealthy influential families had begun preparing for insurrection within the Vatican itself. On 19 September, four nights before the victory at Cremona, the Colonna family, one of the most important in Rome, formed a treacherous union with Hugo de Moncada (an agent of the emperor) and they turned on the Pope. Imperial troops stormed the city and Clement was forced to barricade himself inside the Castel Sant'Angelo, the almost impregnable fort on the periphery of the Vatican. In order to gain his freedom he was obliged to agree in writing to an uneasy peace with the Holy Roman Empire and the Spanish. This involved a complete withdrawal from Lombardy and the handing back of territorial gains the League had made during the year-long war.

Machiavelli was utterly disgusted. In a letter written from the battlefield in October he reported to a friend, Bartolomeo Cavalcanti, that the Pope had placed himself in a position where he was 'taken like a baby'. He had not acted in the way a pope should behave, because he had not raised funds for his troops and had made the gross error of staying in Rome and making himself vulnerable. Furthermore, he explained, the condottieri employed by the Pope to fight in the north were 'all ambitious and insufferable, lacking anyone who knows how to mitigate the caprices [of the troops] and keep them united so that they become a cacophony of barking dogs'.[16]

Little more than two months after Clement had been freed from the Castel Sant'Angelo, Charles, who could not remain content with the gains he had made, pushed south to threaten Florence itself. Having come from a colder climate beyond the Alps, his forces, augmented by Swiss mercenaries, were quite unperturbed by approaching winter and with very little to stop their advance, many in Florence believed the city would be taken before the end of the year.

The temporary peace created by the Pope's embarrassing capitulation in Rome was shattered the moment he was released from his confinement. The Colonna family were also quickly ditched by their co-conspirators and a wrathful Clement sent a force to destroy all the lands owned by them before regrouping his armies at Modena, fifty miles north of Florence. This was a long way from the original shifting front line of the previous summer, and now the forces of the League were in constant, slow retreat. On 25 November, at the battle of Borgoforte, near Mantua, the best soldier fighting for the League, the condottiere Giovanni de' Medici (a great-grandson of Lorenzo the Magnificent and son of Caterina Sforza) was wounded in the thigh by a musket ball and died five days later. This was a terrible blow and it weakened further still the lame and disorganised armies that were defending Italy.

In his *History of Italy*, written years later, Francesco Guicciardini described 1527 as 'full of atrocities and events unheard of for many centuries: overthrow of governments, wickedness of princes, most frightful sacks of cities, great famines, a most terrible plague almost everywhere in Italy; everything full of death, flight and rapine'.[17]

During the early months of this dreadful year Machiavelli was away from home at the front, feeling cold and older than his years. Depressed and frustrated with the way the strange, brooding conflict had gone so terribly wrong for the League, he also shared with his countrymen the fear that Florence would be ravaged by Charles's forces. For the first time since the dark days when Julius II threatened the Florentine Republic, this new conflict not only placed at risk Florentine sovereignty, but also endangered the very lives of his family.

Throughout this fearful time Machiavelli wrote often to his

family and his letters are filled with an affection he had rarely demonstrated before. Marietta was staying at the country estate with their youngest child, Totto, who was no more than six months old at the time and ill (he was to die a few months into the year). With them was the couple's daughter, Bartolomea, their eldest son, Bernardo, and the two younger boys, Guido and Piero, who were studying in the city; the second son, Lodovico, was away on business in the Levant.

Little is known of Machiavelli's family and we have only the bare bones of their lives drawn together from scraps of incomplete state records and a few letters that have survived half a millennium, but the correspondence from this fraught period in their lives does offer a glimpse of who they were. Guido, the second youngest after Totto, was eleven or twelve in 1527. Although documents recording details of his birth have been lost, it is known that the boy was of poor constitution, studious and bookish. The brightest of Machiavelli's children, and the most like his father, Guido was intellectually precocious and had a literary bent. Of the others, Bernardo is thought to have been rather awkward and slow-witted. Almost nothing is recorded of Piero, aged thirteen in 1527, but his brother Lodovico, as well as being the most businesslike of the sons, had also gained a reputation as an aggressive individual who had run into trouble with the authorities on many occasions during the mid-1520s. Bartolomea, Machiavelli's only daughter, was later to marry well and her husband, Giovanni Ricci, became his father-in-law's literary executor.

From the front Machiavelli wrote a stream of letters to his wife and to his favourite son, Guido. Along with chatty advice and exchanges of family news about mules and gifts he promised to bring them when he returned home, he asked Guido to give his love to his mother for him and to look after himself. He advised the boy repeatedly to keep up with his studies and assured him that if he did this then one day he would be 'a man of good standing'.[18] He also gave the family what assurances he could about the progress of the war. In reply Guido reported: 'We are not worrying about the lansquenets [soldiers of the emperor] any more because you have promised us to try and be with us if anything should happen. And so . . .,' he ends, 'Madonna Marietta is no longer worried.'[19]

However, by early April Machiavelli was clearly disheartened by the whole sorry affair and keen to get away from the confusion and the horrors of the front. 'Greet Madonna Marietta for me . . .,' he asked Guido, 'and tell her I have been expecting – and still do – to leave here any day; I have never longed so much to return to Florence as I do now, but there is nothing else I can do.'[20]

Indeed there was nothing Machiavelli could do. He had struggled and argued, he had tried his hardest to make a foolish and indecisive pope see sense. He had fought to get backing to organise properly a force that could have held its own against the armies arrayed against it. All of this had come to little. But then, exactly as he had described in his analyses of war and politics, *fortuna* and the schemes of better strategists than Clement were to quickly move things on, taking him, his family and the fate of Florence (and indeed all of Europe) with them.

Thanks in part to Machiavelli, the Imperial forces did not attack Florence as many expected them to do. During the spring Machiavelli and his greatest ally, Guicciardini, had succeeded in diverting a large military force from the front line to the protection of Florence. At the same time, through his work with the Curators of the Walls, Machiavelli had ensured that the city walls offered a formidable barrier to any expected attack by Charles's forces. Both of these factors were instrumental in making any move on Florence a tough option. Marching along the banks of the Arno, during the final days of April, Bourbon's forces reached as far as Montevarchi, forty miles from the walls of Florence. From there they turned abruptly south and, to the surprise of almost everyone, headed with all speed straight for Rome.

The sack of Rome by Bourbon's forces was considered at the time to be a calamity, a savaging of the iconic centre of the Catholic faith matched only by the invasion of the Barbarian hordes in the fifth century. And indeed it was done with a disregard for history, religion and human life that had much in common with the Goth and Visigoth marauders a thousand years earlier. But no one could seriously deny the Pope had it coming.

Bourbon reached Rome on 4 May, four days after heading south, but by then he was already two days ahead of a heavily armed division sent after him by the commanders of the League. An assault on the gates of Rome at Borgo and Santo Spirito on 6 May met with some resistance from a small force defending the city and Bourbon was killed in the first wave. Undeterred, the army pushed on hard and broke through into Rome, where they met little resistance. Raping, burning and pillaging, the troops displayed a savagery horrible to behold. According to one anonymous contemporary authority: 'The Lutherans rejoiced to burn and to defile what all the world had adored. Churches were desecrated, women, even the religious, violated, ambassadors pillaged, cardinals put to ransom, ecclesiastical dignitaries and ceremonies made a mockery, and the soldiers fought among themselves for the spoil.'[21]

Luigi Guicciardini (brother of Francesco Guicciardini) was an eyewitness to events and reported:

Many were suspended for hours by the arms; many were cruelly bound by the private parts; many were suspended by the feet high above the road, or over water, while their tormentors threatened to cut the cord. Some were half buried in the cellars, others nailed up in casks, while many were villainously beaten and wounded; not few were cut all over their persons by red-hot irons. Some were tortured by extreme thirst, others by insupportable noise and many were cruelly tortured by having their own good teeth drawn. Others again were forced to eat their own ears, or nose or their roasted testicles.[22]

Clement went into hiding before the first blow was struck, locking himself away in the Castel Sant'Angelo for the second time in nine months, while all around him Rome was burned and defiled. For eight days the invaders ravaged the city, an act that was not sanctioned by the Holy Roman Emperor, Charles V, who eventually arrived to rescue the besieged Pope and bring some sort of order to the devastated city.

When news of the Pope's fate reached Florence, it spelt the end of Medici rule. For months Clement's grip on power in his homeland had been slipping away. His representative in Florence, Silvio Passerini, the Cardinal of Cortona, who was regent for the two illegitimate Medici heirs, Ippolito and Alessandro, had escaped the threat of all-out revolution in late April thanks only to the intelligent intervention of the great diplomat Francesco Guicciardini. Guicciardini had succeeded in staving off a bloody rebellion against the Medici, but both sides, the Medici and the rebels (made up of students and the young sons of some of the most powerful Florentine families), had failed to appreciate what he had done. Because of this, tensions remained high in the city, and when word of the sack of Rome finally reached Florence on 11 May, the Florentines were stunned. Cortona was quickly forced to hand over power and a reformed Great Council, modelled on the Savonarola paradigm, was hastily convened.

Still deluding himself that he had any say in the matter, Clement 'agreed to a change of constitution in Florence'. This was a statement that Machiavelli mocked mercilessly, claiming that the fool of a pope had given away something he no longer owned. On 17 May Cortona and the young Medici scions were exiled from Florence, one Niccolò Capponi was elected gonfalonier of justice for a year, the Council Hall, which had been closed up and left to gather dust for almost fifteen years, was reopened, and Florence returned to being a republic once more.

Machiavelli had witnessed the destruction of Rome. With Guicciardini he had acted as a broker for peace in the city and had helped to arrange the rehabilitation of the Pope, who was protected now by Charles V, conqueror of Rome and the most powerful man in the world. When this work was completed, during the last week of May, Machiavelli was granted leave to return to Florence, and with a small group of government officials and men at arms he made his way slowly back home.

Machiavelli was a very intelligent man and possessed an almost superhuman ability to see the consequences of political action. And although these were particularly confused and volatile times, there can be little doubt that he was greatly disturbed by the latest change of government in Florence. He should have rejoiced at the return of a republic, but he knew he could expect very little from the new, young republicans who had seized power. It is said that on his homeward journey, as he travelled through Tuscany and the villages outside Florence, he was heard to sigh and his mood became ever more grave just as most citizens were celebrating the fall of the Medici.

His return was a blend of pain and relief. He was delighted to be reunited with his family after so long and relieved that they had all come through the war unscathed. But at the same time he was immediately made aware of just how unwelcome he was to the new leaders of Florence. 'Everyone hated him because of *The Prince . . .*,' one historian has claimed, 'the Piagnoni [supporters of Savonarola] regarded him as a heretic, the good thought him sinful, the wicked thought him more wicked or more capable than themselves, so that all hated him.'[23] Worse still, the new government not only hated him for what it viewed as his scurrilous book, but also perceived him as a friend of the Medici.

It was the cruellest of ironies. Here stood a man who had been nothing other than a republican and a dedicated patriot his entire life, who had done everything he could for the Republic, who had been tortured, abused and cast out by the Medici, who had lost his livelihood and his brilliant career thanks to the whims of those whom this new government had exiled; in short, a man who had worked ceaselessly for Florence. And, although Machiavelli almost certainly realised he was returning to face humiliation and more pain, when the hammer blow came, on 10 June, it broke his will. That day a Medici ally, the former First Secretary to the newly defunct Otto di Pratica, was given the job of Secretary to the Second Chancery and Machiavelli was passed over.

Machiavelli was almost certainly ill long before he returned home. During the eighteen months of the campaign to stop Charles, he had been travelling almost without a break. He had endured long spells on the battlefield and had lived with squalor, disease and filth before the walls of cities besieged by the League. He had experienced death and destruction on a scale seldom witnessed for at least a generation. He had risked plague and the weapons of the enemy and had seen all his plans and ideas cast aside by the ineffectual and incompetent rulers he served.

He may have lived a little longer if *fortuna* had been on his side, if his countrymen had understood him and comprehended what he really stood for. But that was not to be. Within days of his final rejection, with the majority of influential figures in Florence seeing him as a pariah, he took to his sickbed suffering from what is now believed to have been acute peritonitis brought on by an infected ulcer. He died on 21 June, loved by only his family and a few close friends.

13

Machiavelli's Legacy

In the collected correspondence of Niccolò Machiavelli there is a strange letter which is purported to have been written by his son Piero the day after his father died. It is addressed to Piero's second cousin, Francesco Nelli, and reads:

> My dear Francesco, I have the lamentable duty of informing you that our father Niccolò died on the 22nd of this month [sic], from pains in the belly caused by some medicine he took on the 20th. [During the last eighteen months of his life Machiavelli swore by some quack pills that had been recommended to him by a friend.] He allowed Brother Matteo, who kept him company until his death, to hear the confession of his sins. Our father left us in the deepest poverty, as you know. When you come back up here, I shall tell you a good deal face-to-face. I am in a hurry and shall tell you nothing else except that I send my regards. Your relative, Piero Machiavelli.[1]

The strangest thing about this letter is Piero's mention of the fact that Niccolò Machiavelli made a final confession of his sins before he died because, from what we know of Machiavelli's opinions on religion, this act seems quite out of character.

It has been suggested that the letter is a fake, created to soften posthumously Machiavelli's dark image as an antichrist. Indeed such things were not uncommon during the sixteenth century.[2] The most famous example is a letter that was supposed to have been written by Savonarola to his father but was revealed as a fake during the eighteenth century.[3] Subscribers to this hypothesis point to the fact that the author of the letter gets wrong the date of Machiavelli's death, and suggest that this mistake is more likely to have come from the pen of a con artist than from that of the dead man's son.

This, though, is circumstantial evidence and there are no hard facts to support the idea that Piero's letter is a fake. If it is, it was certainly created by a follower of Machiavelli's, perhaps a distant descendant who found his or her ancestor's morals and religious proclivities unpalatable. Machiavelli's immediate family would not have been involved in such a contrivance. To them Niccolò was not the 'evil' and 'corrupt' author of *The Prince*, the man whom the misinformed and the misguided perceive as an advocate of brutality and ungodly power games. To Marietta Niccolò had been a loving, if distant and unfaithful husband. To his sons and daughter he was a mysterious, but nevertheless caring figure, who cut a dash through the tiny world in which they lived.

A more likely explanation for the incongruous reference is that the letter is not a fake at all and that Piero was merely reporting the real facts but simply made a mistake about the date because he was very upset, and that his father did indeed take a final confession. This would be more in keeping with Machiavelli's character than a refusal to acknowledge the priest. Machiavelli certainly had no respect for the Church, but he did respect and love his family; and Marietta, in particular, was a devout and God-fearing woman. In these circumstances Niccolò would have gone through the ritual (an almost universally accepted custom of the time) simply to appease his family, for they would have feared for his soul even if he had not feared for it himself.

Of course, a great many people have believed that Machiavelli had no soul to risk. Even before his death, what was to become his most famous work, *The Prince*, had tarnished his name and established him, quite without justification, as some sort of heretic, or devil.

Circulated among the intelligentsia in the form of a plagiarised Latin edition first printed in Naples in 1524, *On Principalities* (as it was originally known) was not published as *The Prince* until 1532, five years after Machiavelli's death. By this time his *Discourses on the First Ten Books of Titus Livy* had been published, in 1531, bringing to three the number of his books in print. *The Art of War* was his only book (as distinct from government papers) to be published during his lifetime. But from the start it was *The Prince* that commanded the greatest interest and attracted the most overt misinterpretation.

It is easy to see why *The Prince* became Machiavelli's most famous work. It is short and punchy, radical and direct. But, although it was certain to cause controversy, it was really only after the book became associated with aggressive and influential leaders and statesmen that a wider public began to consider it a work that somehow corrupted readers and encouraged dark impulses.

One historian has said of *The Prince*:

It was received at first almost with indifference; its immediate reception can hardly be called favourable or the reverse; it made its way slowly, as was natural, until it was printed; then religion raised its voice, and opened the era of invective; simultaneously well-intentioned but, we believe, mistaken efforts were made to defend the book on the hypothesis of a secret meaning: then criticism looked back to the author and drew a fancy picture of a cynic and a rogue.[4]

Another contemporary, the historian Benedetto Varchi (a writer in the pay of the Medici), had the gall to say: 'The bad name that he has is due not only to his licentious life but to a little book called *The Prince*.'[5]

Machiavelli was, as another observer has pointed out, 'made a symbol of wickedness, because he was a great man and because he was unfortunate'.[6] At the other extreme there have been suggestions that Machiavelli's first biographer, Pasquale Villari, did not even like his subject. '[He] admires his protagonist . . .,' remarked a later chronicler, Pistelli, 'but has no affection for him.'[7] Such are the fruits of misinterpretation.

As may be considered fitting, the reputation of Machiavelli and his most famous book was linked closely with changes that took place in the political and religious structure of Europe following his death in 1527. After the sacking of Rome, Clement VII was forced to accede land and powers to the victorious Charles V. Until this time the Catholic Church had not officially recognised the Spanish king as Holy Roman Emperor, but one of the conditions of the truce with Clement was that this oversight was to be amended. As a result, Charles was crowned Emperor by Clement himself in Bologna in 1530.

The Third Republic of Florence did not last long. As soon as Clement had regained his political equilibrium, he wisely did everything he could to remain friends with Charles and made the restoration of Florence to Medici rule one of his primary objectives. After a long, dreadful siege, the Third Republic fell in August 1530 to Spanish troops led by Prince Philbert of Orange, and the Pope installed his nephew, the illegitimate Alessandro de' Medici, as the city's new ruler.

But the greatest changes in Europe in the early sixteenth century came about as a result of the religious ferment precipitated by Martin Luther, the rebellion against Rome of Henry VIII of England, and the Counter-reformation, the ultimately fruitless efforts of the Catholic Church to hold back the tide of revisionism and revolution. Within this new Europe Machiavelli was hated by Catholics because his ideas were considered anti-Christian, and he was loathed by Protestants because they believed that Catholic leaders, in particular the radical Catherine de' Medici, had based their bloody policies on Machiavelli's words. This was an odd conclusion to reach because thirteen years before Catherine de' Medici instigated the killing of more than fifty thousand Protestants in France during the St Bartholomew's Day Massacre of 1572, *The Prince* had been placed on the Index Librorum Prohibitorum (Index of Prohibited Books) by Pope Paul IV.

This is indicative of the bad press *The Prince* has received (and amazingly still receives in some quarters). In 1569, three years before the Medici sanctioned the murder of Protestants in France, the word 'Machiavellian' had appeared in an English dictionary, where it was defined as: 'Practising duplicity in statecraft or in general conduct', and it was from about the last third of the sixteenth century that, for a wide spectrum of people throughout the world, the name 'Machiavelli' became inextricably linked with his ideas. By the time *The Prince* was translated into English, in 1640, poor Niccolò was identified with 'Old Nick', the Devil himself.

Although *The Prince* was not published in England until over a century after Machiavelli's death, it had already been widely circulated in Italian and in Latin. There are two pieces of evidence to support this. First, the concept of Machiavellianism had reached the compilers of the English dictionary some eighty years earlier; and second, the major English writers and dramatists of the late-sixteenth and early-seventeenth centuries made very clear references to Machiavelli and his theories.

Christopher Marlowe was probably the first English dramatist to refer to Machiavelli. In *The Jew of Malta*, written in 1590, he wrote Machiavelli himself into the play and had an actor who took the part deliver a Prologue which begins:

'I am Machiavelli,
And weigh not men, and therefore not men's words.
Admired I am of those that hate me most;
Though some speak openly against my books,
Yet will they read me, and thereby attain
To Peter's chair; and when they cast me off,
Are poisoned by my climbing fellows.
I count religion but a childish toy,
And hold there is no sin but ignorance.'

Interestingly, although by this time Machiavelli's image was tarnished and badly contorted, Marlowe made no clear judgements about him or his ideologies. It is also striking that the playwright understood his opinion of religion and had genuine insight into his personal philosophies: Machiavelli did indeed hold that 'there is no sin but ignorance'.

The dramatist who appeared to have been most interested in Machiavelli was Shakespeare. Not only did he make direct references to Machiavelli in three of his plays, but he based several of his most powerful characters on the idealised prince Machiavelli had portrayed. In addition he employed the concepts of *virtù* and *fortuna*, principles close to Machiavelli's heart and integral to the philosophical infrastructure of his political writing.

For Machiavelli, *virtù* and *fortuna* were not simply influences on the individual, but controlled the very destiny of nations (whether republics or principalities) through the leaders who suffered or triumphed at the hands of these forces. Shakespeare appreciated this fully. One of the best examples of a Machiavellian character in his plays is Fortinbras in *Hamlet*. Like some condottiere of Machiavelli's Italy, the man is led by *virtù*. He campaigns against Denmark and is held back by the political manoeuvring of Claudius. Yet, in spite of such adversity, he carries on regardless, struggling against the Poles, and with *fortuna* on his side he eventually wins through at precisely the right moment to take the Danish crown.

Shakespeare's plays abound with characters who appear to follow Machiavellian principles. We need only think of Richard II, Richard III or indeed Lady Macbeth. But perhaps one of the best examples is the character of the villain Iago in *Othello*, a man who uses the force of his will to overcome all obstacles. When Iago convinces the relatively innocent Roderigo to continue working with him, Roderigo protests: 'What should I do? I confess it is my shame to be so fond; but it is not in my virtue to amend it.' Iago replies:

> 'Virtue! A fig! 'Tis in ourselves that we are thus or thus. Our bodies are our gardens, to which our wills are gardeners; so that if we will plant nettles or sow lettuce, set hyssop and weed up thyme, supply it with one gender of herbs or distract it with many, either to have it sterile with idleness or manured with industry, why, the power and corrigible authority of this lies in our wills. If the balance of our lives had not one scale of reason to poise another of sensuality, the blood and baseness of our natures would conduct us to most preposterous conclusions; but we have reason to cool our raging motions, our carnal stings, our unbitted lusts, whereof I take this that you call love to be a sect or scion.'

Machiavelli might well have written such an exchange himself if he had attempted a serious play after the success of his comedies *Mandragola* and *Clizia*. His influence on Shakespeare is even clearer in the Bard's creation of two of his most powerful characters, Richard II and Richard III. Their scheming and ambition may be compared directly with extracts from *The Prince*. For example, Shakespeare heeded well Machiavelli's advice that 'a prince is always compelled to injure those who have made him the new ruler . . . since [he] cannot satisfy them in the way they had taken for granted'.[8] Into the mouth of Richard II he placed the words:

> *'Northumberland, thou ladder wherewithal*
> *The mounting Bolingbroke ascends my throne,*
> *The time shall not be many hours of age,*
> *More than it is, ere foul sin, gathering head,*
> *Shall break into corruption. Thou shalt think,*
> *Though he divide the realm and give thee half,*
> *It is too little, helping him to all;*
> *He shall think that thou which knowest the way*
> *To plant unrightful kings, wilt know again,*
> *Being ne'er so little urged another way,*
> *To pluck him headlong from the usurped throne.'*[9]

In *Henry VI* Shakespeare modelled the actions of the Duke of Gloucester on Machiavellian principles, this time using Machiavelli's description of how a successful leader and ruler must show versatility and flexibility. Machiavelli wrote: 'He [a prince] should appear to be compassionate, faithful to his word, kind, guile-less, and devout. And indeed he should be so. But his disposition should be such that, if he needs to be the opposite, he knows how . . . And so he should have a flexible disposition, varying as fortune and circumstances dictate.[10] Taking this as his cue, Shakespeare has Gloucester declare:

> *'I'll play the orator as well as Nestor,*
> *Deceive more silly than Ulysses could,*
> *And, like a Sinon, take another Troy.*
> *I can add colours to the chameleon,*
> *Change shapes with Proteus for advantages,*
> *And set the murderous Machiavel to school.*

Can I do this, and cannot get a crown?
Tut, were it farther off, I'll pluck it down.'[11]

We should not be too surprised to see the shadow of Machiavelli cast over so much of Shakespeare's writing, for, as we have seen, he described reality as he saw it. He was a chronicler of human weaknesses and strengths. Shakespeare, the great shepherd of human archetypes, a master at dissecting the human condition, filled his plays with the most human of characters, whether good, evil or merely flawed.

By the seventeenth century Machiavelli's work was beginning to gather advocates as well as vitriol and hatred. The late-seventeenth-century writers James Harrington and Algernon Sidney both came out in support of Machiavelli; Harrington in *Oceana* (1656) and Sidney in his *Discourses Concerning Government* (1698). Then, a generation later, in his *Cato's Letters*, the respected intellectual John Trenchard cast aside the traditional view of Machiavelli. By considering the Italian's other serious works, particularly *The Discourses* and *The Art of War* as well as *The Prince*, Trenchard made his peers realise that there was more to Machiavelli than the misreadings of his most famous work.

For freethinkers like Spinoza, Montaigne and Francis Bacon, men who provided the inspiration for the later founders of the Enlightenment, Machiavelli had exposed what they considered 'first principles' in the analysis of human nature and the society of men. *Virtù*, *fortuna* and, most especially Machiavelli's revelation that, because men are naturally selfish and unprincipled, society will always tend towards corruption and degeneration, rang true to them. No longer fettered by the wishful thinking of the Classical philosophers and partially freed from the confines of religious orthodoxy, many of these revolutionary thinkers saw the honesty and clarity in Machiavelli's writing, qualities that so many before them had either ignored or dismissed.

However, even during the Enlightenment of the late-seventeenth and early-eighteenth centuries there were many who saw Machiavelli's ideas as completely negative and malign. In 1739 Frederick the Great, himself a famous political despot, wrote a disparaging tract entitled *Réfutation du Prince de Machiavel* (sometimes referred to as simply *Antimachiavel*). This, though, was seen, even at the time, as little more than a rather transparent attempt to make his own people believe he was a more liberal leader than he really was. Frederick's views were, for the most part, overshadowed by the intellectual heavyweights of the Enlightenment, who were supportive of many Machiavellian considerations. Locke, Hobbes and Hume all wrote favourably of certain of the author's ideas, and, in keeping with the spirit of their own philosophies, they were much taken with the fact that he had been describing the world as it is rather than how people wished it to be.

Machiavelli would have expected this, for he more than anyone realised the timeless quality of his ideas. Because he addressed human characteristics and portrayed what he had observed, his ideas have not only remained untouched by the advancing centuries but have been constantly requisitioned by successive generations, who tailor them to suit their needs.

Hegel, the champion of the nation state, interpreted Machiavelli's republicanism as a model for his own vision. But Machiavelli would have disagreed with him over a major tenet of his thought. Hegel saw the creation of the nation state as the ultimate achievement of humanity, a blending of the spiritual, the political and the practical. Machiavelli considered humanity too frail for such an idea. Human beings were too mired in self-interest to ever be capable of forming an ideal republic. Machiavelli's nation states or republics were never meant to last for ever.

Francis Bacon, the great advocate of the advancement of science and a believer in the 'conquest of Nature', applied Machiavelli's ideas to his own emerging philosophy. In 1620 he wrote: 'Things are preserved from destruction by bringing them back to their first principles' is a rule in Physics; the same holds good in Politics (as Machiavelli rightly observed), for there is scarcely anything which preserves states from destruction more than the reformation and reduction of them to their ancient manners.'[12]

In their own way the leaders of the French Revolution and the initiators of the English Civil War also applied what Bacon called 'the reformation and reduction . . . to ancient manners' in their struggles against monarchism. Like many others before and after their time, they read Machiavelli in a way that suited them. Karl Marx also cherry-picked from Machiavellian ideology. His goal, the liberation of the working class, may be seen as having its roots in Machiavelli's interest in giving power to the citizenry, a concept he had explained in meticulous detail in *The Discourses*.

There were, however, two fundamental flaws in the way Marx tried to adapt Machiavellianism. First, and most importantly, Machiavelli did not believe that the state should be controlled by the people. His democratic vision was limited and primitive, and had much in keeping with the proto-democratic practices of the time. Sixteenth-century Florence and Venice possessed the most sophisticated political systems ever configured up to that time, but the 'democratic system' of these governments bore little relationship to what we in the twenty-first century call democracy. Both states were ruled by a small elite group who placed in power wealthy, land-owning men from within their own ranks. The people – labourers and farmers, tradesmen and soldiers (and, of course, women) – were all excluded.

In Machiavelli's vision of an ideal government, the people worked *with* the ruler. Civic virtue and civic pride served to keep the community stable. The ruler treated the people fairly but needed to be strong under threat and capable of ruling with an iron fist if circumstances required it. In modern parlance Machiavelli's vision of an ideal state was a form of communitarianism. This vision has been adapted to form the basis of many twenty-first-century societies through the growth of liberal democracy, the political system that evolved from the English parliamentary model. The major difference between Machiavelli's ideal state and the modern democracies of the West today is the level of public participation in government. Machiavelli could never have visualised a system in which every adult was entitled to vote for their leaders and where the leaders relied on the people in order to maintain their political careers.

The other way in which Marx and Machiavelli differed greatly was in the stance each took over the unique value of any one particular political vision. For Marx there was one and only one way in which a state could prosper and remain stable. This required all political power to be placed in the hands of the Proletariat. Machiavelli never claimed that his ideal model was the only way for a state to function successfully. Within his guidelines many styles of government are possible. In this way his thinking was centuries ahead of its time, for today relativism, pragmatism and pluralism are watchwords for the liberal democracy that has (with a few wrong-footings) maintained a stable West for more than half a century.

In recent decades Machiavelli has been commandeered by the leaders of industry, and this has prompted the publication of a growing collection of books applying his philosophy to the commercial world and big business. A quick glance at Amazon.com reveals a slew of titles offering guidance the Machiavelli way. *What Would Machiavelli Do?* (Stanley Bing), *Turning the Tables: A Machiavellian Strategy for Dealing with Japan* (Daniel Burstein), *The Machiavellian Manager's Handbook for Success* (Lynn F. Gunlicks), *Profile of the Entrepreneur, or, Machiavellian Management* (Alan F. Bartlett) and even *Machiavellians: Who They Are and Why They're Out to Get You* (R. Christie).

The success of such titles has led to more lateral applications of Machiavellianism, giving us: *The Machiavellian's Guide to*

Womanising (Nick Casanova), *The Princess: How Daddy's Little Girl Can Survive and Thrive in the Machiavellian New Millennium* (Robert Franklin), and one that, if he had seen it, would surely have been a particular favourite of Machiavelli's: *A Machiavellian Vision of the Ministry: A Guide for Professional Leaders of Voluntary Organisations* (Brandon L. Lovely).

Some of these books are fun and some really may assist the aspiring power broker, but to the biographer they simply reinforce the genius of the man who seeded these works. They illustrate the universality of Machiavelli's thought and the brilliance with which he distilled human characteristics and fundamental motivations. They reiterate the timeless quality of Machiavelli's ideas and the fact that he was dealing with universals, general guidelines that have a million applications.

Far more misguided than efforts to apply Machiavellian ideas to business is the attempt that is sometimes made to point to characters in history, or even to particular events, and claim that these were influenced directly by ideas expressed in *The Prince* or *The Discourses*. Only rarely do such comparisons bear up to more than a superficial probing.

The earliest claim to such a connection came from an English cardinal named Reginald Pole, who, in an essay written in 1538, just eleven years after Machiavelli's death, declared his belief that Henry VIII had been motivated to break with Rome thanks to the ideas contained in *The Prince*. Pole believed that Henry's chancellor, Thomas Cromwell, had read *The Prince* as early as 1529 (before it had even been published officially) and had been so taken with it that he advised the king to read it. It was Machiavelli's book, Pole claimed, that encouraged Henry to hold his ground against Clement VII over his desire to divorce Catherine of Aragon, and emboldened him to call for the dissolution of the monasteries and plant the seeds for the creation of the Anglican Church.

A generation later the French Huguenot Innocent Gentillet

published a hugely popular book called *Contre-Machiavel* in which he placed the blame for the St Bartholomew's Day Massacre squarely on the shoulders of Machiavelli, while the principal instigator of the horror, Catherine de' Medici, was considered almost to have been hypnotised by the Italian's evil words.

Although they make for an interesting parlour game, claims that Hitler, Mussolini, Pol Pot or Stalin were inspired to do the things for which they became infamous because they were influenced by *The Prince* are equally misguided. It is true that Napoleon once declared that '*The Prince* is the only book worth reading' and is said to have kept a copy under his pillow; but, the fact is, all tyrants acquainted with Machiavelli were tyrants first and readers of *The Prince* second. It must always be remembered that Machiavelli was describing what he had observed during many years of political service and combined this with his exceptional knowledge of Classical history. It is ridiculous to turn this around and to suggest that any powerful political figure was ever more than superficially influenced by reading *The Prince*. None of them has been influenced by Machiavelli any more than they have been inspired by their individual knowledge of world history and the behaviour of long-dead radical leaders. To see the truth of this, we need only consider the fact that Machiavellian tactics are no more prevalent today than they were during his lifetime or during the long, sordid pageant of human life before Machiavelli was born.

What is undeniable is that Machiavelli has had a huge influence on political science and the analysis of human social history. Without delving too deeply into this matter, it is possible to see how Machiavelli's work offers two valuable tools for our understanding of the world. First, armed with a knowledge of the author's philosophy, we may observe (just as he did), particular Machiavellian moves and strategies as they are played out by figures on the world stage. Second, unlike modern political theories, Machiavelli's political philosophy has an ally in history. We can see the ebb and flow of society, the evolutionary current of civilisation, and we may note how, during the course of five hundred years, trends have always followed Machiavellian rules.

One way to illustrate this is to turn *The Prince* and *The Discourses* inside out. What I mean by this is that Machiavelli constructed his books on direct experience and years of study. From these he was able to distil general rules. These principles are universals, and, as I have said, it is puerile to suggest that any statesman or business leader learns from Machiavelli as if they had never imagined a Machiavellian move before reading his words. But, *after the event*, and employing a process that is no less scientific than observing the behaviour of subatomic particles in a cloud chamber or bacteria under the microscope, we may see how these people have behaved as prescribed by Machiavellian rules.

There are seven clear Machiavellian rules we may consider:

1. *History is written by the winners*. This, like all lessons drawn from Machiavelli, may be illustrated with enough examples to fill a library, but in recent times one of the best is the United States presidential election in 2000. George W. Bush's victory is widely perceived to have been secured on contentious legal grounds, and many believed and still believe, that he should never have reached the White House. However, after the event, after Bush had been inaugurated as the forty-third president, the way he got there had become completely irrelevant. Those who oppose Bush would argue that the way he came to power is not an irrelevance and some will go to their graves insisting that the Democrats were robbed or that the wishes of the majority of American people were ignored, that democracy failed. But such protests mean nothing. History is written by the winners.

2. *People can never be trusted*. This is an axiom many apply in their daily lives, but it is also a guiding principle for the politician and the business icon. Secrecy and spying date back to the origins of civil-isation. In order to preserve the stability of a nation state, leaders

cannot afford the luxury of trusting others. It is for this reason that the concept of the treaty was created. But as civilisation has become more sophisticated, so too have the controls placed on agreements and treaties. The engendering of trust and the maintenance of some form of political honesty between governments were among the original purposes of the League of Nations, and its successor the United Nations. Such organisations are, of course, only partially successful.

3. *A successful leader must be both a lion and a fox.* Some leaders hide this plurality of character remarkably well, others less so. Adolf Hitler was a lion who used his military forces to crush and over-whelm his enemies, but he was also a fox in the way he manipulated his own party and the German people. Margaret Thatcher's handling of the Falklands War of 1982 is a perfect illustration of how a leader needs to use force and cunning. Controversy still hangs over the sinking of the Argentinian ship the *Belgrano* (the act that pushed Britain and Argentina into war). However, many believe that the British leader ordered the attack knowing British forces would prevail in any military conflict and that a victory would secure her a second term as Prime Minister, turning round her low poll rating at home. If this is true, it was a brilliant act of cunning.

4. *A leader must have luck on his or her side, and must be prepared to make the most of it.* Machiavelli illustrated this perfectly with the example of Cesare Borgia, who was destroyed by the unexpected death of his father. Although Cesare had been careful to prepare for almost any eventuality, in 1503 he was assailed by more misfortune than even he could handle. In modern times a great example of a leader having fortune on his side and capitalising on it is provided by the retreat from Dunkirk in the summer of 1940. British and French troops were trapped by Hitler's occupation force in the north-west corner of France. Instead of going in for the kill, Hitler held back. This allowed Churchill to carry out his radical evacuation plan and save the British and French armies.

5. *There are times when a society relies entirely on the actions of a strong leader*. This has been shown to be true on many occasions. Dangerous times often push great leaders to the fore and give rare individuals a chance to grasp the opportunity to become princes and guide their nation through an emergency. Winston Churchill is a great modern example of such a prince, whose personal role was crucial to the survival of Great Britain in 1940.

6. *Always maintain a strong military and always use your own people as soldiers*. Again, this general rule has been proven irrefutably true throughout history. When a nation attacks another purely in pursuit of expansionist goals or as a pre-emptive move, the forces must be well trained and experienced, but, crucially, they must be well looked after. Unless a military force is fighting for its life or for the freedom of the nation, they need other reasons to fight. This may come from rigorous discipline, indoctrination or because of financial incentive; few soldiers fight simply for ideology. Similarly, when defending against an attack from an enemy, if the defensive force is made up of citizens of the nation under attack they will defend the state with far greater energy and urgency than would a mercenary force. This is especially true if the citizenry believe in their leaders and the state was stable and the people happy before the war began.

7. *A nation has to be united to remain strong*. Any nation that is internally unstable will be at a grave disadvantage during times of war and will not reap the greatest benefits from periods of peace and prosperity. Machiavelli considered nothing more important than continued national stability. Today it is clear to see that the wealthiest and most successful nations on earth are those that have the most stable political systems. Nations torn apart by tribal conflict or ethnic intolerance cannot hope to compete with stable nations and they fall further behind very rapidly.

Machiavelli did not live to see a unified Italy, the dream that had acted as the spur for his most widely read book. Indeed Italy was not united and independent until the Risorgimento of 1871, created under the guidance of the republican patriots Mazzini and Garibaldi. Nevertheless, Machiavelli's ideas were crucial to the evolution of other nations. The most significant example is the creation of the American constitution. Taking as their starting point Machiavelli's insistence that all human beings act selfishly and are motivated primarily by self-interest, the founding fathers realised the importance of producing a mixed constitution in which neither a relatively small number of wealthy patricians nor a large number of plebeians could dominate. In this way the constitution has acted as a brake on forces that naturally pull in different directions and this has helped to steer America away from either fascism or communism.

One of the founding fathers of America, Alexander Hamilton, expressed it well when, in a pamphlet written in 1775, he quoted the Scottish philosopher David Hume: 'Political writers [most especially Machiavelli] have established it as a maxim, that, in contriving any system of government, and fixing the several checks and controls of the constitution, every man ought to be supposed a knave; and to have no other end in all his actions, but private interest.'[13]

Machiavelli's description of an ideal state and the application of rules necessary to create and sustain it were meant for his homeland, his beloved Italy. But the fact that his analysis has held true for half a millennium and successfully described the way many societies have evolved has led some to consider him a prophet. The first to suggest such a thing was his friend Filippo da Casavecchia, who declared that Machiavelli was 'the greatest prophet that the Jews or any other generation ever had'.

However, I believe that Machiavelli himself, although perhaps flattered by Casavecchia's words, would not have considered himself in this light at all. Indeed it seems to me that such a misconception about the true nature of Machiavelli's work lies at the very root of why his name has been so maligned through the centuries. Machiavelli did not invent Machiavellianism, he observed it, and as long as humans are humans they will behave in the way Machiavelli described. As one modern historian has put it: 'If modern Machiavellism should be questioned, as indeed it should, the questioning must begin with modernity itself. For one thing should be clear by now: by attacking Machiavelli one cannot save the world from the Machiavellism of modernity.'[14]

So, having dissected the legacy of Machiavelli's work and ideas, what may we conclude about Machiavelli the man?

It is my assertion that Machiavelli was a remarkably honest man. To the casual observer this may seem a ridiculous notion; we are, after all, talking about a man who was unfaithful to his wife, worked for the enemies of the regime he had once served and wrote of the merits of duplicity. I will not repeat the explanations for each of these apparent anomalies, but I will reaffirm my conviction that Machiavelli was honest, for he practised the most important form of honesty: he was honest to himself.

Machiavelli was flawed, and he knew it. He loved women and could never remain faithful to Marietta, whom he cared for and for whom he did his best. His was an independent soul, he was a poet first, a diplomat second, he was the very embodiment of the humanist ideal. He did not believe in an orthodox God and he had no respect whatsoever for orthodox religion; indeed he perceived it as a cancer.

It was, then, almost inevitable that such a man would formulate the tenets for which he has become famous. His experience and education, along with his belief in the total freedom of the intellect, added flesh to a vision of humanity that was very clearly a reflection of himself, warts and all. Central to his philosophy was the concept that we only have one life, that we should enjoy ourselves, that there is no afterlife, no heaven and no hell, only the material world.

Machiavelli might well have imagined that his work would find resonance in the generations that followed his. During his lifetime he gained almost no recognition for his brilliance, and perhaps, as he lay dying, his only hope came from a conviction that his ideas would one day lead to a better Italy and a better world. It is therefore supremely ironic that posterity has painted an image of Machiavelli that is at once inaccurate and unjustified. I like to think, though, that if he could have known what the future would make of his name, Niccolò Machiavelli might have simply shrugged his shoulders and offered a knowing smile, for he knew the ways of the world.

Appendix I

The Principal Works of Machiavelli

Dates refer to period of composition.

Political and military analysis

Discorso sopra le cose di Pisa (1499)

Del modo di trattare i popoli della Valdichiana ribellati (1502)

Del modo tenuto dal duca Valentino nell'ammazzare Vitellozzo Vitelli, etc. (*Description of the Method Used by Duke Valentino to Kill Vitellozzo Vitelli, etc.*) (1502)

Discorso sopra la provisione del danaro (1502)

Discorso dell' ordinaire lo Stato di Firenze alle Armi (1506)

Rapporto delle cose dell'Alemagna (1508)

Il decennale secondo (1509)

Ritratti delle cose di Francia (1510)

Discorsi sopra la prima deca di T. Livio (*Discourses on the First Ten Books of Livy*), 3 vols. (1513–18)

Il Principe (*The Prince*) (1513–14)

Dell'arte della guerra (*The Art of War*) (1518–20)

Discorso sopra il riformare lo stato di Firenze (1520)

Sommario delle cose della città di Lucca (1520)

Frammenti storici (1525)

Provvisione per la Istituzione dell'Ufficio de' cinque Provveditori della Mura della Città di Firenze (Provision for the Creation of the Office of Five Superintendents for the Walls of the City of Florence) (1526)

History

Vita di Castruccio Castracani da Lucca (*The Life of Castruccio Castracani of Lucca*) (1520)

Istorie fiorentine (*Florentine Histories*), 8 vols. (1521–5)

Poems, plays and other fiction

Il decennale primo (*The First Decennial*) (poem in terza rima, 1504)

Andria (comedy translated from Terence, 1513)

Mandragola (*The Mandrake*) (prose comedy in five acts, with prologue in verse, 1513 or 1514)

L'Asino (*The Ass*) (poem in terza rima, 1517)

Belfagor arcidiavolo (*The Devil Who Took a Wife*) (novella, *c.* 1517)

Clizia (comedy in prose, 1524)

Appendix II

The Life and Times of Machiavelli

***c.*1440**: Printing with movable type is invented. Florence has its first printing press in 1471.

1452: Leonardo da Vinci is born in Florence.

1469, 3 May: Niccolò Machiavelli is born in Florence, the son of Bernardo Machiavelli and Bartolomea di Stefano Nelli.

1475: Cesare Borgia is born.

1469–92: Lorenzo de' Medici (Lorenzo the Magnificent) is *de facto* ruler of Florence.

1492: Columbus discovers the New World.

1494: King Charles VIII of France invades northern Italy.

1494–8: Theocracy of Savonarola in Florence.

1496: Machiavelli's mother dies.

1498: Machiavelli becomes Secretary to the Second Chancery in Florence.

1499: Machiavelli is sent to Forlì to negotiate with Catherine Sforza.

1500: Machiavelli's father dies.

1500: First legation is sent to the French court, where Machiavelli meets King Louis XII and the Cardinal of Rouen, Georges d'Amboise.

1502: Machiavelli marries Marietta Corsini and meets Cesare Borgia for the first time.

1502, Summer: Machiavelli's first child, Primerana, is born.

1502, Summer: Piero Soderini is made 'gonfalonier for life'.

1503, January: Machiavelli returns to Florence.

1503, August: Pope Alexander VI dies.

1503, October–December: Machiavelli is in Rome to witness the fall from power of Cesare Borgia and the ascension to the papacy of Julius II.

1504: Second legation is sent to France.

1506: Machiavelli establishes the first citizens' army in Florence in two hundred years.

1507: Cesare Borgia dies.

1508: Machiavellli is sent to the court of the Emperor Maximilian I.

1509: Pope Julius II creates the League of Cambrai to attack Venice.

1510: Third legation is sent to France.

1511: Pope Julius II creates the Holy League to fight against France.

1512: The French are forced out of Italy. The Medici, assisted by a Spanish army, return to power in Florence. Piero Soderini is deposed and Machiavelli is dismissed from office. He retires to his country estate at Sant'Andrea.

1513, February: Machiavelli is tortured and imprisoned by the Medici, but released on 12 March on the election of Giovanni de' Medici as Pope Leo X.

1513–14: Machiavelli writes *The Prince*.

1515: Francis I of France takes the throne.

1513–18: Machiavelli writes *Discourses on the First Ten Books of Livy*.

1515: Machiavelli writes *Mandragola*.

1518, Summer: *Mandragola* is performed for the first time in Florence.

1519: Leonardo da Vinci dies.

1520, July: Machiavelli is offered the commission to write *Florentine Histories*.

1521: *The Art of War* is published.

1521: First war between France and Spain on Italian soil. Emperor Charles V of Spain takes Milanese territory from the French.

1521: Pope Leo X dies and is succeeded by Adrian VI (Adrian Boyers).

1523: Pope Adrian VI dies and is succeeded by Clement VII (Giulio de' Medici).

1524: Francis I of France retakes Milan.

1524: Machiavelli meets and falls in love with Barbara Salutati Raffacani, an actress.

1525, January: *Clizia* is performed for the first time.

1525: Machiavelli is fully rehabilitated by the Medici and returns to political life. From April 1525 to May 1527 he acts as military adviser for Florence.

1527, May: Rome is sacked by the troops of Charles V. Machiavelli witnesses the devastation.

1527 May–June: Machiavelli is viewed with suspicion by the new republican government of Florence and passed over by the new rulers.

1527, 21 June: Machiavelli dies at Sant'Andrea.

References

Introduction: A Man Misunderstood

1 Niccolò Machiavelli, *Discourses on Titus Livy*, ed. Bernard Crick, Penguin, 1970, Book 3.

Chapter 1: Love, Not Money

1 Niccolò Machiavelli to Francesco Guicciardini, 19 May 1521, *Machiavelli and His Friends: Their Personal Correspondence*, trans. and ed. James B. Atkinson and David Sices, Northern Illinois University Press, De Kalb, Illinois, 1996, p.341.

2 Niccolò Machiavelli to Francesco Guicciardini, 17 May 1521, ibid., p.336.

3 Francesco Guicciardini to Niccolò Machiavelli, 18 May 1521, ibid., p.338.

4 Niccolò Machiavelli to Francesco Vettori, 18 March 1513, ibid., p.223.

5 The baptismal archives of Santa Maria del Fiore, *Libri dei Battesimi*, state that Niccolò Piero Michele, son of Messer Bernardo Machiavelli, was born at 4 p.m. on 3 May and christened on the 4th.

6 Archivo di Stato, Florence, Gonfalone Nicchio, 1480, f.128.

7 *Libro di Ricordi di Bernardo Machiavelli*, ed. Cesare Olschki, Le Monnier, Florence, 1954. The original is now housed in the Biblioteca Riccardiana, Florence.

8 Catherine Atkinson, *Debts, Dowries and Donkeys: The Diary of Niccolò Machiavelli's Father, Messer Bernardo, in Quattrocentro Florence*, Peter Lang, Berlin, 2002, p.69.

9 Giovan Battista Nelli, *Discorsi di Architettura del Senatore*, Florence, 1753, p.8.

Chapter 2: Machiavelli's Europe

1 Nicolai Rubenstein, 'Cradle of the Renaissance', in *The Age of the Renaissance*, ed. Denys Hay, McGraw Hill, New York, 1994, p.12.

2 Translation of the German text of the *Oratio*, in 'Die Kultur des Humanismus', Reden et al., Mout, Munich, 1998, p.46.

3 Pico dell Mirandola, 'Oration on the Dignity of Man', cited in Roger Masters, *Fortune Is a River: Leonardo da Vinci and Niccolò Machiavelli's*

Magnificent Dream to Change the Course of Florentine History, Plume, New York, 1999, p.19.

4 Niccolò Machiavelli, *Florentine Histories*, ed. Laura Banfield and Harvey Mansfield, Princeton University Press, 1990, Chapter VII, p.6.

5 Ibid., Chapter VIII, p.36.

6 Niccolò Machiavelli, *Discourses on Titus Livy*, ed. Bernard Crick, Penguin, 1970, p.413.

7 *Florentine Histories*, Chapter VIII, p.9.

8 'Cradle of the Renaissance', p.18.

Chapter 3: In at the Deep End

1 Niccolò Machiavelli to Ricciardo Becchi, Florence, 9 March 1498, *Machiavelli and His Friends: Their Personal Correspondence*, trans. and ed. James B. Atkinson and David Sices, Northern Illinois University Press, De Kalb, Illinois, 1996, p.8.

2 Niccolò Machiavelli, *The Prince*, Chapter VI, p.52.

3 Mario Martelli, 'Preistoria (medicea) di Machiavelli', *Studi di filologia italiana*, vol. 29, 1971, pp.377–405.

4 Niccolò Machiavelli to unknown figure, 1 December 1497, *Machiavelli and His Friends: Their Personal Correspondence*, p.7.

5 Pasquale Villari, *The Life and Times of Niccolo Machiavelli*, Scholarly Publications, Houston, Texas, 1972, p.34.

6 Niccolò Machiavelli, *Le Opere*, 6 vols., 1873–7, Vol. II, ed. P. Fanfani and G. Milanesi, Florence, 1873, p.127.

7 See Roberto Ridolfi, *The Life of Niccolò Machiavelli*, trans. Cecil Grayson, Routledge and Kegan Paul, London, 1954, p.29.

8 Letter from Niccolò Machiavelli to an anonymous Chancery Secretary in Lucca, Florence, early October 1499, in Niccolò Machiavelli, *Tutte le opere storiche e letterarie*, ed. Guido Mazzoni and Mario Casella, G. Barbera, Florence, 1929, p.787ff.

9 Ibid.

10 Quoted in Maurizio Viroli, *Niccolò's Smile*, Farrar, Straus and Giroux, New York, 2000, p.42.

11 Niccolò Machiavelli, *The Prince*, Chapter XII.

12 *Le Opere*, Vol. I, ed. P. Fanfani and L. Passerini, p.LX.

13 Ibid., Vol. III, ed. L. Passerini and G. Milanesi, p.91ff.

14 Ibid., p.201.

Chapter 4: Running with the Devil

1 Niccolò Machiavelli, *The Prince*, Chapter III.

2 Ibid.

3 Agostino Vespucci to Niccolò Machiavelli, 14 March 1506, *Machiavelli and His Friends: Their Personal Correspondence*, trans. and ed. James B. Atkinson

and David Sices, Northern Illinois University Press, De Kalb, Illinois, 1996, p.121.

4 Agostino Vespucci to Niccolò Machiavelli, 25 August 1501, ibid., p.40.

5 Luca Ugolini to Niccolò Machiavelli, Florence, 11 November 1503, *Machiavelli and His Friends: Their Personal Correspondence*, p.87.

6 Johannes Burckhard, *Liber Notarum ab anno MCCCCLXXXIII usque ad annum MDVI*, Collezione Rer. Ital. Script., Città di Catello.

7 *The New Advent Encyclopaedia of Catholic History* website: http://www.newa vent.org/cathen/01289a.htm

8 Niccolò Machiavelli, *The Prince*, Chapter XVIII.

9 Agostino Vespucci to Niccolò Machiavelli, Rome, 16 July 1501, *Machiavelli and His Friends: Their Personal Correspondence*, p.38.

10 For example, letter of 25 August 1501 from Vespucci to Machiavelli. Quoted in above, p.41.

11 *Liber Notarum ab anno MCCCCLXXXIII usque ad annum MDVI*.

12 Quoted in Giuseppe Portigliotti, *The Borgias*, trans. Bernard Miall, George Allen and Unwin Ltd, London, 1928, p.192.

13 Quoted in Roger Masters, *Fortune Is a River: Leonardo da Vinci and Niccolò Machiavelli's Magnificent Dream to Change the Course of Florentine History*, Plume, New York, 1999, p.76.

14 Niccolò Machiavelli, *Le Opere*, 6 vols., 1873–7, Vol. IV, ed. L. Passerini and G. Milanesi, Cenniniani, Florence, 1874, p.4ff.

15 Letter signed by Soderini but written in Machiavelli's hand and dated 26 June 1502. Niccolò Machiavelli, *Le Opere*, Vol. IV, pp.8–15.

16 Quoted in *Letters of Francesco Guicciardini*, 10 vols., ed. Counts Piero and Luigi Guicciardini, Florence, 1857–67, Vol. II, p.43.

17 Niccolò Machiavelli, *Legazioni e Commissarie*, 3 vols., ed. Sergio Bertelli, Feltrinelli, Milan, 1964, Vol. I, p.345.

18 Agostino Vespucci to Niccolò Machiavelli, 14 October 1502, *Machiavelli and His Friends: Their Personal Correspondence*, p.48.

19 Biagio Buonaccorsi to Niccolò Machiavelli, Florence, 26 November 1502, *Machiavelli and His Friends: Their Personal Correspondence*, p.73.

20 Biagio Buonaccorsi to Niccolò Machiavelli, Florence, 21 December 1502, ibid., p.78.

21 Biagio Buonaccorsi to Niccolò Machiavelli, Florence, 22 December 1502, ibid., p.79.

22 Niccolò Machiavelli to the Signoria, 1 and 3 November 1502, 'Legazioni al Duca Valentino', Niccolò Machiavelli, *Chief Works*, trans. Allan Gilbert, Duke University Press, Durham, North Carolina, 1965.

23 Ibid., p.77.

24 Piero Soderini to Niccolò Machiavelli, 22 December 1502, *Lettere familiari*, p.96.

25 Niccolò Machiavelli to the Ten of War, 26 December 1502, Niccolò Machiavelli, *Le Opere*, Vol. IV, p.241ff.

26 Niccolò Machiavelli, *The Prince*, Chapter VII.
27 Ibid., p.253ff. Letter from Niccolò Machiavelli to the Ten of War, 31 December 1502.
28 Niccolò Machiavelli to the Ten of War, 30 October 1503, *Le Opere*, Vol. IV, p.312.
29 Niccolò Machiavelli, *The Prince*, Chapter VII.
30 Ibid., 4 November 1503, p.326ff.
31 Ibid., 30 November 1503, p.424ff.
32 Quoted in Portigliotti, *The Borgias*, p.206.
33 Niccolò Machiavelli to the Ten of War, 28 November 1503, *Le Opere*, Vol. IV, p.437ff.
34 Ibid., 26 November 1503, p.436.
35 Dispatch from Julius II dated 1 December 1503, quoted in Portigliotti, *The Borgias*, p.208.

Chapter 5: Machiavelli's *Cause Célèbre*

1 Francesco Guicciardini, 'Storie Fiorentine', ed. R. Palmarocchi, in *Scrittori d'Italia, Opere di Francesco Guicciardini*, Bari, Laterza, 1931, Vol. VI, p.251.
2 *Machiavelli and His Friends: Their Personal Correspondence*, trans. and ed. James B. Atkinson and David Sices, Northern Illinois University Press, De Kalb, Illinois, 1996, p.58 *et passim*.
3 Piero Soderini to Niccolò Machiavelli, 14 November 1502, ibid., pp.68–9.
4 Niccolò Machiavelli, *The Prince*, Chapter IX.
5 Niccolò Machiavelli, *Le Opere*, Vol. 1, ed. Corrado Vivanti, Einaudi-Gallimard, Turin, 1997, p.15.
6 Ibid., p.16.
7 Ibid., p.15.
8 Francesco Soderini to Niccolò Machiavelli, 29 May 1504, Niccolò Machiavelli, *Lettere familiari*, ed. Edoardo Alvisi, Sansoni, Florence, 1883, p.115.
9 Francesco Soderini to Niccolò Machiavelli, 29 May 1504, *Machiavelli and His Friends: Their Personal Correspondence*, p.101.
10 Quoted by Francesco Guicciardini, *Storie Fiorentine dal 1378 al 1509*, ed. Roberto Palmarocchi, Laterza, Bari, 1933, p.897.
11 Biagio Buonaccorsi, *Summario*, trans. Francesca Roselli, quoted in Roger Masters, *Machiavelli, Leonardo and the Science of Power*, University of Notre Dame Press, Notre Dame, Indiana, 1998.
12 Ercole Bentivoglio to Niccolò Machiavelli, 25 February 1506, *Machiavelli and His Friends: Their Personal Correspondence*, p.119.
13 Francesco Guicciardini, *Storia d'Italia*, ed. Emanuella Scarano, Unione Tipografico-Editrice Torinese, Turin, 1981, Book VI, p.11.
14 Francesco Soderini to Niccolò Machiavelli, 26 October 1504, *Machiavelli and His Friends: Their Personal Correspondence*, pp.106–7.

15 Niccolò Machiavelli, *Discourses on Titus Livy*, ed. Bernard Crick, Penguin, 1970, Book I, p.53.

16 Leonardo da Vinci, *Codex Atlanticus*, Ambrosiana Library, Milan, 45r.

17 Ibid, 284r.

18 Niccolò Machiavelli, *Le Opere*, 6 vols., 1873–7, Vol. V, ed. L. Passerini and G. Milanesi, Cenniniani, Florence, 1876, p.142ff.

19 Letter from Leonardo Bartolini to Niccolò Machiavelli, 21 February 1506, *Machiavelli and His Friends: Their Personal Correspondence*, p.118.

20 Francesco Soderini to Niccolò Machiavelli, 4 March 1506, ibid., p.120.

21 Luca Landucci, *A Florentine Diary from 1450–1516 (Continued by an Anonymous Writer Till 1542)* with notes by Iodoco del Badia, trans. Alice de Rosen Jervis, J.M. Dent, London, 1927, p.218.

Chapter 6: Travels with a Papal Warlord

1 Instructions from the Signoria to Machiavelli, 25 August 1506, in Niccolò Machiavelli, *Le Opere*, 6 vols., 1873–7, Vol. V, ed. L. Passerini and G. Milanesi, Cenniniani, Florence, 1876, p.154ff.

2 Niccolò Machiavelli to the Ten of War, 28 August, ibid.

3 Niccolò Machiavelli to the Ten of War, 13 September 1506, *Le Opere*, Vol. V, p.184ff.

4 Niccolò Machiavelli, *Discourses on Titus Livy*, ed. Bernard Crick, Penguin, 1970, Book I, p.27.

5 Niccolò Machiavelli to the Ten of War, 3 October 1506, Niccolò Machiavelli, *Le Opere*, Vol. V, p.210ff.

6 Niccolò Machiavelli, *The Prince*, Chapter XI.

7 Niccolò Machiavelli to Giovan Battista Soderini, 28 September 1506, *Machiavelli and His Friends: Their Personal Correspondence*, trans. and ed. James B. Atkinson and David Sices, Northern Illinois University Press, De Kalb, Illinois, 1996, p.134.

8 Niccolò Machiavelli, *Discourses*, Book I, p.27.

9 Niccolò Machiavelli to the Ten of War, 5 October 1506, Niccolò Machiavelli, *Le Opere*, Vol. V, p.215ff.

10 Biagio Buonaccorsi to Niccolò Machiavelli, 1 September 1506, *Machiavelli and His Friends: Their Personal Correspondence*, p.127.

11 Biagio Buonaccorsi to Niccolò Machiavelli, 6 October 1506, ibid., p.141. 6 October 1506.

12 Alamanno Salviati to Niccolò Machiavelli, 13 November 1502, Pasquale Villari, *Niccolò Machiavelli e i suoi tempi illustrati con nuovi documenti*, 3 vols., Le Monnier, Florence, 1877–82, Vol. II, p.608n.

13 Niccolò Machiavelli to Luigi Guicciardini, 8 December 1509, Niccolò Machiavelli, *Le Opere*, Vol. 3, ed. Franco Gaeta, Unione Tipografico-Editrice Torinese, Turin, 1984. It is quite likely that this story was a complete fiction, or at least a great exaggeration, a playful story for his friends.

14 Niccolò Machiavelli to Francesco Vettori, 4 February 1514, *Machiavelli and His Friends: Their Personal Correspondence*, p.278.

15 Niccolò Machiavelli, *Mandragola*, opening song.

16 Giovan Battista Soderini to Niccolò Machiavelli, 26 September 1506, *Machiavelli and His Friends: Their Personal Correspondence*, p.137.

17 Biagio Buonaccorsi to Niccolò Machiavelli, 6 October 1506, ibid., p.140.

18 Francesco Soderini to Niccolò Machiavelli, 15 December 1506, Niccolò Machiavelli, *Le Opere*, Vol. V, p.161ff.

Chapter 7: The Rough with the Smooth

1 Niccolò Machiavelli, *The Prince*, Chapter XXIII.

2 Francesco Guicciardini, *The History of Florence*, trans. Mario Domandi, Torchbooks, Harper, New York, 1970, p.271.

3 Alessandro Nasi to Niccolò Machiavelli, 30 July 1507, Niccolò Machiavelli, *Lettere familiari*, ed. Edoardo Alvisi, Sansoni, Florence, 1883, p.169.

4 Niccolò Machiavelli, *The Prince*, Chapter X.

5 Letter of 23 February 1508, Machiavelli, *Le Opere*, 6 vols., 1873–7, Vol. V, ed. L. Passerini and G. Milanesi, Cenniniani, Florence, 1876, p.289ff.

6 Niccolò Machiavelli, *Legazioni e Commissarie*, 3 vols., ed. Sergio Bertelli, Feltrinelli, Milan, 1964, Vol. I, pp.400–1.

7 The Ten to Niccolò Machiavelli, 15 February 1509, *Le Opere*, Vol. V, p.347ff.

8 Alamanno Salviati to Niccolò Machiavelli, 29 April 1506, ibid., p.409.

9 Agostino Vespucci to Niccolò Machiavelli, 8 June 1509, *Machiavelli and His Friends: Their Personal Correspondence*, trans. and ed. James B. Atkinson and David Sices, Northern Illinois University Press, De Kalb, Illinois, 1996, p.180.

10 Filippo Casavecchia to Niccolò Machiavelli, 17 June 1509, ibid., p.181.

11 For more on this see Robert Black, 'Machiavelli, Servant of the Florentine Republic', in *Machiavelli and Republicanism*, ed. Gisela Bock, Quentin Skinner and Maurizio Viroli, Cambridge University Press, 1990, p.98.

12 Alamanno Salviati to Niccolò Machiavelli, 4 October 1509, *Machiavelli and His Friends: Their Personal Correspondence*, p.186.

13 Niccolò Machiavelli, *The Prince*, Chapter II.

14 'Report on the State of Germany', 17 June 1508, in *Le Opere*, Vol. V, pp.313–22.

15 Biagio Buonaccorsi to Niccolò Machiavelli, 28 December 1509, *Machiavelli and His Friends: Their Personal Correspondence*, pp.192–3.

Chapter 8: Trapped

1 Niccolò Machiavelli to the Ten of War, 18 August 1510, Machiavelli, *Le Opere*, 6 vols., 1873–7, Vol. VI, ed. L. Passerini and G. Milanesi, Cenniniani, Florence, 1877, p.69.

2 Francesco Guicciardini, *The History of Florence*, trans. Mario Domandi, Torchbooks, Harper, New York, 1970, p.54.

3 Niccolò Machiavelli, *The Prince*, Chapter XXV.
4 Francesco Vettori to Niccolò Machiavelli, 3 August 1510, *Machiavelli and His Friends: Their Personal Correspondence*, trans. and ed. James B. Atkinson and David Sices, Northern Illinois University Press, De Kalb, Illinois, 1996, p.199.
5 Niccolò Machiavelli, *Legazioni e Commissarie*, 3 vols., ed. Sergio Bertelli, Feltrinelli, Milan, 1964, Vol. III, p.1228.
6 The Ten to Niccolò Machiavelli, 2 September 1510, *Le Opere*, Vol. VI, p.107.
7 Niccolò Machiavelli, *Legazioni e Commissarie*, Vol. III, pp.1227–8.
8 Ibid., p.1258.
9 Francesco Guicciardini, *Storia d'Italia*, ed. Emanuella Scarano, Unione Tipografico-Editrice Torinese, Turin, 1981, Book X, p.14.
10 Luca Landucci, *A Florentine Diary from 1450–1516 (Continued by an Anonymous Writer Till 1542)* with notes by Iodoco del Badia, trans. Alice de Rosen Jervis, J.M. Dent, London, 1927, p.249.
11 Niccolò Machiavelli to an unknown noblewoman, after 16 September 1512, *Machiavelli and His Friends: Their Personal Correspondence*, pp.214–16. This appears in a letter from Machiavelli to an unknown noblewoman. The identity of the recipient has long puzzled historians and there is no clear evidence to say who the noblewoman might have been. The most likely recipient is Isabelle d'Este of Mantua, sister-in-law of the former Duke of Milan, Ludovico Sforza.
12 Niccolò Machiavelli, *Lettere familiari*, ed. Edoardo Alvisi, Sansoni, Florence, 1883, p.212.
13 Niccolò Machiavelli to an unknown noblewoman, after 16 September 1512, *Machiavelli and His Friends: Their Personal Correspondence*, pp.214–16.
14 Niccolò Machiavelli, *Discourses on Titus Livy*, ed. Bernard Crick, Penguin, 1970, Book II, p.27.
15 Ibid., Book III, p.3.
16 Niccolò Machiavelli to an unknown noblewoman, after 16 September 1512, *Machiavelli and His Friends: Their Personal Correspondence*, pp.214–16.
17 Niccolò Machiavelli to Giovanni de' Medici, 29 September 1512, *Machiavelli and His Friends: Their Personal Correspondence*, Letter D, p.424.
18 Niccolò Machiavelli, *Le Opere*, Vol. I, p.XXXIIIff.
19 Quoted in Pasquale Villari, *Niccolò Machiavelli e i suoi tempi illustrati con nuovi documenti*, 3 vols., Le Monnier, Florence, 1877–82, Vol. I, p.648.
20 Niccolò Machiavelli, *Tutte le opere storiche e letterarie*, ed. Guido Mazzoni and Mario Casella, G. Barbera, Florence, 1929, pp.871–2.
21 Ibid., p.872.
22 Niccolò Machiavelli to Francesco Vettori, 18 March 1513, *Machiavelli and His Friends: Their Personal Correspondence*, p.222.

Chapter 9: Exile

1 Niccolò Machiavelli to Francesco Vettori, 18 March 1513, *Machiavelli and His Friends: Their Personal Correspondence*, trans. and ed. James B. Atkinson

and David Sices, Northern Illinois University Press, De Kalb, Illinois, 1996, p.223.

2　Niccolò Machiavelli to Francesco Vettori, 30 March 1513, ibid., p.224.

3　Niccolò Machiavelli to Francesco Vettori, 10 December 1513. Niccolò Machiavelli, *Tutte le opere storiche e letterarie*, ed. Guido Mazzoni and Mario Casella, G. Barbera, Florence, 1929, p.884ff.

4　Niccolò Machiavelli to Francesco Vettori, Niccolò Machiavelli, *Lettere familiari*, ed. Edoardo Alvisi, Sansoni, Florence, 1883, p.241.

5　Niccolò Machiavelli to Giovanni Vernacci, 4 August 1513, *Machiavelli and His Friends: Their Personal Correspondence*, p.244.

6　Francesco Vettori to Niccolò Machiavelli, 18 January 1514, Niccolò Machiavelli, *Lettere familiari*, p.323.

7　Niccolò Machiavelli to Francesco Vettori, 10 December 1513. Niccolò Machiavelli, *Tutte le opere storiche e letterarie*, p.884ff.

8　Dante, *Paradise*, Canto XVII, pp.55–60.

9　Niccolò Machiavelli to Francesco Vettori, 19 December 1513, Niccolò Machiavelli, *Lettere familiari*, p.311.

10　Niccolò Machiavelli, *The Prince*, Chapter VI.

11　Niccolò Machiavelli to Francesco Vettori, 10 June 1514, *Machiavelli and His Friends: Their Personal Correspondence*, p.290.

12　Francesco Vettori to Niccolò Machiavelli, 30 December 1514, Niccolò Machiavelli, *Lettere familiari*, p.387.

13　Roberto Ridolfi, *The Life of Niccolò Machiavelli*, trans. Cecil Grayson, Routledge and Kegan Paul, London, 1954, p.162.

14　Niccolò Machiavelli to Francesco Vettori, 3 August 1514, *Machiavelli and His Friends: Their Personal Correspondence*, p.292.

15　Ibid.

16　Niccolò Machiavelli to Giovanni Vernacci, 15 February 1516, *Machiavelli and His Friends: Their Personal Correspondence*, p.314.

17　Niccolò Machiavelli to Giovanni Vernacci, 10 September 1516, ibid., p.396.

18　Niccolò Machiavelli to Giovanni Vernacci, 8 June 1517, ibid., p.398.

19　Niccolò Machiavelli, *The Prince*, Chapter VI.

Chapter 10: *The Prince*

1　Letter from Niccolò Machiavelli to the Magnificent Lorenzo de' Medici, Preface to *The Prince*.

2　Niccolò Machiavelli, *The Prince*, Chapter VII.

3　Ibid.

4　Ibid., Chapter XXVI.

5　Ibid., Chapter VII.

6　Ibid., Chapter III.

7　Ibid., Chapter XV.

8　Ibid., Chapter XIV.

9 Niccolò Machiavelli, *Discourses on Titus Livy*, ed. Bernard Crick, Penguin, 1970, Book I, Preface; p.97.
10 Ibid.
11 Ibid., Chapter XVII.
12 Ibid., Book III, p.38.
13 Ibid., Chapter XVII.
14 Ibid.
15 Ibid., Chapter XXII.
16 Ibid., Chapter XVIII.
17 Ibid., Chapter VIII.
18 Niccolò Machiavelli, *The Prince*, Chapter XV.
19 Isaiah Berlin, 'The Originality of Machiavelli', in *Against the Current*, ed. H. Hardy, Clarendon Press, Oxford, 1981, pp.29–75.
20 Niccolò Machiavelli, *Discourses*, Book II, p.55.
21 Niccolò Machiavelli, *The Prince*, Chapter III.
22 Ibid., Chapter XXV.
23 Ibid.
24 Ibid., Chapter XVIII.
25 Ibid.
26 Ibid., Chapter XII.
27 Ibid.
28 Niccolò Machiavelli to Francesco Vettori, 16 April 1527, *Machiavelli and His Friends: Their Personal Correspondence*, trans. and ed. James B. Atkinson and David Sices, Northern Illinois University Press, De Kalb, Illinois, 1996, p.416.

Chapter 11: Rehabilitation

1 Niccolò Machiavelli, *The Golden Ass*, Chapter I, line 103; Chapter 3, line 76.
2 Quoted in Professor F.W. Kent, 'Gardens, villas and social life in Renaissance Florence', 1994, www.arts.monash.edu.au/visarts/diva/kent.html
3 Niccolò Machiavelli, *Discourses on Titus Livy*, ed. Bernard Crick, Penguin, 1970, Book II, Preface.
4 Ibid., Book I, Chapter 10.
5 Pasquale Villari, *Niccolò Machiavelli e i suoi tempi illustrati con nuovi documenti*, 3 vols., Le Monnier, Florence, 1877–82, Vol. II, p.313.
6 Niccolò Machiavelli, *Mandragola*, Prologue.
7 Filippo Strozzi to Lorenzo Strozzi, 17 March 1520, in Oreste Tommasini, *La vita e gli scritti di Niccolò Machiavelli*, 2 vols., Loescher, Rome, 1883 (Vol. 1), 1911 (Vol. 2), Vol. 2, p.1081.
8 Niccolò Machiavelli to Francesco del Nero, 10 September 1520, *Machiavelli and His Friends: Their Personal Correspondence*, trans. and ed. James B. Atkinson and David Sices, Northern Illinois University Press, De Kalb, Illinois, 1996, p.329.

Chapter 12: The Final Years

1 Cardinal Salviati to Niccolò Machiavelli, 6 September 1521, *Machiavelli and His Friends: Their Personal Correspondence*, trans. and ed. James B. Atkinson and David Sices, Northern Illinois University Press, De Kalb, Illinois, 1996, p.342.

2 Niccolò Machiavelli to Francesco Guicciardini, 17 May 1521, ibid., p.336.

3 Niccolò Machiavelli to Guicciardini, 30 August 1524, ibid., p.351.

4 Niccolò Machiavelli to Francesco Vettori, 10 June 1514, ibid., p.290.

5 Filippo de' Nerli to Francesco del Nero, Niccolò Machiavelli, *Le Opere*, Vol. 3, ed. Franco Gaeta, Unione Tipografico-Editrice Torinese, Turin, 1984, p.541.

6 *Opere politichie e letterarie*, Giannotti (ed.), Le Monnier, Florence, 1850, Vol. 1, p.228.

7 Niccolò Machiavelli to Francesco Guicciardini, 16 October 1525, *Machiavelli and His Friends: Their Personal Correspondence*, p.368.

8 Francesco Guicciardini to Niccolò Machiavelli, 7 August 1525, ibid., p.360.

9 Francesco Vettori to Niccolò Machiavelli, 8 March 1525, Niccolò Machiavelli, *Lettere familiari*, ed. Edoardo Alvisi, Sansoni, Florence, 1883, p.437.

10 *Archivio Storico Italiano*, Florence, 'Carte Strozziane, 1st ser.', pp.105–8.

11 Desjardin, *Négociations diplomatiques*, Vol. II, p.840.

12 Niccolò Machiavelli to Francesco Guicciardini, 15 March 1526, *Machiavelli and His Friends: Their Personal Correspondence*, p.381.

13 Francesco Guicciardini to Niccolò Machiavelli, Niccolò Machiavelli, *Lettere familiari*, p.468.

14 Francesco Guicciardini to Roberto Acciaiuoli, 18 July 1526, Niccolò Machiavelli, *Le Opere*, Vol. 3, Turin, 1984, p.593.

15 Roberto Acciaiuoli to Francesco Guicciardini, 7 August 1526, ibid.

16 Niccolò Machiavelli to Bartolomeo Cavalcanti, 6 October 1526, *Machiavelli and His Friends: Their Personal Correspondence*, p.403.

17 Francesco Guicciardini, *The History of Italy*, trans. and ed. Sidney Alexander, Macmillan Publishing, New York, 1969, p.174.

18 Niccolò Machiavelli to Guido Machiavelli, 2 April 1527, Niccolò Machiavelli, *Le Opere*, Vol. 3, Turin, 1984, p.624.

19 Guido Machiavelli to Niccolò Machiavelli, 17 April 1527, *Machiavelli and His Friends: Their Personal Correspondence*, p.416.

20 Ibid.

21 Quoted in *The Cambridge Modern History*, ed. A.W. Ward, G.W. Prothero, and Stanley Leathes, Cambridge University Press, 1904–12, Vol. II, p.55.

22 Luigi Guicciardini, *The Sack of Rome*, trans. and ed. James H. McGregor, Italica Press, New York, 2003, p.87.

23 Quoted in Roberto Ridolfi, *The Life of Niccolò Machiavelli*, trans. Cecil Grayson, Routledge and Kegan Paul, London, 1954, p.248.

Chapter 13: Machiavelli's Legacy

1   Piero Machiavelli to Francesco Nelli, 22 June 1527, *Machiavelli and His Friends: Their Personal Correspondence*, trans. and ed. James B. Atkinson and David Sices, Northern Illinois University Press, De Kalb, Illinois, 1996, p.425.

2   This was first postulated by Oreste Tommasini, in Vol. 1 of *La vita e gli scritti di Niccolò Machiavelli* (*The Life and Writings of Niccolò Machiavelli*), Loescher, Rome, 1883.

3   *Savonarola Lettere*, ed. Roberto Ridolfi, Olschki, Florence, 1933, p.XXII.

4   L. Arthur Burd, Introduction to *The Prince* by Niccolò Machiavelli, Clarendon Press, Oxford, 1891.

5   *The Private Correspondence of Niccolò Machiavelli*, trans. and ed. Orestes Ferrara et al., Johns Hopkins Press, Baltimore, Maryland, 1987, p.120.

6   Gino Capponi, *Storia della repubblica di Firenze*, 2nd edn., G. Barbera, Florence, 1876, Vol. III, p.191.

7   E. Pistelli, *Profili e caratteri*, Sansoni, Florence, 1921, p.67.

8   Niccolò Machiavelli, *The Prince*, Chapter VIII.

9   William Shakespeare, *Richard II*, 5.1.55–65.

10 Niccolò Machiavelli, *The Prince*, Chapter XV.

11 William Shakespeare, *Henry VI*, Part III, 3.2.188–95.

12 Francis Bacon, 'De Dignitate et Augmentis Scientiarum', in *Francis Bacon: A Selection*, ed. Sidney Warhaft, Macmillan, 1965, p.413.

13 Hamilton was quoting from David Hume, 'On the Independence of Parliament', Gerard Stourzh, *Alexander Hamilton and the Idea of Republican Government*, Stanford University Press, Stanford, California, 1970, p.77.

14 Anthony Parel, *The Machiavellian Cosmos*, Yale University Press, New Haven, Connecticut, 1992, p.213.

Bibliography

Atkinson, Catherine, *Debts, Dowries and Donkeys: The Diary of Niccolò Machiavelli's Father, Messer Bernardo, in Quattrocentro Florence*, Peter Lang, Berlin, 2002

Atkinson, James B., and Sices, David (trans. and eds.), *Machiavelli and His Friends: Their Personal Correspondence*, Northern Illinois University Press, De Kalb, Illinois, 1996

Bock, Gisela, Skinner, Quentin, and Viroli, Maurizio (eds.), *Machiavelli and Republicanism*, Cambridge University Press, 1990

Bull, George, *Michelangelo: A Biography*, Penguin, London, 1995

Capponi, Gino, *Storia della repubblica di Firenze*, 2nd edn., G. Barbera, Florence, 1876

Cardini, Franco, *Europe 1492*, Facts on File, New York, 1989

Chamberlin, E.R., *The World of the Italian Renaissance*, Book Club Associates, London, 1982

Cronin, Vincent, *The Florentine Renaissance*, Pimlico, London, 1967

Curry, Patrick and Zarate, Oscar, *Introducing Machiavelli*, Icon Books, London, 1997

Da Grazia, Sebastian, *Machiavelli in Hell*, Princeton University Press, Princeton, New Jersey, 1989

Ferrara, Orestes et al. (trans. and eds.), *The Private Correspondence of Niccolò Machiavelli*, Johns Hopkins Press, Baltimore, Maryland, 1987

Gilbert, Allan (ed.), *Machiavelli: the Chief*, Duke University Press, Durham, North Carolina, 1965

Gilmore, Myron P. (ed.), *Studies in Machiavelli*, Sansoni, Florence, 1972

Guicciardini, Counts Piero and Luigi (eds.), *Letters of Francesco Guicciardini*, 10 vols., Florence, 1857–67

Guicciardini, Luigi, *The Sack of Rome*, trans. and ed. James H. McGregor, Italica Press, 2003

Hale, J.R., *The Literary Works of Machiavelli*, Oxford University Press, London, 1961

Hart, Michael, *The 100*, Simon and Schuster, New York, 1993

Jensen, De Lamar, *Renaissance Europe: Age of Recovery and Reconciliation*, D.C. Heath and Co, Toronto, 1992

Landucci, Luca, *A Florentine Diary from 1450–1516 (Continued by an Anonymous Writer Till 1542)* with notes by Iodoco del Badia, trans. Alice de Rosen Jervis, J.M. Dent, London, 1927, p.218

Levey, Michael, *Florence: A Portrait*, Pimlico, London, 1997

Machiavelli, Niccolò, *Chief Works*, trans. Allan Gilbert, Duke University Press, Durham, North Carolina, 1965

Machiavelli, Niccolò, *Discourses on Titus Livy*, ed. Bernard Crick, Penguin, 1970

Machiavelli, Niccolò, *Le Opere*, 6 vols. (Vol. I ed. P. Fanfani and L. Passerini; Vols. II–VI ed. L. Passerini and G. Milanesi), Cenniniani, Florence, 1873–7

—— *Florentine Histories*, ed. Laura Banfield and Harvey Mansfield, Princeton University Press, Princeton, New Jersey, 1990

—— *Legazioni e Commissarie*, 3 vols., ed. Sergio Bertelli, Feltrinelli, Milan, 1964

—— *Lettere familiari*, ed. Edoardo Alvisi, Sansoni, Florence, 1883

—— *Le Opere*, Vol. 3, ed. Franco Gaeta, Unione Tipografico-Editrice Torinese, Turin, 1984

—— *Tutte le opere storiche e letterarie*, ed. Guido Mazzoni and Mario Casella, G. Barbera, Florence, 1929

Martines, Lauro, *April Blood: Florence and the Plot Against the Medici*, Jonathan Cape, London, 2003

Masters, Roger, *Fortune is a River: Leonardo da Vinci and Niccolò Machiavelli's Magnificent Dream to Change the Course of Florentine History*, Plume, New York, 1999

Masters, Roger, *Machiavelli, Leonardo and the Science of Power*, University of Notre Dame Press, Notre Dame, Indiana, 1998

Masters, Roger, *Machiavelli's Sexuality* (a paper kindly sent to me by Professor Masters of Dartmouth College, New Hampshire, USA)

Micheletti, Emma, *The Medici of Florence*, Becocci Editore, Florence, 1998

Norwich, John Julius, *A History of Venice*, Penguin, London, 1982

Parel, Anthony, *The Machiavellian Cosmos*, Yale University Press, New Haven, Connecticut, 1992

Portigliotti, Giuseppe, *The Borgias*, trans. Bernard Miall, George Allen and Unwin, London, 1928

Ridolfi, Roberto, *The Life of Niccolò Machiavelli*, trans. Cecil Grayson, Routledge and Kegan Paul, London, 1954

Rubenstein, Nicolai, *The Age of the Renaissance*, ed. Denys Hay, McGraw Hill, New York, 1994

Stourzh, Gerard, *Alexander Hamilton and the Idea of Republican Government*, Stanford University Press, Stanford, California, 1970

Tommasini, Oreste, *La vita e gli scritti di Niccolò Machiavelli*, 2 vols., Loescher, Rome, 1883 (Vol. 1), 1911 (Vol. 2)

Villari, Pasquale, *The Life and Times of Niccolo Machiavelli*, Scholarly Publications, Houston, Texas, 1972

Vasari, Giorgio, *Lives of the Most Famous Artists*, 10 vols., trans. Gaston du C. de Vere, Macmillan and the Medici Society, London, 1912–14

Viroli, Maurizio, *Niccolò's Smile*, Farrar, Straus and Giroux, New York, 2000

Ward, A.W., Prothero, G.W., and Leathes, Stanley (eds.), *The Cambridge Modern History*, Cambridge University Press, 1904–12

Warhaft, Sidney (ed.), *Francis Bacon: A Selection*, Macmillan, 1965

White, Michael, *Leonardo: The First Scientist*, Time Warner Books, London, 2000

—— *The Pope and the Heretic: The True Story of Courage and Murder at the Hands of the Inquisition*, Time Warner Books, London, 2002

Index